Also by
JACK CAVANAUGH

Tunney

The Gipper

Season of '42

GIANTS AMONG MEN

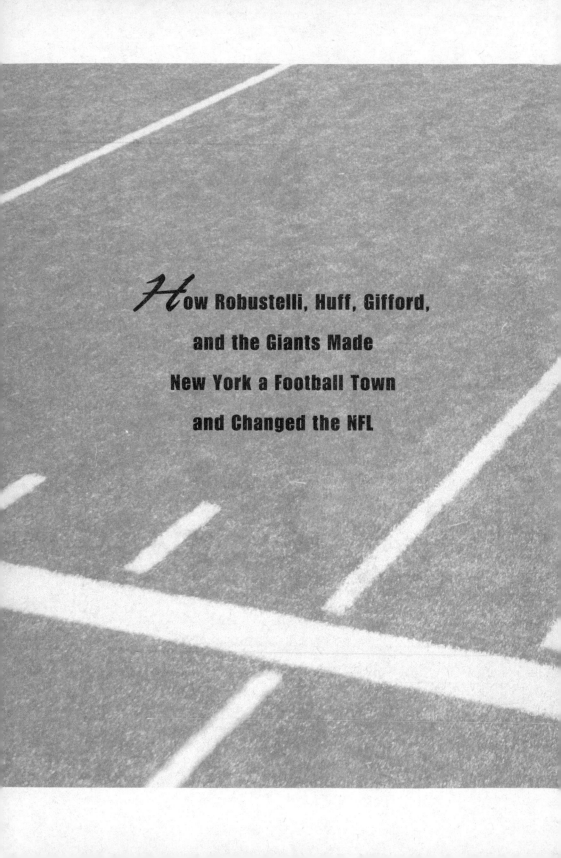

How Robustelli, Huff, Gifford, and the Giants Made New York a Football Town and Changed the NFL

GIANTS
AMONG MEN

Jack Cavanaugh

SPORTS
PUBLISHING

Visit our website at www.sportspubbooks.com.

10 9 8 7 6 5 4 3 2

Library of Congress Cataloging-in-Publication Data is available on file.

Cover design by Tom Lau

Cover photograph: AP Images

Print ISBN: 978-1-68358-080-5
Ebook ISBN: 978-1-68358-081-2

Printed in the United States of America

To Marge, John, Tara, Lance,
and our wonderful grandsons,
Rogan Jack and
Tanner Patrick Wells

When I joined the Giants, what impressed me most was the intelligence of the players, both on and off the field, and how close they were. They were very talented players, but they were also very bright guys. That's why so many of them became so successful later on—players like Andy Robustelli, Frank Gifford, Sam Huff, Y. A. Tittle, and Kyle Rote. It was a pleasure and a lot of fun playing with that very smart bunch of guys and playing under assistant coaches—*assistant* coaches, mind you—like Tom Landry and Vince Lombardi.

—PAT SUMMERALL
placekicker for the Chicago Cardinals and the
New York Giants, and nationally known
television sportscaster

CONTENTS

═══

The Talk of the Town

A lot of them hung out at places like Toots Shor's and P. J. Clarke's, rubbing elbows with people such as Jackie Gleason, Ernest Hemingway, Joe DiMaggio, Frank Sinatra, and Ed Sullivan. And to most of the patrons of such popular Manhattan restaurants in the mid- and late 1950s and early 1960s, they were as big in the celebrity world as any of the show business figures with whom they associated. Some of their names were Frank Gifford, Sam Huff, Charlie Conerly, Kyle Rote, Y. A. Tittle, Andy Robustelli, and Pat Summerall, and they were all readily recognizable to most New Yorkers and visiting celebrities, whether it was at the "21" Club, Mike Manuche's restaurant, Eddie Condon's jazz club, or walking along Fifth or Madison avenues.

They played football for the New York Giants when the Giants actually were a New York team, playing in the Bronx and not in New Jersey; when the United States was at peace; when the last general to be elected president, Dwight Eisenhower, himself a onetime football player at West Point, was in the White House; when the Paramount, Roxy, and Capitol theaters still offered stage shows to go with their feature movies in Times Square; when nightclubs like the Copacabana and the Latin Quarter were flourishing; when Lindy's was still a showbiz hangout on Broadway complete with Damon Runyon–like *Guys and Dolls* characters; and when the Giants had a grip on the city that has not since been surpassed—not by the Yankees, the Mets, the Knicks, the Rangers, or even the three Giants teams that won the Super Bowl while playing across the Hudson River in New Jersey, far removed from Yankee Stadium. There, players like Rosey Brown, Del Shofner, Emlen Tunnell, Alex Webster, Jim Katcavage, Jimmy Patton, Ray Wietecha, Dick Lynch, Rosey Grier, and Jack Stroud captured the sporting hearts of New Yorkers. It was also an era when the NFL rosters included the likes of Jimmy Brown, Johnny Unitas, Norm Van Brocklin, Paul Hornung, Bart Starr, Gino Marchetti, Otto Graham, Gene "Big Daddy" Lipscomb, Ray Nitschke, Jimmy Taylor, Raymond Berry, Lenny Moore, George Blanda, Bobby Layne, Elroy "Crazylegs" Hirsch, Marion Motley, Jerry Kramer, Dick "Night Train" Lane, and the incomparable yet notorious Hardy Brown, whose unique and devastating shoulder tackle made him the most feared and despised player in the NFL.

It also was an era during which face masks first appeared, when the goalpost was situated on the goal line, when placekickers approached the ball straight ahead and not at an angle, when the passing game came into full flower, and the sixty-minute player became a vanishing breed.

Apart from their overall talent, the Giants of the mid- and late 1950s and early 1960s were distinctive in a number of other ways. For one thing, six of them—Brown, Gifford, Huff, Robustelli, Tittle, and Tunnell—along with two assistant coaches, Tom Landry and Vince Lombardi, have been elected to the Pro Football Hall of Fame. For another, this was hardly just another collection of inarticulate jocks who merely dealt with the public and ultimately retired and disappeared. This was a most remarkable and memorable group whose quarterback in the early sixties (Tittle) was a relatively slight and bald-headed man who looked like a typical middle-aged fan; and whose star running back and later a receiver (Gifford) was a handsome former All-American from Southern California whose good looks earned him roles in more than two dozen movies and numerous television commercials.

Collectively, it may have been the smartest football team ever assembled, producing a large number of coaches and a boardroom full of self-made millionaires in an era when the average National Football League salary was about $15,000. Indeed, they were so well known for their intelligence that the Giants organization, founded by a legal bookmaker and New York sportsman named Tim Mara in 1925, and run by the Mara family into the third millennium, became known as "Mara Tech." It might well have been called Broadcast Prep, too, since so many Giants of that era went on to become sports broadcasters, most notably Gifford and placekicker Pat Summerall, for years the preeminent NFL play-by-play announcer. And if the Giants organization was Mara Tech for players, it was the Sorbonne for assistant coaches. Indeed, no team has ever simultaneously had two football legends as the Giants did when Landry and Lombardi served as the offensive and defensive coaches, respectively, in the 1950s. Nor has any other NFL team ever had as its head coach, as the Giants did in the 1960s, a small, former left-handed quarterback from Brooklyn College who was too small to play for his high school team yet spent five seasons as a backup quarterback in the NFL and who, except for an incongruous Southern accent, was a quintessential New Yorker. Allie Sherman succeeded Lombardi as the team's offensive coordinator in 1959 and became the head coach in 1961.

In the opinion of many football historians, the defining moment in NFL history was the 1958 championship game between the Giants and the Baltimore Colts at Yankee Stadium. One of the first NFL games shown on network television to a national audience, the epic encounter, often called "the greatest football game ever played," is largely credited with popularizing the league around the country and solidifying it as a major sports attraction—not only with spectators, but with network television executives and national advertisers. By then, though, the Giants had already achieved a fan breakthrough in New York after thirty years of trying—and being overshadowed and outdrawn by college teams from Fordham University, New York University, and, especially, Army—when in 1956 they won their first championship since 1938. That season the Giants set a team attendance record at Yankee Stadium, to which they had moved from the old Polo Grounds, just across the Harlem River. And it was that year that Giants fans, smitten by the great defensive unit that the team had assembled, and which the innovative Landry coached, began to inspire the players at crucial junctures of games with cries of "*Dee-fense!*"—the first time that such a collective exhortation had been heard at NFL games.

By late fall of 1956, the Giants had become the talk of the town, idolized by both longtime and new fans, and drawing near-capacity crowds to Yankee Stadium after the Yankees had just won another championship by beating the Brooklyn Dodgers in the World Series. Suddenly, major political figures, network and advertising moguls, show business stars, and nationally known New York sports columnists such as Red Smith and Jimmy Cannon were lionizing the Giants. For the team and its growing legion of fans, it was the beginning of an ardent love affair that probably reached its most passionate peak between 1956 and 1963, when the Giants won six Eastern Conference championships. Indeed, at a time when the New York Yankees had once again played in back-to-back World Series, the Giants found themselves sharing lockers with Yankee stars such as Mickey Mantle, Yogi Berra, and Whitey Ford.

What made the Giants of the late fifties and the early sixties unique and, arguably, more special than the Green Bay Packers, Cleveland Browns, and Chicago Bears, the other dominant teams of that era? In large measure it was the meshing of individual talents into a cohesive unit under Jim Lee Howell and then Sherman. Moreover, the team was characterized by a rare togetherness, the very essence of the word *team,* both on and off the field. Veterans such as Conerly and Robustelli, both of whom had seen action in the Pacific during World War II, blended in perfectly with superb young players like Gifford and Rote. Helping enhance team unity further, most of the players lived relatively close together, mainly in New York City and in nearby suburbs in Westchester County and Connecticut. Along with their wives, most of whom became close friends on their own, they socialized frequently. After home games, for example, the laconic quarterback Conerly and his wife would host cocktail parties in their apartment at the Concourse Plaza Hotel, where, at one point, almost half of the team lived during the season. After the parties, most of the players and their wives or girlfriends would board a subway train and ride more than one hundred blocks to midtown Manhattan to have dinner at Toots Shor's or at "21" or some other favorite restaurant, and then end the evening at P. J. Clarke's or at the famed Copacabana nightclub or some other Manhattan nightspot, where they would often be greeted with cheers.

More than forty years later, many of them were still recognized on the streets of Manhattan, while most Giants players went unnoticed in public, apart from stars like Lawrence Taylor, Phil Simms, Eli Manning, Tiki Barber, and Michael Strahan, all of whom spent more time in New Jersey than they did in New York. In the early 1990s, three decades after he had retired, Andy Robustelli was walking along Madison Avenue when he was approached by two men who recognized the Hall of Fame defensive end from nearby Stamford, Connecticut. Beaming, they greeted Robustelli warmly and then shook his hand. Asked if that happened often, old number 81 said, "It still happens, and I find it hard to believe."

At the head of this close-knit family was Timothy J. Mara, a native New Yorker who started taking legal bets at New York racetracks in the days before pari-mutuel wagering became legal in New York State. It was he who seized on a happenstance opportunity to buy a nonexistent New York franchise in the newly formed National Football League for $500 after a boxing manager declined an offer to do so because he was busy guiding a handsome former marine named Gene Tunney to win boxing's world heavyweight championship. More than three-quarters of a century later, the team, worth hundreds of millions of dollars, was still owned primarily by the Mara family. But in all of those years, few, if any, other team developed a closeness to surpass that enjoyed by the Giants of the mid- and late fifties and early sixties, in large measure, admittedly, because they played in the nation's media capital and had been embraced by fledgling television networks and their top executives, many of whom became fans.

That the Giants also had so many personable and outstanding players further helped capture the imagination and hearts of New Yorkers at a time when most of the team's fans lived in New York City. They, along with this collection of extraordinarily intelligent and talented players, helped make the Giants of the late 1950s and early 1960s a team for the ages and New York a pro football town.

GIANTS AMONG MEN

1

Return to Winooski Park

$\mathscr{S}$entimentality was never one of Andy Robustelli's strongest suits. Only when it was relevant to a conversation might he mention having grown up in a predominantly Italian neighborhood on the West Side of Stamford, Connecticut, in a six-family tenement. Nor would he talk much about his service during World War II as a teenage water tender and gunner aboard the destroyer escort *William C. Cole*, a small, top-heavy fighting ship that saw considerable action in the South Pacific. Later in his life, the same thing would be true of his playing days in the National Football League, which, glorious as they were, he was disinclined to talk about. Indeed, whenever anyone would bring up his Hall of Fame career or anything relating to football, Robustelli, who by then had become the head of a highly successful business conglomerate, would usually say, "I'm a businessman now, not a football player, and I'd much rather talk about business."

Despite that lack of sentimentality, Robustelli could not help but feel a twinge of nostalgia when he drove onto the campus of Saint Michael's College in the Winooski Park section of Colchester, Vermont, to join the New York Giants of the NFL in late July of 1956 after having been traded by the Los Angeles Rams—indeed, offered to the virtually incredulous Giants because he'd had the audacity to ask the Rams if he could report to training camp a few days late after his wife had given birth to their fourth child. Such was the way of the world in the twelve-team NFL of 1956, when players' salaries aver-aged less than $10,000, there was no players' association, free agency did not exist (meaning that players, no matter their stature or the length of their tenure, had no say as to which teams they played for), and players negotiated their own contracts. As Robustelli was to re-call in 2007, during his thirteen years in the NFL, not a single player ever held out. "It was a different time," he said. "Nobody was making much money, and you might ask for more than what they offered, but you usually signed a contract even after you got to training camp."

One of Robustelli's teammates with the Giants, Alex Webster, said it often was a take-it-or-leave-it situation as far as management was concerned. "There were only twelve teams and about four hun-dred players when we were playing," Webster, an outstanding run-ning back, recalled. "That meant a lot of good football players were available who would be willing to play for less than guys in the NFL, and the owners knew it. So when it came to salaries, you didn't have much choice. So you usually took what they offered. But I must say that the Giants were very good in that respect."

But if Robustelli remembered Winooski Park, followers of the Saint Michael's football team certainly remembered him as a foot-ball and baseball player for Arnold College who once drove a baseball into the centerfield fence, five hundred feet from home plate, and his prowess as a two-way end and sometimes linebacker while playing against Saint Michael's teams from 1947 to 1951. Then, too, it was at Saint Michael's in October of 1950 that Robustelli, as a twenty-four-year-old senior at Arnold, broke his leg on the second-to-last play of what turned out to be his final college football game—and, it appeared to him and even his biggest supporters, his last football game, period. "I had some pleasant and unpleasant memories about the place, but I surely never expected to be back practicing with the Giants on the same field where I had broken a leg," Robustelli recalled.

The thirty-year-old Robustelli was hardly the only new player turning out for the opening training camp session on the small but picturesque Saint Michael's campus, but he was one of the most pop-ular among fans, along with All-Pro halfback Frank Gifford, thirty-five-year-old quarterback Charlie Conerly, and Kyle Rote, who in 1953 had been converted from halfback to a wide receiver because of injuries to both knees suffered during his first two years with the Giants.

Certainly none of the other sixty-odd players reporting for pre-season practice had ever played at Saint Michael's, but they were an astonishingly talented group. Defensive tackle Dick Modzelewski had been obtained from the Pittsburgh Steelers after playing with the Washington Redskins and at the University of Maryland. Halfback Gene Filipski, after being caught up in a 1951 cribbing scandal at West Point, attended Villanova University and had been traded to the Giants by the Cleveland Browns a few weeks before Robustelli's arrival. Defensive back Ed Hughes had been a teammate of Robustelli's with the Rams after playing at North Carolina State University and the University of Tulsa.

Two weeks after training camp began, they would be joined by the rookies: running back Henry Moore, the Giants' number one draft choice, who would wind up carrying the ball only twice for a net loss of 2 yards in his rookie year before being traded to the Baltimore Colts; defensive linemen Robert Lee "Sam" Huff and Jim Katcavage; punter Don Chandler and offensive end Hank Burnine, who had played at Arkansas, West Virginia, Dayton, Florida, and Missouri, respectively. They all had been selected to play in the then-annual College All-Star Game against the previous year's NFL champion—in this case, the Cleveland Browns, who demolished the All-Stars 28–0. They all had heard of Robustelli, but not of his alma mater; Arnold College, which, like Saint Michael's, played on the lowest rung of the college football ladder and was barely known even in Connecticut, though it had existed since 1921—first in New Haven and then on the shores of Long Island Sound in the town of Milford, about ten miles from New Haven—as a physical education school with an enrollment of about five hundred students. At that Arnold had resurrected its football program in 1947 after abandoning it during World War II.

How Robustelli wound up at Arnold was pure happenstance. Unrecruited after playing one season of football at Stamford High School in Connecticut, and not at all during three years in the Navy during World War II, Robustelli considered attending a prep school in Stamford for a year to prepare for college while playing baseball and football. "I lived nearby and ran into Andy and Mike Sette (another Stamford athlete), as they were leaving St. Basil's prep on a summer day in 1947," Carmine Tosches, a former teammate of Robustelli's at Stamford High, recalled. "By then I had enrolled at Arnold, and when I told them that Arnold was re-instituting a football program that fall, they became interested and went up and enrolled at Arnold the next day." It turned out to be a fortuitous meeting for Tosches, since he became the starting quarterback at Arnold and Robustelli his primary receiver while also starring on defense.

In one of the most remarkable success stories in NFL history, Robustelli in 1951 made the improbable jump from little Arnold College to a starting position as a defensive end with a Los Angeles Rams team that not only won the NFL championship but is still re-garded as one of the best professional football teams of all time. It was comprised of such perennial All-Pros as Bob Waterfield, Norm Van Brocklin, Elroy "Crazylegs" Hirsch, and Tom Fears, as well as Tank Younger, the first player from a historically all-black school— in his case, Grambling State University—to play in the NFL; "Dea-con Dan" Towler; and Glenn Davis, the former Army star halfback and Heisman Trophy winner. Though Robustelli had been named to the Associated Press's Little All-America team while at Arnold, not many football people noticed or were impressed, given that Arnold's opponents usually included similarly small schools such as Saint Mi-chael's, American International College, New Haven State Teachers College, Wagner College, Montclair State, and Adelphi College. One of those who had noticed, though, was Lou DeFilippo, a former Giants guard from New Haven, who had become an Eastern scout for the Rams in addition to coaching the line at Fordham.

DeFilippo was one of about a hundred part-time scouts—or "bird dogs," as they were called—whom the Rams had hired to seek out talent at small schools like Arnold. The idea belonged to Dan Reeves, the co-owner of the Rams and a visionary who was convinced there was a wealth of unknown football talent in the hundreds of small col-leges under the radar of the national media and thus unpublicized, and, on a national scale, unnoticed. Reeves's efforts got a further boost when Tex Schramm, a former sports editor in Austin, Texas, whom he had hired as a publicity man, got the idea of sending out letters to football coaches at hundreds of small colleges in the coun-try, asking them to list the five best players their teams had played against that year. Robustelli almost assuredly was listed in some of the responses, but indications are that DeFilippo was largely responsible for bringing the end from Arnold College to the Rams' attention.

In his reports, DeFilippo had raved about the 220-pound

Robustelli's pass-catching ability, his deadly tackling, his remarkable punt-blocking skills, and his speed and agility. "He'd be good against anybody," DeFilippo was to report to the Rams, "and he's definitely worth a look." Eventually the Rams took a look, dispatching end coach Red Hickey, who later became the head coach of the San Francisco 49ers, to Winooski Park to watch Robustelli in what became his last college game. As it was, he saw Robustelli enjoy one of his best games, catching a half dozen passes, making about twice as many tackles, and blocking several punts before breaking his leg. Hickey had seen more than enough and gave the Rams hierarchy a rave review, adding that Lou DeFilippo knew what he was talking about. As a result, the Rams proceeded to pick Robustelli in the nineteenth round of the 1951 NFL draft, in which each team selected thirty players. All eighteen players that the Rams chose ahead of Robustelli were from nationally known schools, but only eight made the team.

None of the veteran Rams expected the unknown rookie to make the talent-laden squad. No way was he going to beat out Crazylegs Hirsch or Tom Fears at offensive end or veterans Jack Zilly and Larry Brink at defensive end. But Zilly, the right end, broke a leg during training camp, giving Robustelli the chance to validate everything Lou DeFilippo and Red Hickey had said about him.

But Robustelli had not played organized football until his senior year at Stamford High School. And after playing one season at a military prep school on Long Island in 1943, he had not suited up again until four years later, after his discharge from the navy. The young man was so unsure whether or not he should try out for the Rams that he accepted an offer from the New York Giants baseball team to try out at the Polo Grounds in June of 1951. A third baseman who hit both for average (nearly .400) and power at Arnold College, Robustelli so impressed Giants scouts that he was offered a contract to play with the Giants' Class AA Southern Association team in Knoxville, Tennessee, for $400 a month. The offer was tempting, especially since Robustelli had grown up as an ardent Giants baseball fan.

By then, too, Robustelli had sought out the advice of J. Walter Kennedy, a public relations executive in New York and sports columnist for the *Stamford Advocate* with strong connections in the sporting world, as to whether he should accept the Rams' invitation to training camp. Kennedy, who would go on to become mayor of Stamford and then commissioner of the National Basketball Association, advised against it, recommending instead that Robustelli, by then the father of a year-old son, accept an offer to teach physical education and coach football at a high school in Meriden, Connecticut. "Stick to the teaching and coaching by all means," Kennedy told Robustelli. "You've got a wife and a baby, so you can't afford to gamble on something as chancy as professional football—certainly not with your small-college background."

That night, Robustelli, still undecided, told his father, Lucien, a neighborhood barber who charged twenty cents for a haircut, what Kennedy had told him. "He didn't really understand sports," Robustelli later explained, "but he said, 'You've got to take a chance. If you don't, you'll spend the rest of your life wondering whether you could have made it. But then, you've got to make up your own mind.' "

And make up his own mind Robustelli did: to take a chance, as his father had suggested. He decided that he was capable of playing at any level, and that if necessary, he could raise his game even higher than it had been at Arnold College. After telling his mentor, Kennedy, of his decision, Robustelli flew to California on July 17, on what most Stamford sports followers thought was a quixotic adventure—a big fish from a little pond would be diving into a sea full of sharks. No way, most of his Connecticut friends thought, was Robustelli going to make it with a team that had played in the previous year's NFL championship and was favored to win the title in 1951.

—

After less than a week at the Rams' training camp site, three thousand miles from his wife and infant son, Robustelli found himself increasingly homesick and discouraged at what he perceived to be his own lack of progress on a team that had eleven ends in camp. Three of them were perennial All-Pros, including Fears, who had led the NFL in pass receptions and yards gained in 1950, and Hirsch, who would do the same in 1951. Indeed, Hirsch had been an outstanding running back before a series of serious injuries prompted Clark Shaughnessy, then the Rams' coach, to switch him to flanker—a position where an offensive end, rather than lining up alongside a tackle, lines up closer to the sidelines, and thus alone. After watching Hirsch catch a pass from Bob Waterfield in full stride against the Bears and then zigzag more than fifty yards for a touchdown, Bears coach George Halas, an NFL pioneer who had seen it all, said, "Almost without realizing it, we have reached the point where the pass-catching end has replaced the running back as a long-distance threat. There wasn't a back in the league who could have done what Hirsch did."

Robustelli found himself spending most of his time on defense during his first two weeks in camp. Perhaps, he thought, that was why the Rams had drafted him in the first place, albeit so low. No doubt Lou DeFilippo and Red Hickey had noticed that while Robustelli had become best known at Arnold (and among its opponents) for his pass catching, they had raved about his defensive skills—in particular, his extraordinary punt blocking. But Robustelli did not know that. And so, after another sleepless night, he went to coach Joe Stydahar, the Hall of Fame tackle for the great Chicago Bears teams of the 1930s and 1940s, and told him of his insecurity as a Rams prospect, of his homesickness, and how he was thinking of going back to Connecticut and becoming a teacher and coach. "I was so unsure of my chances that I hadn't even unpacked my bags," Robustelli said.

After glaring at Robustelli for a few seconds, Stydahar did what for him was easy: He exploded.

"If you go home now, you'll be cheating yourself, and that Polish wife of yours will hit you over the head with a broomstick!" Stydahar boomed. "And she *should* do that if you don't stick it out and give it a fair shot. You can't quit now, and I won't let you quit. Now get the hell out of here."

Though Robustelli's wife, Jeanne, was actually Slovak, those were still strong words, even by Stydahar's standards. But it was clear that the old Bears tackle cared about Robustelli and felt that the rookie with the serious-looking mien had a good chance to make the team. Comforted by what Stydahar had said, Robustelli called his wife and told her he was going to stick it out and that he just might make it after all. A few days later, Zilly broke his right leg and was lost for the season. It would mark a turning point for the long-shot end from Arnold College.

In his first full scrimmage as Zilly's replacement at right end, Robustelli was outstanding, spinning around the left tackle to sack and otherwise harass the quarterbacks and recording a number of other tackles. He was even more impressive in the Rams' first exhibition game, a 56–6 pasting of the Chicago Bears at the Los Angeles Coliseum, in which Robustelli played right end and on the kickoff- and punt-return teams.

Meanwhile, Zilly went out of his way to help Robustelli. "Jack was great, spending hours with me and teaching me a lot," Robustelli recalled. So much so that the following year, Zilly was traded to the Philadelphia Eagles.

Not only did Robustelli make the Rams—for the munificent salary of $4,200—he was named an All-Pro defensive end four straight years following his first season, when he was named the NFL's rookie of the year.

—

That Robustelli was now with the Giants, in 1956, had come about by a fortuitous circumstance. After Jeanne gave birth to their fourth child in July of 1956, Robustelli asked Rams head coach Sid Gillman if he could delay his arrival at training camp until his wife returned home from the hospital—obviously unaware that sensitivity was not one of Gillman's better traits. Two years into his first coaching job in the NFL, after having been an assistant at Army and a head coach at the University of Cincinnati, Gillman had quickly become a hard-liner. No, he told Robustelli, he could not have a few more days in Stamford, regardless of whether his wife was still in the hospital with her baby. "I've got a team to worry about, not your family," Robustelli recalled Gillman telling him.

"Well, I've got some kids to worry about, and I've got to do what's right for me," said an upset Robustelli. "And what the hell, it's only a couple of days."

Gillman, unmoved, replied, "I don't care if it's a couple of days or not. You get your ass out here. That's all I can tell you."

"Sid," Robustelli said, "I'll be out there as soon as my home situation is settled."

Whereupon Gillman hung up on his $7,000-a-year All-Pro defensive end.

Several days later, with his wife and new baby home from the hospital, Robustelli was preparing to leave for the Rams' training camp when he got a phone call from Wellington Mara, the youngest son of Giants owner Tim Mara. "I've been talking to the Rams about you, and they're willing to trade you," a delighted Mara told a stunned Robustelli. "I know that you're thirty years old, but do you think you could play two or three more years? If so, we'd certainly love to have you play for us."

Robustelli's initial reaction was one of dismay. He liked playing for the Rams and had fit in well with one of the NFL's best-ever teams. But he finally said to Mara, "They really want to trade me, huh? I find that hard to believe. As for me continuing to play, I'll try to play as long as I can, but I don't know how long that might be. But then, as you know, I got a late start and have only been in the league for five years."

But as the conversation went on, Robustelli became convinced that the Giants wanted him—obviously far more than the Rams did. "I appreciate your calling, Mr. Mara, and if you can do it, go ahead and make the deal."

A day later, on July 27, Mara did, obtaining one of the league's best defensive ends for a first-round draft choice; it turned out to be wide receiver Del Shofner, who, ironically, would wind up with the Giants in 1961. A three-paragraph Associated Press story in the next day's *New York Times* quoted coach Jim Lee Howell as saying that Robustelli had become available because of his "increasing reluctance to leave his Stamford, Connecticut, home and play on the West Coast." That quote was half right. With each passing year, as his family grew in size, Robustelli had become more reluctant to leave Stamford, but he had never expressed a desire to leave the Rams.

For the Giants, it was a deal made in heaven, and one of the best the team has ever negotiated. It also turned out to be a blessing for Robustelli, whose family ties—fittingly—had forced a trade that would now have him playing his home games at Yankee Stadium, less than an hour's drive from his home. Maybe he had always dreamed of playing for his favorite team, the New York baseball Giants, but, hey, those Giants were soon to leave New York for California, and the New York football Giants were on the verge of becoming one of the best NFL teams of all time.

2

Huff as in Tough

*G*iven all of the college facilities the Giants football team could have trained at in the New York metropolitan area, Saint Michael's College in faraway Vermont seemed an odd place to set up training camp. But then, before coming to the bucolic campus at Saint Michael's, more than three hundred miles from New York, they had trained even farther away: at Willamette University in Salem, Oregon; Gustavus Adolphus College in Saint Peter, Minnesota; and at University of Wisconsin-Superior. "I think the Maras had the team train as far away as possible because of how lousy they were," said Robert Daley, the Giants' public relations director from 1953 through 1958, only partially in jest.*

Though he was never told so, Don Smith, who succeeded Daley as the team's public relations director, said he thought the Maras had the Giants train in Vermont, Oregon, and Minnesota, rather than in the New York area, so that there would be fewer distractions, if any, for the players when they were permitted to leave camp after dinner. Apparently the deeply religious Maras also thought that training at Catholic colleges might somehow benefit the players spiritually. What's more, the Maras enjoyed seeing a number of college administrators, priests, and professors, along with the

*That may have been true in 1953, the year Daley started, when the Giants went 3–9 after training in Minnesota, but they'd had winning seasons the three previous years and also in 1954 and 1955.

occasional seminarians and nuns who watched practices in between heading to classes or offices.

Whether there was any correlation between training at Roman Catholic schools and the Giants' ultimate successes never has been established, but Wellington Mara thought so. Of course, it also made it convenient for Mara, who lived in dormitories with the players and coaches and worked out regularly with the team, usually catching punts or retrieving practice field goal attempts, to go to the campus chapel for Mass every morning with the team's offensive coordinator, his Fordham University classmate Vince Lombardi.

However, training at such remote outposts as Salem, Oregon, and Winooski Park, Vermont, also had drawbacks. Perhaps the most severe was the absence of New York sportswriters—and, consequently, little coverage of a Giants team that never sold out its home games at the Polo Grounds where the Giants had played since 1925, but in 1956 would move into Yankee Stadium. Both Robert Daley and Don Smith said it was rare for a New York writer to show up when the Giants were training hundreds, and even thousands, of miles from New York.

"About the only time a writer from a New York paper would turn up at Saint Michael's was when he happened to be on assignment in Boston or somewhere else nearby," said Smith, who had covered the Giants for the *Long Island Star-Journal* before becoming the team's public relations director. "First of all, the NFL still hadn't caught on big, even in the early 1950s. You also had three baseball teams in New York at the time, and the media focus was strictly on baseball right into October, when the Yankees and the Brooklyn Dodgers usually were in pennant races"—as were the baseball Giants several times in the early 1950s—"or playing in the World Series. So for years, the Giants played their first three or four games on the road with only occasional coverage by the New York papers; usually the *New York Times* and the New York *Herald Tribune*."

Another downside of the location was its modest accommodations. After having savored the rather luxurious training facilities in Redlands, California, with the Rams, Robustelli was somewhat taken aback by the locker rooms at Saint Michael's, which were adjacent to the boiler room in the basement beneath the school's dining hall. Spartan to the core, the cramped locker rooms had brick walls and wooden floors and were outfitted with about thirty-five YMCA-like metal lockers arrayed in front of several rows of benches.

"You'd come into a room on a hot day that was even hotter inside, and then go into a shower room that was even hotter," Sam Huff recalled years later. "At that, there were only a few showers, so we had to share them. Then you'd get dressed and walk out sweating and even hotter than when you came in. If you tried to get today's players to change and shower in such conditions, they'd probably go on strike."

But the Burlington Chamber of Commerce, eager to publicize the college town of Burlington, Vermont, and its surroundings as potential summer vacation venues (the area had no problem drawing thousands of skiers during the winter months), had been trying for three years to convince a professional football team to conduct its preseason training in the area. Finally, in 1956, the Giants showed interest. Several team representatives visited Saint Michael's, which had offered the Giants the use of its football field, locker rooms, dining hall, and housing in Alumni Hall, a new dormitory that was completed shortly before the team arrived. Impressed with the campus, the facilities, and the overall peace and tranquility, the Mara family agreed to spend what would be the first of two consecutive preseasons at Saint Michael's. Wellington Mara had to be even further impressed when the new dormitory was formally opened and blessed by Burlington bishop Edward Francis Ryan the very morning of the day the first wave of players arrived on July 23.

Having just arrived fresh from the College All-Star Game, Huff and the four other rookies were called on to play in the team's annual intrasquad game at Centennial Field at the University of Vermont in Burlington. Playing both middle guard and linebacker, as Tom Landry alternated between 5-2 and 4-3 defensive combinations, Huff was all over the field, making more than a half dozen tackles. He also figured in what turned out to be the play of the game. As Don Chandler took the snap from center to punt, Huff broke past his blocker and literally snatched the ball off of Chandler's foot just before he made contact and raced forty yards for a touchdown, to the delight of a crowd of around five thousand. Further demonstrating his versatility, Huff then kicked the extra point in his team's 13–6 victory. It was, to say the least, an impressive debut for the rookie from West

Virginia.

Even so, Huff, after a few weeks in camp, worried that he did not fit into the Giants' plans. Tom Landry was in the process of developing a new defense wherein the two ends and the two tackles would form the defensive line (rather than the customary six or seven "down linemen") with three linebackers playing directly behind them. The revolutionary new defense would feature a middle linebacker, a position that Landry assigned to a former All-American from Georgia Tech named Ray Beck, a second-round draft pick by the Giants in 1952. Having played nose guard at West Virginia, the cocky and supremely confident Huff thought that he was perfectly cut out to play middle linebacker. And although he understood Landry's preference for the experienced and able Beck, he was too impatient to wait for a chance that just might come, as had happened to Robustelli with the Rams.

Making matters worse for Huff, the heralded rookie made a gaffe shortly after his belated arrival in Winooski Park. Eager to practice some placekicking, which he had done at West Virginia, Huff assumed, on the basis of the gray hair he saw beneath a baseball cap, that he had spotted a Giants coach.

"Hey, Coach, where are the kicking balls?" he called out.

The object of Huff's query turned out to be Charlie Conerly, who, fire in his eyes, turned to Huff, glared at him for a moment, then said, "Don't you ever dare call me coach again, you smart-ass rookie." Huff said he was sorry for the mistake but knew he had alienated the Giants' veteran quarterback, who was already sensitive about his less than youthful appearance. "I could laugh about it with Charlie later," Huff would say, "but it definitely wasn't funny at the time, and I was pretty embarrassed."

And things would only get worse. Far and away the most interesting development during the Giants' monthlong stay at Saint Michael's College was the introduction of Landry's new 4-3 defense. For years, teams had put either six or seven defensive players on the scrimmage line, with one or two linebackers and three defensive backs. By the early 1950s, though, most NFL teams were using what had become known as the "Eagle" defense, which consisted of a five-man line with two linebackers who played behind the ends. The defense was named after the Philadelphia Eagles, whose coach then, Earle "Greasy" Neale, was the first to use it in the 1940s. In passing situations, Frank "Bucko" Kilroy, the All-Pro two-way lineman who spent thirteen years with the Eagles, would move from his middle guard, or nose tackle, position on the front line to a standup position a few yards back to protect against a pass. In such alignments, the Eagles were, almost unwittingly, using what would become a proto-typical NFL defense.

With teams passing more and more each season, Landry reasoned that it made more sense to have as many as seven players behind the front line on a regular basis. So his alignment would include two ends and two tackles as down linemen, backed by three linebackers—left, right, and center—and two cornerbacks and two safeties, whose main purpose was to protect against the deep forward pass. The key player in the Landry defensive system, which he conceded was patterned after the Eagle defense, was the middle linebacker, who stationed himself about two yards behind where the middle guard usually played.

Some skeptics thought that Landry's "4-3" made the defense more vulnerable to a strong running game. Landry, though, theo-rized that a good linebacking corps, playing directly behind the front four, would lend more than enough run support and would also be in position to defend against short passes.

Huff, among others, reveled in the new concept. "I had played middle guard in college, so I was usually in the middle of the defense. But I was bent over in a stance, looking right into the opposing cen-ter's helmet," Huff said. "Now, when I played center linebacker"—Beck left Winooski Park as the starter at the position, but Huff would get his chances—"I was standing up, and I could see everything—and I mean everything, since I have peripheral vision." Not to mention cockiness, quickness, intelligence, and a killer instinct that seemingly made him an ideal candidate for the position.

However, only a few weeks after Huff reported to training camp, he overheard line coach Ed Kolman and another coach discussing rookies, including him, and how they might fit into the Giants' scheme.

"What are we going to do with this kid Huff?" one coach asked.

"I really don't know," the second coach replied. "He's a step too slow for offensive guard, and he's too light to play defense. Two hun-dred thirty-five pounds isn't enough weight for this league."

Huff walked away feeling that he most likely would be cut before the Giants left training camp. Despite solid play during practices, Huff became increasingly discouraged, as did punter Don Chandler. Finally, in late August, shortly before the team was to break camp, Huff and Chandler decided to leave. "There was a song called 'Detroit City' that was very popular at the time, and one of the lyrics—'I want to go home'—really used to get to us," Huff said. "And one day we heard it once too much, and I said, 'That's it. Let's leave.'" Chandler was more than willing.

Feeling that they owed it to the Giants, both players decided to turn in their playbooks to head coach Jim Lee Howell. Howell wasn't in his room, but Lombardi, who shared the room with Howell, was. As Huff recalled, "He called us every name in the book." Undeterred, Huff and Chandler went back to their rooms to pack. As Huff did, Ed Kolman came to his room, urging him to stay. "I told him I couldn't take Jim Lee Howell anymore, and that I was tired of him yelling and screaming at me," Huff said. Kolman, at his persuasive best, said, "Sam, you can be a star in this game and a great player, but you've got to stay in camp and stick it out. And I'll talk to Jim Lee and ask him to get off your back."

His shaken confidence restored by Kolman's words, Huff agreed to stay, but Chandler, still determined to leave, convinced another rookie, Jerry Harkrader, to drive him to the Burlington airport. Huff went along, mainly to try to get Chandler to change his mind, but the Giants' rookie kicker was adamant. As they sat in the waiting room at the airport, Lombardi burst in, having raced there in his station wagon. Furious, he unleashed a tirade at both Huff and Chandler. "Now, hold on! You may not make this club, Chandler, but you're sure as hell not quitting on me now! And neither are you, Huff, in case you've got any ideas of running out. Now get the hell back to Saint Michael's and be at practice tomorrow morning!"

Huff and Chandler did not have to be told twice by the red-faced Lombardi. They returned immediately to their dormitory rooms. Years later they remained grateful to Lombardi for convincing them to stay. "In a way, what we did worked," Huff said, "because from then on Howell stayed off our backs."

In later eras, such a scenario would seem impossible to imagine. But sports agents did not exist, and players, whether rookies or veterans, negotiated their salaries on their own, usually in one-on-one bargaining sessions or by phone. In the case of the Giants, players found Wellington Mara, who was in charge of player personnel, a hard bargainer. Players might ask for more than was offered but in the end knew that they had no choice.

Huff recalled his introduction to negotiating for a one-year contract as a rookie in 1956. Meeting Mara face-to-face for the first time, Huff was offered $5,000. "I told him I couldn't play for that little, since I had a wife and child to support," said Huff, who married while in high school.

"Well, what will you play for?" Mara asked.

"I told him I'd like at least seven thousand, and he said that might be possible," Huff recalled. "But then I told Well Mara that I wanted to run it past my coach at West Virginia, Pappy Lewis, to see what he thought," Huff recalled. "So, while Well Mara waited, I called Pappy."

" 'Mr. Mara wants me to sign for seven thousand. What do you think?' " I asked Pappy.

"Son, that's like stealing money," replied Lewis. "You get right back over there and sign that contract before he changes his mind."

Huff, following his old coach's instructions, did just that, securing for himself about $1,000 more than the average rookie's salary.

As for negotiating more shrewdly, the mechanics simply didn't exist. "I can never recall a player holding out during the six years I was the team's public relations director in the 1950s," Bob Daley said. "It just didn't happen." Said Robustelli, "I never remember anyone holding out while I was with the Rams or the Giants."

Then, too, free agency had not yet arrived in the NFL, and veteran players not only didn't have the option of going to another team, but, like rookies, were bound to the team with which they had contracts. In effect, especially with rookies, it was a take-it-or-leave-it situation, and talented rookies either took what was offered or, in some cases, signed with teams in the relatively new Canadian Football League for even less money. "You really didn't have much of a choice," recalled Robustelli.

"You didn't hold out, because you were scared of what might happen," said Dick Modzelewski, who never missed a game—180 in all—during fourteen seasons in the NFL. "You knew that if you didn't show up for training camp, they'd get someone else. Besides that, we were very disciplined, and that included getting to training camp on time."

Charlie Conerly, one of the NFL's best quarterbacks, was earning around $18,000 in 1956, which made him one of the highest-paid players in the league. "Whatever the Maras offered, I usually accepted," Conerly said. "The exception was my last year, when I wanted to be the highest-paid player in the league, and Wellington Mara offered me the thirty thousand dollars I asked for."

—

On August 20, Huff and the Giants' new front four of Robustelli, Katcavage, Modzelewski, and Roscy Grier, who had joined the Giants the year before, excelled as the team won its first exhibition game, beating the Baltimore Colts, 28–10, in Boston. It was there that the Giants first got to see a rookie quarterback for the Colts named John Unitas, who was harried throughout by Modzelewski in particular.

"Will you look at the goofy-looking son of a bitch," Charlie Conerly said to Frank Gifford when they saw the slender, slope-shouldered Unitas, with his crew cut and high-top shoes and his unusual follow-through passing motion. "Wonder where he came from?" Conerly wasn't the only one at Nickerson Field, once the home of the Boston Braves before they moved to Milwaukee, to wonder where in the world this quarterback came from. But both he and Gifford were soon very impressed.

Though it was only their first preseason game, it was clear that the Giants were much improved over the team that had gone 6-5-1 the previous season, particularly on defense. And with a veteran backfield of Conerly, Gifford, Alex Webster, and Mel Triplett, an experienced and solid offensive line, plus Gifford, Ken MacAfee, and Kyle Rote as the primary receivers, the offense clearly was going to be one of the best in the National Football League.

Training where they did and possessing promise as a team, the Giants gained thousands of new fans during their monthlong stay at Saint Michael's. "The Giants coming to Winooski Park was huge for the whole area," said Tony Adams, who at the time was the sports director for WCAX, the CBS television affiliate in Burlington, which in 1956 began to telecast Giants games. "The players were friendly, and the fans, who could watch them work out for free, got to see them close-up." They also got to hear Howell and Lombardi yell at their charges. "Lombardi was the loudest," Adams recalled. "I recall him screaming at Alex Webster, 'Alex, I told you to hit that hole! Run that play over until you do!' "

Fans also got to see some of the players close-up at the Mill, a popular bar only a short distance away from the Saint Michael's campus, where some of the Giants went following dinner at the campus dining hall. "There was never any trouble of any kind involving the players," Adams said. "And those who went to the Mill knew they had to be back by the eleven o'clock curfew." They also knew that Jim Lee Howell himself often would conduct a bed check at Alumni Hall, where the players, coaches, and other staff members stayed. Maybe the locker room was cramped, hot, and dismal, but the dormitory accommodations were above average for a training camp.

On August 23, with the squad pared down to forty-five players*, the Giants broke camp at Saint Michael's, leaving by bus for Albany, New York, where they would board a New York Central Railroad train for Wisconsin to play their second of six exhibition games.

"They made a lot of friends in the Burlington area, and even though the Patriots now play in Massachusetts, which is a lot closer than New York, the Giants still have a tremendous amount of fans around here more than fifty years after they first trained at Winooski Park," Tony Adams later said. "And you could tell they were going to be a very good team, especially with the new players they had."

This time around, Robustelli would leave Winooski Park in good shape, not on a stretcher with a broken leg. Though they would have to play eight more games on the road before doing so, the Giants also would be moving into a new and larger home, Yankee Stadium, after thirty years at the Polo Grounds. Just maybe, the Maras thought, the Yankees' winning tradition would rub off on the much-improved New York Giants football team and its new defensive right end from little Arnold College.

---

*The maximum during the season would be thirty-three compared with the forty-five that it gradually became in 1991 and remained into the twenty-first century.

3

Mr. High-Low and the Former Bomber Pilot

*N*o other coach in football history ever had two more illustrious assistants than Jim Lee Howell, the Giants' head coach, had in 1956. Since he was named to succeed Steve Owen as head coach in 1954, Howell's assistant coaches had been Tom Landry—an All-Pro defensive back for the Giants from 1950 through 1955, the year he was a player-coach—and Vince Lombardi. "With Tom and Vince, all I have to do is make sure the footballs are all blown up, send in the punter on fourth down, and decide whether to kick off or receive," Howell would often say in paying tribute to his talented assistants.

Not exactly. As brilliant and creative as Landry and Lombardi were, Howell ran the overall show. A towering six-foot-six former Giants end and then an assistant coach after serving as a captain in the Marine Corps during World War II, Howell had a commanding presence. Some players thought that he tried to succeed through intimidation, but it was also clear that he knew how to run an organization. "He was strict and ran the team like a CEO, delegating an awful lot of responsibility to Landry and Lombardi," Bob Daley said of Howell, "and that made sense, considering how good both Landry and Lombardi were as coaches." Pat Summerall, who joined the Giants in 1958, agreed. "Jim Lee was the glue who held the team together," he said.

Frank Gifford, though, had a contrary view of Howell, who coached the ends when Gifford joined the Giants in 1952. A favorite target of Howell's barbs even though he was the team's most versatile player and biggest star, Gifford felt that Howell disliked him because of his movie roles and because he occasionally did television commercials. At a team meeting during the 1957 season, on the Monday after a loss in which Gifford had missed a key block, Howell thundered, "We have some of these California hotshots who've gotten so big during the off-season that they're not a part of the team anymore. They've just got their minds on being movie stars." Coming as it did after Gifford had been named the NFL's MVP, the outburst shook him, and he finally walked away close to tears. Even some of his teammates cringed at Howell's diatribe.

Another time, following a practice at Fordham University, Howell unloaded in similar fashion in his booming Southern drawl. "And then there's Mr. Hollywood, number sixteen, the most valuable player in the National Football League. Right now he's the worst player on this football team." Recalling the incident, Sam Huff, no fan of Howell's either, said, "It was absolutely embarrassing, and I believe there were tears in Frank's eyes, although he didn't say a thing. And all of us were just squirming. The whole thing was totally uncalled for, because we all knew that Frank was going to be there when it counted in a game to make the big plays for us."

Yet most of the Giants seemed to like Howell, who owned and ran a cattle farm in Arkansas in the off-season and whose first two teams had posted winning records following a disastrous 3-9 season in 1953, the team's last year under Steve Owen. "He was an absolutely impartial and fair man who never played favorites," said tackle Rosey Grier, who often endured Howell's wrath for coming to camp far overweight or for gaining too much weight during the season—or both. "I loved the man."

Tom Scott, an All-Pro linebacker with the Philadelphia Eagles before joining the Giants in 1959, said that Howell spared virtually no one with his bellowing barbs during practice. "You're no All-Pro here, Scott!" he recalled Howell often yelling at him when he flubbed an assignment on the practice field. "I never took it personally, because he yelled at just about everybody except maybe Charlie Conerly." And that could have been because Conerly had been around since 1948 and had usually been blamed, unfairly, when the team lost.

Robustelli thought Howell was a good administrator who did an excellent job of delegating authority. "Jim Lee was very gracious with outsiders, and he would praise assistants without any hesitation or fear that they were usurping his role as head coach," Robustelli said. So much so that Howell was the first head coach to have the offensive and defensive coordinators meet with their teams separately to watch game films and to discuss future opponents. Indeed, Howell would be the first one to concede that having Landry and Lombardi as his chief assistants made life much easier for him. An example: Kyle Rote recalled how, while walking down a hallway in the team's training camp dormitory at Saint Michael's College one night, he saw both Landry and Lombardi watching film in their rooms. "Then when I walked past Jim Lee's room, I saw him lying in bed reading a newspaper," Rote said.

Besides being aware that he had two brilliant assistant coaches and pretty much leaving them to their own devices, Howell was not above deprecating his own abilities. For example, Howell was asked once whether, having coached at Wagner College, he had remembered Robustelli from when his Arnold College team played Wagner. "I recall him," Howell said. "But I couldn't have been overly impressed, since I didn't even tell the Giants that he was worth looking at. I guess that gives a line on what a smart talent scout I am."

Gifford's other complaint was that Howell was not a good strategist and lacked imagination as a coach. "Right from the first day on the job, Jim Lee Howell functioned as more of a figurehead than a head coach," Gifford was to say, adding that Howell "knew little or nothing about the tactics of pro football." That seemed an unkind cut, given that Howell had spent eight seasons as a two-way end for the Giants and a half dozen more as an assistant coach in charge of the offensive ends—while doubling as head coach at Wagner College on Staten Island, where Howell and his wife lived during the football season—before being named the Giants' head coach in 1954.

In return, years later, Howell conceded that he had not been impressed with Gifford during his early practice sessions as a rookie because he got the impression he wasn't going all out. "He had such a smooth, easy stride that it looked as if he was loafing," Howell said. "Matter of fact, some of the guys called him 'Tippy Toes.' If he hadn't been our first draft choice, we might have released him." Which was further proof that whatever Howell's talents were, they didn't include scouting.

At that, Gifford was not exactly impressed by being recruited by the Giants. For one thing, he has said that when he heard he had been the top draft choice of the Giants, he thought it was the New York Giants baseball team. That seems to have been disingenuous, since Gifford, having gone to college in Los Angeles, knew that the Los Angeles Rams existed; indeed, by 1951, Gifford's last year at USC, the Rams had drawn crowds of more than fifty thousand to the Los Angeles Coliseum, where USC also played its home game. By then, too, Gifford must have known that the NFL included the New York Giants—the football Giants, that is.

Gifford also has said that when he returned to Southern California after his first few seasons with the Giants, friends would ask him where he'd been and what he'd been doing over the last five months or so. That, too, seems unlikely—unless Gifford's friends didn't read newspapers—since the sports sections of the Los Angeles papers reported Gifford's exploits with the Giants. Gifford also said that he had been recruited by the Edmonton Eskimos of the Canadian Football League but decided to accept the Giants' offer of $8,000 for his rookie season because he at least knew where New York was. Living on the West Coast since he had been born, it seems unlikely that Gifford never would have heard of one of Canada's largest cities, especially since Edmonton is located in the Pacific Northwest.

———

The long train trip to Green Bay, Wisconsin, was not Vince Lombardi's first visit to the NFL's smallest city. A few years earlier, Lombardi had found himself and another Army assistant coach snowbound during a recruiting trip to Green Bay—the biggest (or smallest, depending on how one looks at it) anomaly in major league sports—to interview a prospective cadet football player. Turning to his coaching colleague, Lombardi expressed amazement that anyone could live in Green Bay (population: sixty-five thousand), particularly during the winter when the average temperature is about 25 degrees, although it often plunges below 0.

On this train ride, Lombardi had plenty to ponder. Prior to becoming the Giants' offensive coordinator in 1954, he had spent eight years as a football and basketball coach and physics and Latin teacher at a Catholic high school in New Jersey; then two years as a freshman and assistant football coach at his alma mater, Fordham, and then five years as an assistant at West Point. By now, he was beginning to won-

der if he would ever be a head coach. What was it going to take? At
St. Cecilia High School in Englewood, across the Hudson River from
Manhattan, his football team had gone unbeaten four years in a row.
Utilizing the still relatively new T formation, Lombardi's teams beat
some of the best high school teams in the New York metropolitan area
while winning the New Jersey state parochial school championship
in 1943. Still, he was rebuffed repeatedly for college head-coaching
jobs and finally settled for an assistant coach's position at Fordham,
which, by then, was in the process of de-emphasizing football. In
Lombardi's playing days in the 1930s, the Fordham Rams often drew
more than sixty thousand spectators to the Polo Grounds or Yankee
Stadium against such major powers as Tennessee and Pittsburgh, but
by 1947 Fordham was reduced to playing far less formidable opponents before much smaller crowds.

All the same, Lombardi instituted the T formation with his freshman team at Fordham, driving his charges harder than they had ever
been driven—to a point where they outplayed the varsity on several
occasions during weekly scrimmages. Lombardi was convinced that
he knew both how to coach and how to handle young football players, and knew as much, if not more, than a lot of former Fordham
teammates and other coaches younger than him who were getting
head-coaching jobs at top-tier college football programs around the
country. Was he being ignored because of his emotional way of coaching? Or could it be because he was Italian? (There were no coaches
of Italian extraction in the NFL at the time.) Lombardi was hardly
paranoid, yet he felt that for some reason or other, he was being overlooked, while other assistants he knew who were far less creative and
inspiring were getting ahead.

Lombardi's frustrations, exacerbated by his natural impatience,
continued to gnaw at him even during his first few years with the
Giants. When contacted by Wellington Mara late in 1953, Lombardi
thought he was going to be offered the head-coaching job and not the
position of offensive coordinator. Then, only a few weeks after his
first season with the Giants, Lombardi applied for, and was offered,
the head-coaching job at Fordham—only to have the agreement
dissolve when the university announced in mid-December of 1954
that it was dropping football. Shortly thereafter, Lombardi reached
a tentative agreement with Army coach Earl Blaik to return to West
Point as an assistant coach. But that arrangement also fell apart when

Mara, informed of it by Blaik, convinced Lombardi to remain with the Giants, virtually assuring him that he eventually would become the team's head coach.

By contrast, Tom Landry had no aspirations of becoming a head coach, one of many differences between the two men. After excelling as a defensive back with the Giants for six years (the last year as a playing coach at a time when most NFL teams, like the Giants, had only four assistant coaches), Landry became a full-time coach in 1956. Content to work for the Giants from July into December and then return to Texas to sell insurance, Landry had been working toward a master's degree in industrial engineering during the offseason. Having received the degree from the University of Houston in 1952, Landry was looking forward to a career in engineering after his playing days ended, but had been enticed to stay on for the 1956 season by Jim Lee Howell.

"I think my postgraduate training, which stressed coordinating people, helped me as a coach," Landry once said. "My approach was to blend players together as a single unit to establish a strong, solid defense. Under my plan, we hold a position and don't try to force through a block when it's not going to work. That way each player controls a specific area."

If Lombardi practically fit the stereotype of a New Yorker—brash, often loud and impatient, yet quick to laugh—Landry was a prototypical soft-spoken, methodical, and serious man of the Texas plains; in his case the small south Texas border town of Mission, where he had grown up and become a high school football star. Where Lombardi openly showed his emotions, Landry rarely ever changed his somewhat dour expression. When the Giants played flawlessly on defense—even making a dramatic goal-line stand or running back an interception for a touchdown—he remained unflappable. They were *supposed* to do those things, Landry reasoned, and thus there was no cause to celebrate. And if the defense broke down, his expression remained the same.

Jim Lee Howell understood Landry's approach. "Tom is a warm person, but not with his players," said Howell. "He gets impatient with them, and he doesn't pat them on the back. He expects them to go out there and do their jobs. He's also a perfectionist like Paul Brown [then the coach of the Cleveland Browns]. And he's smarter than anyone."

Robustelli, somewhat similar in nature, also appreciated Landry's stoic and sometimes enigmatic style. "Tom tolerated our mistakes because he knew he could correct them, but not during a game," said Robustelli, who had played against Landry while he was with the Los Angeles Rams. "And if we lost a game, Tom didn't get moody like Lombardi, who might go days after the defeat without talking to any of the players. Unlike Vince, who was always trying to motivate his offensive players with his fiery personality, Tom chose to motivate you through preparation, which he thought was the best motivator."

Another key difference, at least in the eyes of many Giants, was their life experience. Landry was born and raised in a small town in Texas's Rio Grande Valley, the son of a mechanic and father of six who bartered automotive work for fruits and vegetables grown by area farmers. After playing one season, in 1942, at the University of Texas, Landry's studies and football with the powerful Longhorns were interrupted for three years when he joined the Army Air Corps in the middle of World War II in February of 1943 and became a lieutenant and copilot. He served aboard a B-17 Flying Fortress bomber that completed thirty missions in Europe. During one mission, Landry's plane ran out of fuel and crash-landed in a stand of trees in Belgium. Like so many American servicemen who saw action during World War II, Landry tended to downplay such dangerous escapades. "Oh, we got a few holes in our bomber once in a while," Landry was prone to saying when asked about his experiences in the Army Air Corps, "but nothing much really happened."

Returning to the University of Texas as a twenty-two-year-old sophomore in the fall of 1946, Landry became the backup quarterback to eventual Pro Football Hall of Famer Bobby Layne before being moved to fullback on a team that recorded victories in the Sugar Bowl in 1948 and the Orange Bowl in 1949. A few weeks after Texas beat the University of Georgia in the Orange Bowl game, Landry married Alicia Wiggs, also a Texan, whom Landry had met on a blind date in 1947 when she was a freshman and Landry a junior at Texas.

After one season with the New York Yankees of the All-America Football Conference in 1949 (the league's last), Landry joined the Giants in 1950 as a defensive back and punter who during his first four years also occasionally played halfback—and part of one game at quarterback—and ran back kickoffs and punts.

If the backgrounds of Landry and Lombardi were vastly different, so too were their personalities. "They were both superb coaches, but they were as different as daylight and dark," Jim Lee Howell said. "They were also very fine people."

Howell, Landry, and Lombardi, along with the rest of the Giants' staff, were among those who showed up every day at 5:30 in the afternoon at training camp for the Five-Thirty Club, a loose-knit organization formed by Jack Mara some time ago. Sportswriters and other members of the media, both locals and visiting writers like Red Smith, W. C. Heinz, Frank Graham, Dan Parker, and Milton Gross from New York papers, were invited to drop in at one of the dormitory rooms at whatever college they were training at from 5:30 to 6:00 p.m. for drinks. The atmosphere was convivial, with general manager Ray Walsh and Jack and Wellington Mara mixing with the writers and friends of the Maras who had come to visit, along with the team chaplain, Benedict Dudley, and the team's legendary doctor, Francis Sweeny, who is believed to have started the club with Jack Mara. The one iron-clad rule was that whatever was said during the half-hour gathering was strictly off the record.

Sweeny, a brother-in-law of former coach Steve Owen, had been with the Giants since their inception and also was the doctor for sports teams at Manhattan College in New York. Very much a part of the team, the five-foot-five Sweeny would pace along the sidelines during a game, screaming at officials and, when the Giants played the Bears, at his archenemy George Halas, who was revered by many but not by "Doc" Sweeny.

"Doc was of the old school who felt that, more often than not, a couple of aspirin or a few belts of Scotch could solve any physical problem," Don Smith said. "And he was dead-set against a player undergoing surgery, especially during the season. I remember a period during the late fifties when Charlie Conerly had a sore right arm and could hardly throw, and an orthopedic doctor said he might have to go under the knife to get it fixed. But Doc overruled the orthopedist and called in a dentist friend of his whose name, and this is the God's truth, was Dr. Croaker. Sure enough Dr. Croaker found that Charlie had an abscessed wisdom tooth. He drained it, and in a couple of days Charlie's arm was fine. But that was Doc Sweeny, who had his own medical theories, and stayed with the Giants for a long, long time."

Bad as the weather in Green Bay was during the winter, the Packers had been just as bad during the fall, not having turned in a winning record since 1947. But when the Giants arrived for the August 25 exhibition game, only five days and a long train trip after their first exhibition against the Colts in Boston, Green Bay had a promising rookie quarterback from the University of Alabama named Bart Starr, who had been overlooked until the seventeenth round of the 1956 draft. Starr performed brilliantly, both with his dexterous fakes and deft short passing game, and the Packers beat the Giants, 17–13, before a paltry crowd of fewer than seventeen thousand spectators. Winning was nice, especially over a team like these formidable Giants, but to the Packers' coach, Lisle Blackbourn, observing his young quarterback and several other promising rookies was far more important.

Still, like most preseason National Football League games, the Giants-Packers exhibition was a precursor of absolutely nothing.* Jim Lee Howell used his regulars sparingly; Charlie Conerly, for example, did not play until late in the second half, when the Giants scored their only touchdown on a 1-yard plunge by Alex Webster after Conerly connected with passes to Frank Gifford and Kyle Rote that gained more than 50 yards. Late entry into games would become the norm for Conerly during the ensuing season because of a new scheme devised by Howell: starting Don Heinrich, now in his third year with the Giants, so that Conerly could observe the opposition's defense and thus make things easier for Conerly when he went into a game. Conerly chafed at the system, since whenever Heinrich played very well, Howell would tend to leave him in the game and, at times,

---

*NFL coaches rarely leave their veteran players on the field for more than a quarter in preseason games, both because they know what they can do and to avoid injuries. Indeed, many NFL players believe that preseason games are too risky. Also, unlike in bygone years—such as the 1950s—when most players had full-time off-season jobs, most modern-day players spend much of their time between seasons working out, since they don't have to work during the off-season to make ends meet, so generally they are in very good shape when they report to training camp in July. It is also commonly believed that the preseason games are played primarily for monetary reasons. By the 1990s, for example, it was common for NFL season ticket-holders to have to pay for a specific number of preseason home games in addition to those played during the regular season, which, by 2007, were costing an average of $100 a game. With almost every player in the NFL earning more than $1 million, and many at least five times that much, team managements were not about to put an end to the cash cow that preseason games had become.

not insert Conerly until sometime in the second half—and in one game, not at all. Conerly, the consummate team player, did not complain, but at one point during the season, he did mention that the players' bench offered the worst possible viewpoint of a game, and thus he gained nothing from watching Heinrich operate the offense.

Green Bay's veteran quarterback, Tobin Rote, who would lead the NFL in passing during the 1956 season, ran 8 yards for the Packers' first touchdown. He then made way for Starr, who guided the home team on a 73-yard drive in the third period and scored what proved to be the winning touchdown on a quarterback sneak from the 1-yard line.

—

With the next two exhibition games scheduled to be played in the Pacific Northwest against the Los Angeles Rams in Seattle and then the San Francisco 49ers in Portland, the Giants entrained for Oregon, where they would set up another training camp, this one at the University of Portland. Indeed, because of Jim Lee Howell's aversion to flying, almost all Giants road trips were made by train while he was the head coach. As at Saint Michael's, the squad, now down to about forty-five players, was housed in a dormitory, ate together in the campus dining hall, endured bed checks, and practiced twice a day at Multnomah Stadium in downtown Portland. The Giants would remain on the University of Portland campus for almost two weeks until leaving for Chicago to play the Bears and then going on to Memphis for a final exhibition game on September 23 against the Chicago Cardinals. By then the Giants would have played six exhibition games over a five-week span, all of them on the road and three in non-NFL cities. After that they could look forward to their first three regular season games—all on the road, in San Francisco, Chicago, and Cleveland—before finally opening at their new home field, Yankee Stadium, against the Pittsburgh Steelers on October 21. Bizarre as this schedule was, it was typical for the Giants of the 1950s, and it would become even more so after the move to Yankee Stadium, since the Yankees were in the World Series every year but two from 1949 through 1964.

Yet the Giants consistently made the best of it. Leaving their West Coast base, the Giants won their next two exhibitions, beating Robustelli's old team, the Los Angeles Rams, 20–10, and the San

Francisco 49ers, 21–14. In what amounted to a homecoming for Don Heinrich, the quarterback delighted a crowd of about twenty-five thousand at his alma mater, the University of Washington, by completing 9 of 17 passes for 101 yards, including one for a touchdown. The following week, Heinrich also played well while Conerly led the Giants to two last-quarter touchdowns in defeating the 49ers before a crowd of almost thirty thousand in Portland—not bad for an NFL exhibition in a city without a professional football team.

By then it was becoming clear that this Giants team was the best in years. Conerly and Heinrich at quarterback and Gifford, Webster, and Mel Triplett as the primary running backs operated behind an outstanding offensive line which included Rosey Brown, Ray Wietecha, and Jack Stroud. With Kyle Rote having developed into an outstanding receiver, the offense was clearly one of the most effective in the NFL. So too was the defense, whose new front four had quickly jelled into a cohesive and punishing unit while playing in front of a superb linebacking corps that included Bill Svoboda, Cliff Livingston, and Harland "Swede" Svare, in addition to Beck and Huff and a secondary comprised of the incomparable Emlen Tunnell, Jimmy Patton, Dick Nolan, Ed Hughes, and another former Ram, Herb Rich. Added to that sterling mix was the impressive punting and occasional placekicking of rookie Don "Babe" Chandler, who, in his second season, would lead the NFL in punting average in 1957.

If other teams were taking notice of this solid team, few of the dozen New York City daily newspapers were. None of them was covering the Giants' exhibitions—not even with part-time stringers—but were relying entirely on the Associated Press, whose accounts were confined almost entirely to offensive play.

But a mere recap couldn't possibly explain the team's improvement. The defense was benefiting manifestly from the presence of new personnel, as well as the introduction of Landry's innovations, but what about the offense? Following a bad start the previous year, the Giants won five of their last six games while averaging 27 points a contest. In large measure, the turnabout occurred because of the introduction of what would become a Lombardi trademark: the power sweep. The concept had, in fact, been developed by Lombardi and the Giants' line coach, Ed Kolman—a native of Brooklyn, like Lombardi, who had been a tackle on the powerhouse Chicago Bears teams of the 1940s. Knowing that Jim Lee Howell was in dire need of an offensive spark,

Lombardi and Kolman proposed the tactic in midseason.

"We think Ed and I have something that will help," Lombardi told Howell.

"Let's have it, then," the coach replied.

Lombardi and Howell then described the power sweep, a play that essentially combined a dose of old-time single-wing blocking with the T formation that Steve Owen had adopted in 1949, plus elements of the Giants' old A formation. It included two running backs who were stationed behind the quarterback but who took snaps directly from the center, the difference being that opposing linemen would be double-blocked at the point where a ball carrier would key on a particular hole in the line or on a run to the outside.

"Everyone is brush blocking in the T these days," Lombardi explained in referring to quick, temporary blocks of an opponent. "So Ed and I thought that if we could put some double-team blocking into our running game, we'd catch a lot of teams by surprise."

The Giants had done just that during their last five games of 1955. Most of the time, the play featured both guards pulling out as blockers around end for either Gifford or Webster, who would follow them, Triplett, and an end and a tackle. The keys in both situations were for the Giants' ends and tackles—depending on which side the sweep was being run to—to double-team the opponent's defensive end, while the guards double-blocked an outside linebacker. The play, later adopted by several other NFL teams, most notably the Green Bay Packers, became the talk of the NFL. "What a difference it made for us at the end of the 1955 season," Howell was to say.

Another consequence of the power sweep was that it further secured the respect Lombardi had fought hard to win. Not many Giants had ever heard of the Seven Blocks of Granite at Fordham, of which Lombardi was one, but they did know that he had never played in the NFL, which all of their other coaches had. So what right, more than a few of them thought, did this obnoxious guy who had only been a high school coach and then a freshman and assistant coach at Fordham and Army have to scream, rant, and rave at players who not only were NFL veterans, but in some cases had spent years in the South Pacific fighting the Japanese or in Europe battling the Germans? Making Lombardi's style all the more disturbing to some veterans was the fact that his defensive counterpart, Landry, never raised his voice while talking to his defensive players.

"Quite a few players were turned off by Lombardi's style at the start," Bob Daley recalled. "Their reaction was sort of 'Who is this guy, anyway?'" Even Lombardi's son, Vince Jr., recalled his father's aggressive, and even belligerent, manner. "I remember once, when the Giants were at Saint Michael's, a spectator called out to Gene Filipski, who was standing near me, and said, 'Gene, is he always that loud?'" he recalled. "Gene was kind of embarrassed and nodded toward me, I guess to indicate the guy was talking about my father. And the guy then said, 'Well, I guess maybe he should know about it.' Of course, I already did."

Making matters worse, Lombardi tried, at the outset, to implement Army's option T, which required the quarterback to run either right or left and then decide whether to throw a pass or pitch the ball to a trailing back. In no uncertain terms, Lombardi soon learned that there was no way that Charlie Conerly, at the age of thirty-three and with sore, battered knees, was going to run an option of any kind.

But sensing the resentment of Conerly, Gifford, and a few others, Lombardi eventually began to drop in to see Giants veterans in their dormitory rooms at Willamette University to get their reactions to his coaching philosophy and to plays he had devised. As Gifford was to recount some years later, Lombardi even went so far as to ask some of the veterans for help. "What he really was telling us was, 'Come on, I need your help,'" Gifford said. And it worked. "That changed the whole tone of our relationship. All of a sudden, we found ourselves wanting to help him. And we discovered that he was a real guy, a warm, funny guy."

It was the second time that Lombardi had ingratiated himself with Gifford. When he joined the Giants at their training camp in 1954, he introduced himself to Gifford and immediately said, "I've looked at a lot of film, and you can forget about playing on defense. From now on, you're my left halfback." As good a defensive back as he was, that was great news to Gifford, who knew that running a football was really his strongest suit.

As time went on, and Lombardi developed a rapport with the veterans, he became more relaxed and more confident. "As he stayed around us more and more, and around the pro game more, the mystique wasn't what he imagined it to be," said Kyle Rote. "Finally, instead of asking us how much we'd like to play in preseason games, he said to us for the first time, 'You're going to play the whole first half and a little of the second half,' and we realized he'd caught up with us."

Where the team's two very different chief assistant coaches were similar—and this helps to further explain the Giants' success—was in their dedication. While Lombardi instructed with passion and gusto, Landry's single-mindedness and focus became legendary. "Tom was a great teacher, and he could become totally preoccupied during the week leading up to a game," said Robustelli, who often rode with Landry to practices at Yankee Stadium. "All we talked about was defense, both to Yankee Stadium and back home to Stamford. That was Tom, totally preoccupied with football and very creative."

Sam Huff also vividly remembered Landry's preoccupation. "My first few years with the Giants, I lived at the Concourse Plaza Hotel near Yankee Stadium and then at the old Excelsior Hotel in Manhattan near Central Park, as did Tom Landry and some of the other Giants," he said. "And quite often at night, Tom would call me and ask me to come up to his apartment to go over some defensive schemes he was considering. Tom was already a genius in his first year as a full-time coach, which was 1956, the year I joined the team. He was very methodical and didn't show any emotion, which led some people to think he was a cold person. But he wasn't; he cared deeply about his players. He once told me that he believed the team reacts the way he reacts, and that if he showed he was upset or emotional when a player got hurt, the players would notice it and would lose their concentration, and so he never wanted any display of emotion by him to break his players' concentration. But Tom really did care about the players. He really did. Only he never showed it."

And certainly Landry didn't understand why Lombardi insisted on showing it so much. "I used to call him Mr. High-Low," Landry once said. "When his offense did well, he would be sky-high, but when they didn't, you couldn't talk to him, maybe not for two or three days." But, contrary to rumors at the time, especially when Landry's defense overshadowed Lombardi's offense, Landry maintained that he and Lombardi had a good relationship.

And together they had good reason to respect each other and to look forward to the 1956 season.

4

The Marlboro Man

*A*mong the Giants' strong nucleus returning from the 1955 season were the two senior members of the team, thirty-five-year-old quarterback Charlie Conerly, who had been on the verge of retiring several times because of the physical punishment he had taken while operating behind a somewhat porous offensive line since joining the team, and Emlen Tunnell, the thirty-four-year-old All-Pro safety walk-on who became a Giant the same year. After that, in succession, had come All-Pro offensive guard Bill Austin; center Ray Wietecha, believed to be the first NFL center to snap the ball to the quarterback in the "no-look" fashion that was eventually accepted universally; offensive linemen Dick Yelvington and Jack Stroud; and Kyle Rote, an All-American halfback from Southern Methodist University and the country's number one draft pick in 1951. Rote, one of the most popular Giants of all time—seven of his teammates were to name sons after him—was a dazzling runner. When knee injuries ended his career as a running back after three seasons in the NFL, he became one of the league's best pass receivers and open-field runners. In 1952 the Giants' first-round draft choice was another All-American running back, Frank Gifford of Southern California.

Others returning from the 1955 squad were quarterbacks Don Heinrich and Bobby Clatterbuck; linebackers Harland Svare, Ray Beck, Cliff Livingston, and Bill Svoboda; the superb offensive tackle Rosey Brown; defensive backs Dick Nolan and Herb Rich; defensive linemen Rosey Grier and Walt Yowarsky; receivers Bob

Schnelker and Ken MacAfee; and running backs Alex Webster, Mel Triplett, and Bobby Epps.

———

Though far from being gregarious, Andy Robustelli soon felt at home with this squad, and not just because he was less than an hour's drive from his hometown in Connecticut. Soon to turn thirty-one on December 6, Robustelli was one of the oldest members of the team. And having already established himself as an All-Pro defensive end with a powerful Los Angeles Rams team, Robustelli found that he was looked at as a leader by the younger defensive linemen: Grier, Katcavage, Modzelewski, and Yowarsky. All of them soon realized that Robustelli was both an inspirational force and a highly intelligent and perceptive player, quick to discern an offensive lineman's weaknesses and a quarterback's intentions, along with being perhaps the quickest and most nimble pass rusher in the NFL. He also had an uncanny knack of picking up a quarterback's cadence. "Quarterbacks often repeat themselves in certain situations, and I would capitalize on it," Robustelli said. "Another advantage I had, I guess, was that I rarely was anxious or nervous before or during a game," he said. And perhaps no defensive end was ever better at blocking punts. "I understand that's one of the main reasons the Rams drafted me—that and the fact that I seemed to recover quite a few fumbles." Many of which, although he wouldn't say so, he had forced.

Friendly and quick to smile, Robustelli blended in well with the rest of the squad, which he soon knew was going to be as good as, if not better than, the Rams team that had traded him away. Making Robustelli feel especially at home was his being reunited with former Rams teammates Harland Svare—who had been perhaps his best friend there—Herb Rich, Ed Hughes, and placekicker Ben Agajanian. "It was like a reunion," Robustelli was to say later. "And I realized right away that all the talk about a 'Giants family' was true; it was a close-knit group in large part because of the Mara family. The guys who had been there for a while couldn't have made me feel more comfortable. And the same was true of the Maras."

Robustelli also soon found that in Tom Landry he had an extraordinarily innovative defensive coach and one of the most creative coaches in the NFL. "Tom was a great teacher, and he never stopped teaching, since he was always coming up with something new," Robustelli recalled. "He made us believers in his four-three defense and everything else he taught us. It was because he had absolute confidence in everything he told us to do, and that confidence carried over to us on the field. He tolerated our mistakes, but not if you screwed up too often in a game, because if you did, he'd bench you. And when we made mistakes collectively during a game, he'd say, 'Okay, you know what you did wrong. Now it's up to you to do it right.' That was it. Tom was no screamer, but he was so preoccupied with his defensive schemes that you could walk right past him, and he wouldn't even notice you. And he wasn't being rude; it was just that he was so caught up in what he was thinking about. He was the same during a game, stoic and always in complete control. It made no difference whether we made a great goal-line stand or allowed a touchdown. He might make some adjustments because of the touchdown, but otherwise he wouldn't say a word."

If Robustelli was a big admirer of Landry's, the feeling was mutual. For one thing, Landry never had to worry about motivating Robustelli. In a way, Robustelli was Landry's presence on the field: a soft-spoken yet stern leader.

"When you analyze Andy Robustelli piecemeal, there's little about him that suggests a great end," Landry once said. "He seems lacking in size, speed, and other traits. But as soon as you put them all together, you have the best there is. The main reason Robustelli's better than anyone else is because he puts more book time into his work than others do. The average star football player is pretty much of an instinctive athlete. Robustelli's more than that. He thinks, not only on the field but in his room at home. Watch him juke an opponent, and you're watching a real master. Terrific speed of mind, hands, and feet make him the best. But without his burning desire, those qualities would be only so-so. He pours in that something extra."

———

If Robustelli soon took on the mantle of the leader of Landry's defense, Charlie Conerly was clearly the leader of the offense, as he had been for almost a decade.

A single-wing halfback at the University of Mississippi, Conerly was one of thousands of college and professional football players whose careers were interrupted by World War II. In Conerly's case, the interruption came after he had spent two years playing for Ole

Miss and joined the marines as a private, eventually rising to corporal. While on duty in the South Pacific, Conerly had a close call that threatened to end not only his football career but his life. On patrol on the island of Guam in 1945, Conerly's rifle was shot out of his hands by a Japanese sniper perched in a palm tree. Remarkably, Conerly was not injured. Years later, Conerly's mother gave his wife, Perian, the mangled gun clip from the rifle that had been blasted out of his hands. Charlie had never told his wife that he'd brought back the damaged gun clip, his only souvenir of his three years in the marines.

While Conerly was in the South Pacific in 1945, his mother sent him a letter from the Washington Redskins informing Conerly that they had drafted him. His college class had already graduated, so he was eligible for the NFL draft. Conerly wrote back, "Tell them I'll be glad to come." Of course, he could not, as an infinitely tougher assignment was at hand. Alex Webster, a teammate of Conerly's for seven years, recalled Conerly telling him, "If a war breaks out in the future, do all that you can to stay out of it. I was scared to death all the while I was in the marines in the Pacific." After that experience, Conerly was to say in later years, the sight of a 250-pound tackle bearing down on him paled in comparison.

Deciding to forgo the NFL at least for a while, Conerly reenrolled at Ole Miss in the fall of 1946 at the age of twenty-five. Declining to take note of the three years spent away from the Mississippi campus, the sports information office merely added one year to his age when he had last played as a sophomore in 1942, making him a twenty-two-year-old junior. "Charlie never lied about his age," Perian Conerly said later. "The sports information people at Ole Miss just made him younger, and then the Giants picked up on it."

She was right. Conerly, when asked, was honest about his age. In 1957, a sportswriter who had described Conerly as an "amazing old pro at thirty-three" in a story, asked the Giants quarterback when he would turn thirty-four.

"Been there," said Conerly, using a minimum of words, as usual. "I'll be thirty-six on September the nineteenth."

Conerly's decision to return to Ole Miss turned out to be beneficial, both for him and the football team, especially during his senior year in 1947, when, as the Rebels' single-wing tailback, he completed 133 of 232 passes, 18 of them for touchdowns, while amassing 1,366 yards, running for 9 touchdowns, and averaging 40.2 yards on 58 punts. No other Division I halfback had a better season, and Conerly was named an All-American. Despite his gaudy statistics, however, the Redskins, with the legendary Sammy Baugh and rookie Harry Gilmer at quarterback, were set at that position and traded him to the Giants. First, though, Conerly passed up a five-year contract offer from Branch Rickey, who was then owner of the Brooklyn Dodgers football team of the struggling All-America Football Conference, which had started in 1946. According to varying newspaper reports, Rickey's offer ranged from $80,000 to $100,000, an unheard of amount for a rookie or even most stars. Years later Conerly was to say that the amounts reported in the press were news to him. "If it had been for that much, I might have signed," Conerly said. In explaining his decision to go with the Giants, he said, "They'll probably be around a while longer, and who knows what will happen to the new league."*

In signing a five-year contract with the Giants for $62,500, one of the most lucrative ever in the NFL at the time, Conerly was aligning himself with a team that, after winning the NFL's Eastern Division title in 1946, had finished last in 1947 with a 2-8-2 record. Both Wellington Mara and Giants head coach Steve Owen had been watching Conerly play in the Delta Bowl on January 1, 1948. In the Giants' first few games in 1948, before the team switched to the T formation, Conerly played left halfback and played it well, running 40 times for 160 yards, an average of 4 yards a carry, and scoring five touchdowns, half of what he would score during his fourteen years with the Giants. Eventually he would supplant the previous year's quarterback, former Columbia University star and native New Yorker Paul Governali. It was rare for a rookie quarterback to become a starter so soon, but, then, Conerly was hardly a typical rookie. He was twenty-seven years old, battle hardened, and possessed of the maturity and poise of a veteran. A slim and lanky six-foot-one-inch 185-pounder, Conerly, if anything, always looked older than his years when he was with the Giants, even when he reached forty. Soft-spoken when he talked—"yep" and "nope" seemed to be his favorite responses at post-

---

*What happened was that it folded after the 1949 season with four of its franchises (the Baltimore Colts, the Cleveland Browns, the New York Yankees, and the San Francisco 49ers) joining the NFL in 1950. That year the league created an Eastern and Western Conference to replace the Eastern and Western divisions.

game press conferences—Conerly had a leathery visage that seemed to evoke a cowboy on horseback on a plain in the Old West. Indeed, Conerly was so symbolic of the Old West that in the 1950s he became one of the first of the Marlboro Men. These male models for Marlboro cigarettes appeared in television commercials, newspaper and magazine advertisements, and on billboards across the country, and came across as quintessentially rugged cowboys of the prairie. Though Conerly's name was not used in the commercials and advertisements, he was recognizable to Giants fans, and, unlike many athletes who endorse products but never use them, Conerly never shied away from admitting that, yes, this particular Marlboro Man did indeed enjoy the product.

With Conerly throwing for more yardage (2,175 yards) and more touchdowns (22) than he would in thirteen subsequent years with the Giants, the 1948 team finished 4-8 while giving up a then–NFL record 388 points. In perhaps his best outing, Conerly completed 36 of 53 passes for 363 yards and 3 touchdowns against the Pittsburgh Steelers, who still managed to win, 38–28. Conerly's overall accomplishments earned him rookie of the year honors and made it evident that the Giants had found the quarterback of their future. But it would be a future of highs and lows, of adulation and disdain, of winning and losing seasons. Conerly would maintain a love-hate relationship with fans and sportswriters and sportscasters, especially during his early years, while establishing a quiet leadership role with the team.

Like many athletes, Conerly had his quirks. One was his relationship, or lack thereof, with rookies in training camp. "Charlie would tell me he had no interest in knowing who a rookie was unless, and until, he made the team," said Don Smith, who succeeded Robert Daley as the Giants' public relations director in 1960. "And even when they did, he didn't talk to the rookies very often." Conerly summed up his attitude toward rookies when he said, "I don't want to waste time talking to them, because most of them aren't going to be around once the season begins." Considering how Chuckin' Charlie (as he was called while at Ole Miss) didn't say much to veterans, either, that attitude was not surprising.

As often happens in football, the quarterback bore the brunt of fans' ire when things went wrong. That he had seen action in the marines during World War II mattered not a whit to many Giants fans. Indeed, when the Giants lost their last two games in Conerly's first year and then lost four of six home games in 1949, when the team finished 6-6, Conerly heard more boos than cheers. The booing subsided, but most certainly did not end entirely, during the next three seasons, when the Giants posted winning records, including a 10-2 mark in 1950 that earned the team a first-place tie in the Eastern Conference. In the eyes of many, including Conerly, those winning seasons were attributable to the changeover to the T formation in 1949, as that was the year that Giants management hired twenty-six-year-old Allie Sherman to teach the still relatively new formation to Conerly.

Despite the Giants' successes in 1950, 1951, and 1952, by which time they were using the T almost exclusively, Conerly was booed often in 1953, when the Giants won only three of twelve games, and Conerly threw a career-high 25 interceptions, compared with NFL lows of 7 in 1950 and 10 in 1952.

"Charlie gets blamed for everything that goes wrong, and every criticism of him is absolutely wrong," said Eddie Price, a Giants running back from 1950 through 1955. "There isn't a better passer in the league than Charlie, but he can't do it alone. Our offensive line is inexperienced and doesn't give Charlie any protection." Price himself was painfully aware of the Giants' inexperienced line, as his rushing average fell from 4 yards a carry in 1952 to 2 yards in 1953, which turned out to be Steve Owen's last year and the last losing season Conerly would endure.

Reflecting on the booing by Giants fans, Conerly, easygoing as always, said years later, "They got pretty rough at times, but, hell, they were paying their money to see us play, and then, too, the booing didn't bother me none."

What did bother him, though, was being booed when he wasn't even playing, as once happened at a hockey game at Madison Square Garden. To Conerly's surprise, he and some other Giants players were introduced by the public address announcer. "It was embarrassing out there in public," Conerly recalled of the booing, which was directed at him. "But, then, I was the quarterback, and they figured when things went wrong, it was my fault." As a result of that episode, Conerly said he and his wife rarely went out in public, except following home games. Then they went to places like Toots Shor's, where Conerly was not likely to be booed. Referring to the occasional public ridicule he endured, Conerly said, "I didn't want my wife to have to put up with that."

—

Following the abysmal 1953 season, Conerly decided, yet again, to retire. He was only thirty-two years old but felt that working the two-hundred-acre farm that he had bought for his parents in his hometown of Clarksdale, Mississippi, was a lot easier on his body than being slammed to the turf repeatedly by 250-pound linemen. That was upsetting news to Jim Lee Howell, who had been named to succeed Steve Owen as the Giants' head coach. Well aware that Conerly was an integral part of the Giants' offense, Howell, himself a Southerner, from Arkansas, went to visit Conerly while he was on a business trip with a friend, demonstrating the use of a new tractor on a farm in Missouri. "I told Charlie I wished he'd change his mind and come back because we needed him," Howell was to say. "Charlie told me he was tired of getting hit so often, but I promised him things would get better." Trying to be as persuasive as possible, Howell then guaranteed Conerly that offensive tackle Rosey Brown and other young linemen such as Jack Stroud, Ray Beck, and Ray Wietecha were bound to be much improved in 1954. And besides, Howell told Conerly as he sat on the tractor, Tom Landry, an outstanding defensive back with whom Conerly was friendly, was to become the team's defensive coach in 1954.

Howell's visit paid off. The coach knew that in making those predictions he was taking a chance and that, in fact, things could get worse. Fortunately, for both men, they got a lot better. In addition to better protection, Conerly found himself with two new rookie receivers, Bob Schnelker and Ken MacAfee, who could go reasonably deep, something the Giants had previously lacked. The pair would catch eight touchdown passes each in 1954. Another new pass catcher, Barney Poole, was the third (and last) Poole brother to play for the Giants—all of them ends—since 1937.

In a remarkable turnaround, the Giants won six of their first eight games. But then, in large measure because of season-ending injuries to Gifford in the ninth game and Conerly in the tenth, the Giants lost three of their last four to finish at 7-5, much improved over their 3-9 record in 1953. In one of the season's most significant developments, Kyle Rote, newly converted to a wide receiver because of his damaged knees, averaged a team-high 19 yards on 29 passes and was selected for the Pro Bowl game. Further bolstering the Giants' offense was the team's new placekicker, Ben Agajanian, who made all 35 of his extra-point attempts and was successful on 13 of 25 field-goal tries. Like Tom Dempsey of the New Orleans Saints—who for a while held an NFL record with a 63-yard field goal in 1970—the thirty-five-year-old Agajanian defied logic as a kicker, since he had lost all but the little toe on his kicking foot in an accident while in college and kicked with a specially made right shoe. Even though Conerly missed the last three games of the season, he threw his one hundredth career touchdown pass in his final game, something that only two other quarterbacks, stars Sammy Baugh and Sid Luckman, had ever done.

Self-effacing as always, Conerly would not put himself in their class. Years later he said, "I don't know if I was a good passer or not, but I could see the field." Conerly went on to say, "I thought I was average. I couldn't throw the ball too far, but, then, I usually never had anybody who could go deep." Which was true until the Giants got Schnelker and MacAfee, and, even more so, Del Shofner near the end of Conerly's career. However, Conerly was being modest when he said he could not throw "too far." When he had to, or chose to, Conerly could fling a football as far as any quarterback. He just had to make sure he had a receiver who could race down 40 or 50 yards fast enough to catch it. As Frank Gifford once said, the team was short on quality receivers when Gifford arrived as a two-way player in 1952. Although Conerly never complained about dropped passes, poorly run routes, or a receiver's inability to catch up with one of his long passes, Gifford speculated that Conerly felt that he, Gifford, was his only reliable receiver, and probably thought to himself, *All I got is Giff, and he ain't much*. But, like the boos he heard so often during his early years with the Giants, Conerly was not about to find fault with anyone but himself.

"Charlie was unflappable, in good times and bad," Robustelli said. "He was a ruggedly handsome, soft-spoken Southern gentleman, and all of us looked up to him because he was a link to the past and had taken so many physical beatings and endured all that booing when he was playing with bad teams."

—

From the standpoint of personnel, the Giants were a lot better in 1955 with the addition of Webster, Triplett, defensive backs Jimmy Patton and Herb Rich, and defensive linemen Rosey Grier, Harland Svare, and Walt Yowarsky. Yet despite the addition of so many quality veterans and promising rookies, the Giants lost four of six exhibition games in 1955—all played on the road as usual—and then, shockingly, their first three league games—also on the road—while the Yankees and Dodgers battled it out in the World Series in New York. Thereafter, though, the Giants lost only two of their last nine games, going without a loss in their final five. Apart from Webster's glittering inaugural year, Conerly threw 13 touchdown passes. Gifford caught four of them, scored three touchdowns rushing, and threw for two more, as he continued to demonstrate his remarkable versatility.

As Conerly was to say at the end of the season, "We were the best 6-5-1 team you ever saw."

5

The Meanest Man in the NFL

$\mathcal{F}$ollowing their peripatetic six-week preseason journey, which took them from Massachusetts to the Pacific Northwest, then to the Midwest, and, finally, to Memphis, the Giants returned to New York for a few days of practice at Fordham University before flying to San Francisco. There the Giants would open the 1956 season against the San Francisco 49ers, who were beginning their seventh season in the NFL after playing in the All-America Football Conference. Flying in a chartered DC-6 was both a luxury and a novelty for the Giants, who, for the most part, had been crisscrossing the country by bus and train, both to cut down on expenses and because of Jim Lee Howell's aversion to air travel.

The 49ers finished 4–8 in 1955, despite having one of the league's best quarterbacks in Y. A. Tittle; three of the NFL's premier runners in Hugh McElhenny (who Andy Robustelli said was, except for Jimmy Brown, the best running back he had ever faced), Joe Perry, and John Henry Johnson; as well as All-Pro tackles Leo Nomellini and Bob St. Clair—all eventual Hall of Famers. Nor could the 49ers' poor performance be ascribed in any way to St. Clair, at six foot nine and 265 pounds the biggest player in the NFL, and one of the league's best offensive tackles. St. Clair, a native San Franciscan, had played at the University of San Francisco with eventual Hall of Famers Gino Marchetti and Ollie Matson. He was also one of the game's most popular, and idiosyncratic characters, renowned among his teammates for eating steaks and all other meat uncooked, along with raw eggs. Playing a position that usually attracted little attention, no matter how good the player was, St. Clair stood out, both because of his extraordinary size, his superb blocking ability, his speed, and his love of hitting. He also excelled on special teams, especially in field-goal situations. Before the 1956 season ended, St. Clair would block an astonishing 10 field goal attempts, almost assuredly a record in a category that the NFL did not tabulate.

Though the 1956 team was essentially the same as the previous season's, San Francisco had a new coach, Frankie Albert, the 49ers' quarterback from 1946 to 1952. A daring and highly capable quarterback, Albert was a small but slick left-handed passer who split the quarterbacking with Tittle during his last two seasons as a player. Though he projected an aura of insouciance on the field, the five-foot-nine-inch Albert inspired his teammates with his talent, creativity, and determination, which made him one of San Francisco's most popular athletes of all time. As the 49ers' quarterback since their founding by San Francisco businessman Tony Morabito, Albert was not about to give way to Tittle when Y. A. was obtained from Baltimore in 1951 after two seasons with the Colts, the first in the All-America Football Conference and the second in the NFL.

"Frank was already a legend in San Francisco after playing at Stanford and then with the 49ers since they started," Tittle recalled, "and he didn't take kindly to someone coming in to play quarterback. I sat on the bench most of the first season, but then the second year, Buck Shaw, our coach, alternated Frank and me. One of us would start a game, and the other one would play the second quarter, and then it would be the same in the second half.

"Eventually, a quarterback controversy developed in the San Francisco papers, as often happens," Tittle said. "In one game, as I went in to replace Frankie in the second quarter, I asked him whether the other team was using a five- or four-man front. And Frank just looked at me and said, 'Don't ask me anything; you're trying to take my job.' I thought he might be joking, but I wasn't sure."

As it developed, Tittle, eight years younger than Albert, wound up with more playing time that season, which turned out to be Albert's last as a player.

From Albert, Tittle learned what later became one of his patented plays, wherein, with his team close to an opponent's goal line, a quarterback fakes a handoff to a running back, then places the football behind his hip, convincing defenses that he no longer has possession, then races around the end for a touchdown, usually running one way while all of the defense is running the other way. A master at the boot-leg, Albert scored most of his 20 touchdowns in the old AAFC and his 7 during his three seasons with the 49ers on the bootleg, whose first exponent had been Bob Waterfield.

"A lot of people thought I was good at the bootleg play," Tittle said years later, "but I couldn't carry Frankie Albert's helmet when it came to bootlegging. Nobody could fool the defense like Frank could. He was only a mediocre passer without a really strong arm. But he was a pretty good runner and a good punter and a very good leader who made football fun."

For Andy Robustelli, Kezar Stadium, in San Francisco's expansive and attractive Golden Gate Park, was a familiar football venue. During his five years with the Los Angeles Rams, he had played there against the 49ers every season, since the two teams, fierce rivals, played each other twice every year. At a time when many NFL teams, including the Giants, considered thirty thousand a big crowd, the Rams-49ers games—probably the most heated rivalry in the NFL—drew huge crowds of up to ninety thousand at the Los Angeles Coliseum and close to sixty thousand at Kezar Stadium in the early 1950s. Apart from the intense rivalry between the two cities in general, the Rams-49ers games also were a big draw because the two teams had more than a few of the biggest marquee names in the NFL. Then, too, in the early 1950s, the 49ers and the Rams were the only major league teams in their respective cities. The baseball Giants and Dodgers would not arrive in San Francisco and Los Angeles, respectively, until 1958, and neither city had a team in the National Basketball Association or the National Hockey League, mainly because most big-league sports teams still did most of their traveling by train, and only went as far west as St. Louis. The general feeling was that from an economic standpoint, having franchises on the West Coast would be prohibitively expensive. So it was that since the founding of the All-America Football Conference in 1946, when the 49ers and the Los Angeles Dons became charter members, only professional football had major league teams in the two archrival cities until 1958.

In a league dominated by the Cleveland Browns, who since being merged with the NFL in 1950 had reached the league's championship game for six consecutive years and won the title three times, the

Giants were hardly a big attraction. Still, the opening game at Kezar Stadium drew a crowd of 41,751, the third-largest of the six NFL opening-day gatherings on Sunday, September 30. And what most of the spectators saw was somewhat alarming, especially at the start, when the Giants scored on their first three possessions.

With the team's second-best quarterback, Don Heinrich, running the offense, the Giants got into the end zone on three quick bursts: a 44-yard pass play involving Heinrich and Alex Webster, and a dazzling 59-yard run and a 17-yard field goal by the versatile Gifford, who was doing the team's placekicking while the regular kicker, Agajanian, was still trying to decide whether to forgo his garbage removal business in Southern California and return to the Giants.

Ahead 17–0 at the end of the first quarter, the Giants widened their lead to 24–0 early in the second quarter when fullback Mel Triplett combined with Heinrich on a 35-yard play. Only a 16-yard touchdown run around left end by McElhenny late in the second quarter prevented the 49ers from leaving the field scoreless in the opening half. Constantly harassed by Robustelli and the rest of the Giants' front four, and the linebackers, running backs McElhenny and Perry had trouble gaining any yardage on the ground and Tittle, under constant pressure, threw often but with little success.

A 1-yard plunge by Triplett midway through the third quarter increased the Giants' lead to 24–7, virtually putting the game out of reach. Tittle got the 49ers to within 10 points when he climaxed a 70-yard drive with a 3-yard touchdown pass to Billy Wilson. But then Triplett put the Giants up by 17 points again on a 12-yard run up the middle late in the fourth quarter before the 49ers scored for the last time on a 3-yard run.

The 49ers, with two of the NFL's best runners, gained only 107 yards rushing against 167 yards by the Giants. Forced to pass as a result, Tittle completed 27 of 47 passes for 288 yards, but was intercepted three times.

It was an impressive victory, and no one was more pleased than defensive coach Tom Landry, no longer in pads and cleats but wearing a suit, tie, and what would become a trademark fedora. On the basis of this opening game, he knew that the Giants now had one of the best, if not the best, defenses in the National Football League. Since none of New York's dozen papers had a writer at the game, the city's dailies had to rely on an Associated Press report, which highlighted the game's scoring and made reference to Bill Svoboda, who "spent most of the afternoon hanging around Tittle's neck." At that, most of the New York papers gave short shrift to the game, burying the AP story on the inside pages of their sports section, while playing up the Dodgers' final-game victory over the Milwaukee Braves at Ebbets Field, which put them in the World Series against the Yankees for the second year in a row.

After boarding the team's charter several hours after beating the 49ers, the Giants flew home to New York, where hardly anyone seemed to be aware of their opening-game victory and where they would have to spend the week practicing at Wellington Mara's and Vince Lombardi's alma mater, Fordham, in the Bronx. The Giants' new home field was occupied as usual in late September and early October by its primary occupant, the New York Yankees, who in 1956 would not relinquish it until the middle of the following week, after a seven-game World Series that included a "perfect game" by Yankee pitcher Don Larsen. In the 1950s, the Giants also occasionally trained at the Bear Mountain Inn near West Point, about forty miles from New York. The Chicago Cardinals were next—on the road, of course—but the key game, both the coaches and players knew, was the one in two weeks in Cleveland.

Otto Graham, the Browns' Hall of Fame quarterback, had retired after the 1955 season at the age of thirty-four after playing in a remarkable ten straight championship games, even though he again led the NFL in passing. With Graham the only starting quarterback the Browns had known since being formed in 1946 in the All-America Football Conference, Cleveland had won the Eastern Conference title every year since joining the NFL in 1950 and had captured the NFL championship the last two seasons. In the title game on December 26, 1955, the Browns crushed the Los Angeles Rams, 38–14, before a crowd of 85,693 at the Los Angeles Coliseum in what was to be Andy Robustelli's last game with the Rams. But even with Graham gone, the Browns were still loaded and were still the team to beat.

—

The Giants boarded a train at Grand Central Terminal in Manhattan at four o'clock for the overnight eighteen-hour trip to Chicago on Friday, October 5, 1956, to play the Cardinals. At the time, Chicago had the distinction of being the only city in the NFL with two teams,

the Bears and the Cardinals, both of them charter members of the
NFL when it was begun in 1922. As was the case with most NFL
teams, the Bears and Cardinals played in major league baseball stadiums—the Bears at Wrigley Field, the home of the Chicago Cubs;
and the Cardinals at Comiskey Park, where the Chicago White Sox
played.

The major differences between the two teams, though, were that
the Bears—the so-called Monsters of the Midway—were consistent
winners and had won five NFL titles, while usually drawing more
than forty thousand spectators to their home games. The Cardinals,
on the other hand, had won only one NFL championship and rarely
drew crowds that exceeded twenty thousand at Comiskey Park, where
one end zone actually bordered on a box seat railing.

As it was, the Cardinals and Giants drew only 21,799 spectators
on October 7, even though the Cardinals' lineup included halfback
Ollie Matson and another future Hall of Famer defensive back Dick
"Night Train" Lane, along with All-Pro players cornerback Lindon
Crow and halfback Johnny Olszewski. At that, the crowd for the
Giants-Cardinals game was about one thousand larger than the Car-
dinals had drawn a week earlier against Cleveland, when the turnout
of 20,966 was the smallest of the six NFL opening games.

Though there was bad news at the gate, there was good news for
the Giants. Hardy Brown, at the age of thirty-two, was nearing the
end of an eight-year career during which he had been the scourge of
the NFL, knocking out scores of opponents and breaking as many, if
not more, noses and jaws with his patented shoulder tackle. Though
only six feet tall and about 190 pounds, Brown had a well-deserved
reputation as the most devastating hitter in the NFL, a hell-bent
linebacker who flattened quarterbacks, running backs, receivers, and
opposing linemen, usually by using his shoulder as a lethal weapon.

Brown's tackling approach was unique, to say the least. As he approached a running back or receiver, Brown would get into a low
crouch, with his right shoulder lower than the left one, then spring
up and drive his right shoulder into the opponent's head. Indeed,
Y. A. Tittle, who played with Brown in Baltimore and San Francisco, called him the toughest football player he had ever met. "Hardy
wasn't a great linebacker and missed a lot with his shoulder tackle,
but when he hit you, you usually didn't get up," Tittle said. "He was
a regular knockout artist and inspired us. I remember how in his first

game with the Colts against the Redskins in 1951, he knocked out all three running backs. Altogether that year, he knocked out twenty-one players. And when I say knocked out, I mean knocked out cold with his shoulder tackle to the point that they had to be carried off on stretchers. I never saw a football player who could hit as hard as Hardy Brown. He broke a lot of noses before players began wearing face masks in the mid-fifties, and then, after players began wearing face masks, busted a lot of them with that vicious shoulder tackle. All of his opponents hated him, and sometimes, to get back at him, a quarterback would call a play that would let Hardy break through, and all ten players would let him have it. But amazingly, I don't ever remember Hardy being hurt, although he himself sent a lot of players to the hospital."

Raymond Berry, the Hall of Fame receiver for the Baltimore Colts, came close to being one of them during his rookie year in 1955. "We were playing the 49ers at Kezar Stadium in San Francisco when, at the end of a play, I instinctively hit the ground," Berry recalled. "Good thing I did, because just then someone came flying right over me. Turned out it was Hardy Brown. If I hadn't hit the ground on my own, who knows what might have happened. Then when I got to the bench, one of my teammates told me that I'd better watch out for Hardy Brown, and I said, 'Thanks for telling me.' "

To a certain degree, Brown's violence on the football field seemed to typify the NFL of the 1950s. Late hits on quarterbacks, forbidden today, were usually overlooked during that decade. Also, until 1955, ballcarriers who weren't in the grasp of a tackler after being knocked down could get up and run again on the same play. That encouraged piling on once a runner was tackled and was out of his tackler's grasp. Then, too, until players began wearing face masks, high tackling—aimed at the head—was very much in vogue, resulting in innumerable broken noses and broken jaws, not to mention the loss of an untold number of teeth.

The 1950s are often looked upon as a relatively somnolent decade, devoid of the large-scale, and often violent, demonstrations of the 1960s, which stemmed both from an incipient civil rights struggle and, later, America's growing involvement in Vietnam. Professional football ran counter to the zeitgeist of the era. Indeed, in the opinion of many players, coaches, media observers, and fans of the era, play in the league was tougher than it's ever been since. The two most

popular theories for the rough play was the competitiveness for roster spots in a league of only twelve teams and a total of just under
four hundred players and the fact that many of the players had been
toughened, even hardened, by their experiences during World War
II or the Korean War.

Tough and rough as players of the fifties may have been, none
was tougher or rougher than Hardy Brown, himself a marine veteran of World War II. On the assumption that no one could inflict
so much damage, and injury, by tackling with his shoulder, George
Halas once had game officials check Brown's shoulder pads before a
game to see whether Hardy had inserted something in the pads. But
they found nothing; Hardy Brown's shoulder pads were perfectly legitimate. Still, the question remained as to why Brown played with
such fury, reveling in vicious hits. Tex Coulter, a Giants lineman
from 1946 through 1952, thought some early family experiences
might have played a part in Brown's on-field demeanor, while Y. A.
Tittle thought that his having been in an orphanage throughout his
boyhood and teenage years might have been a factor in Brown's ferocious play.

Like Brown, Coulter spent time in an orphanage in Fort Worth,
Texas, starting when they were both five years old. By then Brown
had looked on as his father was shot to death in a neighbor's house
in 1928 when young Hardy was four years old. A few months later,
Brown witnessed a family friend shoot and kill one of Hardy's father's
killers. Less than a year later, Hardy's mother sent him and his three
siblings to the Masonic Home School, an orphanage in Fort Worth.
There he met Coulter, who became an All-America tackle with the
national championship Army teams of the mid-1940s after having
played previously at Texas A&M University and Cornell University.
Discipline at the orphanage, which had its own dairy farm and school,
was strict, and corporal punishment was inflicted on children who did
not do their assigned chores.

For Brown and Coulter, the saving grace at the orphanage was
its high school football team, which became one of the best in Texas,
with a huge following throughout the state. "Football gave us self-
worth," said Coulter, a three-time All-Pro while he was with the
Giants who later played five years with the Montreal Alouettes of
the Canadian Football League. "The city boys [in Fort Worth] were
frightened as hell of us. I can't blame them the way Hardy Brown

was—and I was too, to some extent. The goddamn guys would be bleeding all over the place." Indeed, the Masonic Home Team, from a school of about 140 boys and girls, almost all of them orphans, was so good that it regularly beat teams from high schools that had several thousand students. And although the team often fielded as few as twelve players, they often defeated some of the best high school football teams in Texas.

Coulter recalled lining up against his old Masonic Home teammate in a game between the Giants and the 49ers in the early 1950s. "I came out of the huddle and thought I'd say hello to Hardy," said Coulter. "But when I came to the line and looked across at him at his linebacker spot, his eyes looked like they belonged to some caged animal. They were fiery and unfocused, so I kept my mouth shut."

So much for old childhood friendships.

Brown finally left the Masonic Home in 1941, when he was seventeen, to join the marines and fight against the Japanese in the Pacific. After the war, Brown attended Southern Methodist University briefly and then the University of Tulsa, where he was a star blocking back and linebacker. Jim Finks, a quarterback and defensive back for the Pittsburgh Steelers from 1949 through 1955, and later the president of the New Orleans Saints, roomed with Brown at Tulsa and remembered him well. "I think it was in a game against Baylor University that he knocked out the two ends on consecutive plays," Finks said. "That was how hard he hit."

Finks said Brown could get "wild" when he was drinking, which he apparently did often, both in college and while playing in the NFL, but that off the football field he was generally "intelligent, warm, and shy." Tittle, who roomed with Brown for five years while both were with the 49ers, also found Brown a different person off the field. "He was quiet, soft-spoken, and very reserved," Tittle said. "I used to look at him reading a book and wonder how he could be so tough out on the football field. And if you were in a bar with him, inevitably Hardy would wind up in a fight. He could be a good companion, but he could also be mean."

Considering that he had not heard from his mother for the twelve years he was in the Fort Worth orphanage—and then only when he had to get her permission to join the marines—perhaps that deep-seated rage was understandable.

Though only thirty-two years old, Brown showed that he was on the downside of his extraordinary career when the Giants met the Cardinals. Nevertheless, Andy Robustelli warned teammates who had never faced Brown to beware of his unorthodox shoulder tackle. "I remember Andy warning me about Hardy Brown," said Alex Webster, "but he still hit me so hard at one point that he almost knocked me out." Indeed, Brown's ferocious nature had hardly abated, nor had his penchant for head-hunting, but he seemed to have lost a step or two and was no longer the most feared defender in the NFL. The Giants' solid offensive line kept Brown at bay during most of the game and, for the most part, away from the Giants' running backs. It was hardly the Hardy Brown that Robustelli remembered from Brown's glory days with the San Francisco 49ers in the early 1950s. Brown's NFL career ended when the Cardinals released him after the 1956 season. But four years later, after playing briefly with the Hamilton Tiger Cats in the Canadian Football League, working as a bartender in Las Vegas and in construction in Texas, Brown was signed by the Denver Broncos of the new American Football League. Though thirty-six, he played in thirteen of fourteen games before retiring for good. That made Brown and placekicker Ben Agajanian the only players to have played in the NFL, the All-America Football Conference, and the American Football League. Spiralling out of control after his football career ended, Brown drank heavily and eventually was institutionalized by his wife in Stockton, California, where he was diagnosed with dementia and later died in a mental institution in 1991 at the age of sixty-seven. Doctors said his condition was probably caused by excessive drinking, many blows to the head, and traumatic experiences during childhood.

—

That containment of Brown was one of the reasons the Giants, 9-point favorites, led twice in the opening half of the game after scoring two touchdowns. However, the Cardinals countered when quarterback Lamar McHan scored from the 2-yard line following a fumble by Webster and Night Train Lane's 68-yard run following an interception of a Charlie Conerly pass that gave the home team a 14–13 halftime lead. Pat Summerall converted after both Cardinals touchdowns, while Gifford had been wide on his first extra-point attempt, which made the 1-point difference at the intermission.

Much to the Giants' surprise, it was a lead that the Cardinals would not relinquish. McHan, working out of the option, ran more than he threw, amassing more than 100 yards rushing while throwing only seven passes in the game, an extraordinarily low number for an NFL quarterback in the 1950s. Five of those passes were completed, however, for 136 yards, including two on the Cardinals' first two possessions of the second half that resulted in touchdowns, for a 28–13 lead. McHan then put the game out of reach when he ran 13 yards for his second touchdown and the Cardinals' final score with five minutes left in the fourth quarter. That touchdown run overshadowed a third short dash into the end zone by Triplett and a 5-yard touchdown pass by Conerly—who completed 16 of 31 passes for 176 yards—to Ken MacAfee in the last minute of play, narrowing the gap to 35–27. But it turned out to be the Giants' final possession.

It wasn't until after the game that the Giants learned that McHan had received considerable help from the Cardinals' bench, from where coach Ray Richards had transmitted all of the team's offensive plays to the quarterback via a transistor radio hookup. As the Giants were to find out, Richards wasn't the only coach using an electronic communications system to talk to his quarterback, which was not only novel in the NFL but legal. At any rate, the loss did not portend well for the Giants, since their next opponent, again on the road, would be the Browns—whom the Giants had not been able to beat in their last six games.

In the immediate aftermath of the loss to the Chicago Cardinals, the Giants headed for the LaSalle Street Station and an eighteen-hour train trip back to New York, where they would spend most of the following week practicing at their home away from home, Fordham University.

6

Putting Together an
Instant Dynasty

No other professional football team has ever had as remarkable a run as the Cleveland Browns of the mid- and late 1940s and the early 1950s, playing in championship games ten years in a row under one of the sport's most innovative, if indeed not the most innovative, coaches, Paul Brown. And when the Browns met the New York Giants on October 14, 1956, they were heavily favored to extend that streak to eleven straight years, even though their quarterback during all ten of those years, the truly magnificent Otto Graham, had retired following the 1955 season.

The first four of those ten championship games had been played in the All-America Football Conference, all of which the Browns won. But the last six had been in the National Football League, whose title it had won three times—including 1950, the Browns' first year in the NFL. This came much to the astonishment of the League establishment, which had regarded the AAFC as inferior.

Even though the eight-team AAFC did not have the cachet of the far more established NFL, it had an ample supply of very good players during its inaugural 1946 season, including 40 of the 67 players from the College All-Star team that had defeated the Cleveland Rams. Somewhat lost in pro football antiquity, the Cleveland Rams preceded the Browns, playing in the NFL from 1937 through 1945. After that season, Dan Reeves, a Los Angeles stockbroker, and Fred Levy, a Los Angeles businessman, who had bought the team from original owner Homer Marshman, moved the Rams to Los Angeles.

The move, which followed seasons when the Rams rarely drew as many as twenty thousand spectators—and sometimes played in front of crowds smaller than five thousand while posting only one winning season in eight years—made the Rams the first NFL team west of Chicago. But it also meant that they would have to compete with the Los Angeles Dons of the new All-America Football Conference. Ironically, the Rams' last season in Cleveland, in 1945, was their best, with a regular-season record of 9-1 (NFL teams played ten-game seasons then) followed by a 15–14 victory over the Washington Redskins in the NFL championship game—the Rams' only title in Cleveland. In large measure, the turnabout from a 4-6 team in 1944 to a team that, under a new coach, Adam Walsh, lost only one game a year later was due both to the introduction of the T formation and the addition of a rookie quarterback out of UCLA. Bob Waterfield threw 14 touchdown passes that season to tie veteran Chicago Bears quarterback Sid Luckman for the league lead. Waterfield went on to play six seasons with the Rams in Los Angeles and became perhaps as famous for marrying movie star Jane Russell as for his Hall of Fame accomplishments.

Into the Cleveland pro football void stepped the new Cleveland Browns of the AAFC, founded by Cleveland taxi company owner and entrepreneur Arthur (Mickey) McBride, who promptly named Paul Brown as the head coach and general manager. It was an excellent choice, since Brown had been a winner everywhere he had coached: at Washington High School in Massillon, Ohio, where his teams were so powerful that one of them went through an entire season without having to punt; at Ohio State University; and at the Great Lakes Naval Station in Illinois during the recently ended Second World War, where his team included scores of former professional and college stars.

Brown also quickly turned into a winner in pro football, signing a host of players he was familiar with, such as Otto Graham, a single-wing All-American halfback from Northwestern University. Brown had seen him while coaching at Ohio State. The intelligent and hand-some Graham was multitalented: a good enough basketball player to play in the National Basketball League, the predecessor of the National Basketball Association, during the 1945–46 season, and a good enough musician to play the French horn in the Northwestern band, while also being capable of playing the cornet, violin, and piano.

Coach Brown would convert him into a T-formation quarterback.

Others recruited by Brown were tackle Lou Groza, end Dante Lavelli, and guard Bill Willis, all of whom he had coached at Ohio State; recently discharged army veteran and end Mac Speedie, who'd impressed Brown when his Fort Warren, Texas, army team played Great Lakes; fullback Marion Motley, who had played for Brown at Great Lakes; and other outstanding players such as tackle Lou Rymkus and tackle and fullback Lou Saban, who later spent sixteen years as a coach in the American Football League and the NFL. Of all those recruits, the one Brown knew best was guard Lin Houston, who by 1946 had played for Brown at every level: at Massillon's Washington High, at Ohio State, and now with the Browns, where he would remain through the 1953 season.

Motley and Willis had written to Brown asking for tryouts. In response, Motley was first told that the Browns had enough running backs, while Willis never heard back from his old college coach. Eventually Willis was contacted by a sports editor friend of Brown's and invited to camp for a tryout. Several weeks after pretraining camp began in July of 1946, Brown, realizing he could use a back with Motley's talents, asked another friend to contact Motley and ask if he'd like to try out for the Browns. As a married father of four, Motley found the offer tempting, realizing that he would prefer playing in the NFL to working in a steel mill, which he was doing at the time. Whether Brown's hesitation about asking Motley and Willis—through intermediaries—to try out for the Browns was due to a reluctance to sign blacks was never determined. Years later Brown claimed that he'd hesitated in inviting Motley and Willis to camp to ease the pressure on them. Maybe, but from the very start of training camp, it was clear that the Browns needed help at guard, which was Willis's position, and at running back, which was Motley's, and yet they were not invited until weeks later. At any rate, Brown certainly had no regrets about finally asking them to come.

Once he realized what Willis meant to the Browns, Brown once said, "He often played as a middle or nose guard on our five-man defensive line, but we began dropping him off the line of scrimmage a yard because his great speed and pursuit carried him to the point of attack before anyone would block him. Bill was the forerunner of the modern middle linebacker."

Unlike Jackie Robinson, Willis and Motley, two of the first four blacks to play in the AAFC, did not encounter vitriolic racial hatred. But there were still some unpleasant moments. Willis recalled an incident in a game against the Brooklyn Dodgers of the AAFC when a number of white players piled on Motley after he was down. "I started pulling guys off, saying, 'Okay, boys, the play's over,'" Willis recalled. At that point, a Dodgers player who weighed about 250 pounds screamed, "Keep your black hands off me!" Willis stepped back a bit in the event the player tried to hit him, but he kept his hands on the player's shoulder pads before his teammates intervened.

"There were also times when I'd be punched by opponents after a play or called a black SOB," Willis said. "But Lou Groza and Lou Rymkus said to me, 'Don't let anybody excite you. If there's trouble, tell us, and we'll handle it.' After that, I never had to say anything. We were in the trenches together, and the two of them would take care of a guy. It was comforting to have teammates like that. Also, I soon won the respect of my opponents. They found that I could take it and dish it out."

Motley, who became one of the NFL's all-time great fullbacks, thought it took awhile longer to gain that respect. "That kind of crap went on for two or three years until they found out what kind of players we were," he said. "They found that out while they were calling us niggers—I was running for touchdowns, and Willis was knocking the shit out of them."

Motley and Willis were eventually elected to the Pro Football Hall of Fame. They weren't trailblazers in pro football, since Fritz Pollard and Paul Robeson were among about a half dozen blacks who played in the NFL in the 1920s, although none had played in the league since the 1930s. The same year that Motley and Willis were signed by the brand-new Browns, the recently departed Rams recruited two outstanding black players from Los Angeles who had attended UCLA: twenty-eight-year-old halfback Kenny Washington and thirty-two-year-old end Woody Strode, who would play only one season, in 1946, for his new hometown team, catching four passes before retiring. At that, Washington and Strode made it to football's fragmented big league, as it were, a year before Jackie Robinson, another former Bruins football star, broke the color barrier in major league baseball.

Still, by the end of the decade, the NFL and AAFC had only a handful of black players, including the incomparable Giants defensive back Emlen Tunnell, Joe Perry, Tank Younger, and "Deacon Dan" Towler, so called because he would lead the Rams in prayer before every game and eventually became a minister. That would change, incrementally, in the 1950s, the breakthrough decade for blacks in the NFL. Indeed, by 1954 the five leading rushers in the league—Perry, John Henry Johnson, Younger, Towler, and Maurice "Mo" Bassett—were all black.

———

Where the name Browns came from has remained somewhat of a mystery over the years. At the very outset, McBride, the team's owner, wanted it named for Paul Brown, who by the age of thirty-eight—when the Browns were born in 1946—was already something of a legend in Ohio. But Brown balked at the idea, whereupon McBride sponsored a newspaper contest to find a name, offering a $1,000 war bond to the eventual winner. Most of the entrants chose "Browns" after the popular coach, but Paul Brown still declined the offer. Finally, Panthers was chosen. But then the owner of a former Ohio semipro team claimed that he still owned the rights to the name. At that point, McBride convinced Brown to go along, albeit reluctantly, with the name Browns. The name, as it was to turn out, would become even more appropriate in the coming years when a fullback out of Syracuse named Jim Brown joined the team.

If the Cleveland Rams had trouble drawing fans as an NFL franchise, the Cleveland Browns were a box office success from the start, averaging more than sixty thousand fans at home their first two seasons in the new AAFC. Attendance tailed off during their next two, and final, years in the fledgling league, mainly because of their overwhelming dominance. Crowds at Cleveland Municipal Stadium remained relatively small during the Browns' first few years in the NFL, as the team continued to win with relative ease, including, ironically, a 30–28 victory over the Los Angeles Rams in the 1950 NFL championship game.

During one stretch that began in 1947, the Browns went unbeaten through twenty-nine regular-season games along with two championship games, a feat that has never been duplicated in professional football. And in 1948, they went 14-0. Yet the AAFC records were not transferred to the NFL record book as the American Football

League records were when the AFL merged with the NFL in 1970. The reason given at the time was that the AAFC was inferior to the NFL, and thus its records were suspect. That argument was defused immediately, though, by the Browns' performance from the time they joined the NFL. Thus, while Joe Namath's AFL passing statistics are included in the NFL records, the great Otto Graham's are not. Former Cleveland Browns of that era still simmered about this rank injustice more than a half century later.

To Paul Brown, Graham was the essence of the Browns. "Otto was my greatest player because he played the most important position," Brown said of his quarterback who, over the course of 10 professional seasons, had a passing accuracy of 55.7 percent and threw 88 touchdown passes. "I think Graham had the best peripheral vision I've ever witnessed. You know, he was an All-America in basketball, and one year he played with Rochester in the NBA, where he was a tremendous playmaker. I watched him in a game one night, and I wasn't aware of him scoring, yet he ended up with twenty points, and he'd helped everyone else score. His hand-eye coordination was most unusual. And as a football player, find another quarterback who took his team to as many championships."

As with the Giants, the Browns were an extremely close unit. "Money wasn't the prime factor when we played in the fifties," said Graham, who went on to coach the Washington Redskins and later at the Coast Guard Academy in New London, Connecticut, where he also served as athletic director. "We played mostly because we liked to play. They used to say that if I had a killer instinct, I would have been a better quarterback. But I never saw it that way. I played to win, but if we lost, I didn't brood about it. I'd start planning to win the next one."

Perhaps because of the passage of years, Graham became overshadowed by the exploits of latter-day quarterbacks like Johnny Unitas, Terry Bradshaw, Joe Montana, Dan Marino, John Elway, and Brett Favre. But in the opinion of many longtime football observers, Graham not only belongs in that pantheon of quarterbacks but might have been the best ever.

—

By 1955, when the Browns won their third NFL title, attendance had picked up markedly and remained strong in 1956. Far and away the biggest crowd in 1956 turned out for the Browns' third game of the season on Sunday, October 14, when the New York Giants came to town, attracting a gathering of 60,042, the largest assemblage to see an NFL game that weekend. It would turn out to be an epochal game for the Giants, playing their ninth consecutive game on the road since preseason training began in Winooski Park, Vermont, almost three months earlier.

The game would be particularly special for Dick Modzelewski, the Giants' new tackle, who would literally be going head-to-head against his older brother, Ed, the Browns' second-year fullback. Like Dick, Ed had gone to Maryland. It also would be special for rookie halfback Gene Filipski, who had been traded to New York by the Browns for a draft choice during preseason training. Missing from the Browns teams that had dominated the old All-America Football Conference and the first few years in the NFL, besides Graham, were Marion Motley, who had averaged over 5 yards a carry during his first four years in the NFL before being traded to Pittsburgh after the 1953 season; linemen Bill Willis and Lou Rymkus; and end Mac Speedie, who had jumped to the Canadian Football League. Nevertheless, the Browns were a touchdown favorite to beat the Giants in their home opener at the cavernous eighty-thousand-seat Municipal Stadium, also the home of the Cleveland Indians baseball team.

As if they needed an edge, forty-eight-year-old Paul Brown tried to give the Browns one. Like Ray Richards, the coach of the Chicago Cardinals who had upset the Giants the week before, Brown had begun to use a transistor radio hookup to communicate with his new starting quarterback, George Ratterman.* Richards may well have gotten the idea of using a transistor radio from Brown, who came up with more innovations than any coach in football except, perhaps, Yale's Walter Camp. In the late nineteenth century, "The Father of American Football" introduced the center snap, the four-down system, the line of scrimmage, and eleven-man teams, in addition to coming up with the idea of an All-America team at the end of each college football season.

---

*Before joining the Browns in 1952, Ratterman had played with the Buffalo Bills of the All-America Football Conference, the New York Yanks of the NFL, and the Montreal Alouettes of the Canadian Football League. An extraordinary all-around athlete, Ratterman was one of only four athletes to have lettered in four sports at the University of Notre Dame: football, baseball, basketball, and tennis. (Johnny Lujack, who lettered in the same four sports, was perhaps the best known to have done so.)

The erudite, aloof, and inflexible Brown devised playbooks that included a team's offensive plays and were distributed to every player to study. In addition, he insisted that his players take notes in loose-leaf notebooks during classroom sessions akin to college lectures, graded players' game performances based on reviews of game films, conducted periodic tests among his players, sent in offensive plays from the bench, conceived the idea of a "pocket" around the team's passer on pass plays, and revolutionized scouting methods. A strict disciplinarian, Brown also insisted that players wear jackets and ties while traveling and abstain from liquor. Each week Brown also said at a team meeting that married men had to abstain from sex from Tuesday until after the coming Sunday game. That often prompted Otto Graham, then single, to ask Brown whether that edict also applied to single players. He did so with tongue in cheek, wondering if Brown thought that his single players were already celibate. Each time, Brown would glare at his star quarterback and not answer him.

Aware of Brown's latest innovation, Jim Lee Howell, Tom Landry, and Vince Lombardi were prepared to disrupt it. To that end, Bob Topp, an offensive end who did not get into a game in 1956, was equipped with a radio receiver capable of picking up Brown's play calls to Ratterman. Topp then immediately told Gene Filipski, seated alongside him on the Giants' bench, to interpret the calls, since he had been with the Browns during the preseason and knew the team's plays. Filipski did so and quickly called out each play to Andy Robustelli, who then told the rest of the Giants defenders in the huddle what to expect. However, after a few offensive plays were run, Ratterman pointed to his helmet and the crowd, signifying that he could not hear Brown because of the deafening crowd noise. Thereafter, Brown retreated to his old system of sending in plays with Ray Renfro and rookie halfback Preston Carpenter.

"We were tuned in to their wavelength and seemed to hear the plays that Brown was calling in better than Ratterman was," Ray Walsh, the Giants' general manager, said later. "In one instance, Brown called for a pitchout, and after Filipski yelled out the play, we stopped them for a two-yard loss. Finally, after three sequences, they gave up in disgust.

"I guess the Browns thought we might try something like we did," Walsh said. "Before the game, they warned us that it was a ten thousand dollar fine if anyone was found jamming their wavelength.

It seems Cleveland had its own licensed radio station to carry out the experiment." If there was a $10,000 fine for jamming a wavelength, either Brown never found out that the Giants were listening in to his radioed instructions or the Browns just never bothered to file a grievance with the Federal Communications Commission.

Four days later, NFL Commissioner De Benneville (Bert) Bell, aware of what Ray Richards and Paul Brown—among perhaps other coaches—were doing, banned the use of transistor radios and all other electronic devices during league games.* More than fifty years later, signal stealing caused a ruckus of sorts when a cameraman working for the New England Patriots on the sidelines during a game against the New York Jets was caught filming Jets coach Eric Mangini signaling to his players on the field. As a result, Patriots coach Bill Belichick (a former Browns coach, no less) was fined $500,000 and warned not to resort to such trickery again, while the team was fined $250,000 and deprived of a first-round draft pick the following season. By contrast, Bert Bell never took any action against the Giants for in effect stealing signals being phoned in by Paul Brown. But, then, such a theft, like the radioing in of plays, was new to the NFL and no more illegal than calling in the offensive plays.

——

Whether Brown's electronic play calling would have made a difference in the outcome of the 1956 game against the Giants is problematic. But one thing is sure: The visitors from New York amassed 256 yards on the ground. Unable to make much movement rushing, coach Paul Brown instructed Ratterman to pass often. That was easier said than done in light of the fierce rush put on Ratterman, particularly by Robustelli and left end Walt Yowarsky. Though he managed to complete 17 of 25 passes for 156 yards, Ratterman, constantly harried by the Giants' defensive line, was intercepted once and sacked

---

*Two Ohio electronics specialists, John Campbell and George Sarles, convinced Paul Brown to use a small radio receiver that could be installed in a football player's helmet, enabling the coach to send in signals by radio. Brown liked the idea, mainly because he would no longer have to send in each offensive play with a substitute, as he had done for years, and tested it out in a preseason game against the Detroit Lions in the summer of 1956. Satisfied with the results, Brown decided to have his quarterbacks use the "radio helmet" during regular-season games. Thirty-eight years later, in 1994, the NFL permitted teams to use radio helmets for limited communications between sideline coaches and quarterbacks.

about a dozen times—including six times by Robustelli, who consistently spun around Cleveland's All-Pro left tackle Lou Groza or blew through the left side of the Cleveland offensive line.

After a scoreless first quarter, the Giants, led by the running of Gifford, Triplett, and Webster, scored early in the second period when Don Heinrich faked handoffs to Gifford and Triplett, then hit Webster in the end zone with a 9-yard pass to cap a 71-yard drive. Gifford, placekicking in the absence of an injured Ben Agajanian, added the extra point.

Cleveland made it 7–7 at halftime when, after a 38-yard field-goal attempt by Gifford was blocked, Galen Fiss scooped up the ball and raced 55 yards to the Giants' 16-yard line. Six plays later, Ed Modzelewski banged into the end zone from a yard out, and Groza, that rare lineman who also did his team's placekicking, booted the extra point to tie the game. It would be Cleveland's only touchdown of a game in which Modzelewski, the Browns' best runner, gained only 28 yards on 14 carries. By comparison, Webster, Triplett, and Gifford gained 94, 91, and 73 yards, respectively. Gifford also caught four passes for 42 yards, 2 yards more than the Browns gained rushing.

Totally dominating the second half, the Giants scored two touchdowns, both by Webster. The first, from 5 yards out in the third quarter, climaxed a 68-yard drive; the second came on a 34-yard run in the final period to punctuate an 80-yard march that gave the Giants a 21–7 lead. Cleveland's only score of the half came late in the game: Charlie Conerly, appearing prepared to punt from the end zone, took the snap from center and deliberately ran laterally, enabling Junior Wren to tackle him for a harmless 2-point safety, which inevitably made the final score 21–9.

During that second half, the Giants' defense demonstrated clearly that it would be a force to be reckoned with throughout the season. At one point, the Browns reached the Giants' 14-yard line, only to have Ratterman thrown for losses of 10 and 17 yards by Yowarsky and Robustelli, respectively, on successive plays, forcing the Browns to try a 48-yard field goal that went wide. In another instance, the Browns had a first-and-goal at the New York 1-yard line, only to be stopped on four consecutive plunges into the middle of the Giants' line. On the last one, Ed Modzelewski hit the left side of his line and was stopped in his tracks by his younger brother for a 2-yard loss.

"Ed was so furious at me for tackling him and ending the Browns' drive that as I started walking off the field, he picked up the football and threw it at me, hitting me in the helmet," a smiling Dick Modzelewski said. "But I got the last laugh."

Paul Brown conceded that the game had been a mismatch. "They were the better football team than we were because they had the desire," the Browns coach said. "They wanted to win. Also, their defensive line got the jump on our offensive line, and their offensive line outcharged our defensive line."

Giants coach Jim Lee Howell was extremely gracious in victory. "I still consider the Browns the best team in the division," he said after the game. "The difference is they're not head and shoulders above the rest like they used to be."

Hearing that last statement, most sportswriters felt that Howell was alluding to the absence of their former quarterback, Otto Graham, the best quarterback in the team's history. As it developed, Ratterman, his successor, would play only one more game following the Browns' loss to the Giants. In the Browns' next game, in Washington, Ratterman sustained a knee injury that would end his pro football career at the age of thirty. In retirement, he would become a pro football television analyst for ABC and CBS, obtain a law degree, and then be elected a county sheriff in northern Kentucky.

———

For the first time in 1956, several New York newspapers, including the *New York Times* and the New York *Herald Tribune* (second in terms of prestige to the *Times* at the time, and the only paper to have covered the previous week's game in Chicago), had sent writers to a Giants game. In his account of the game, Bill Lauder of the *Herald Tribune* wrote that "the Giants were hurt by the loss of their key man in their defensive line—Ray Beck—but you never would never have known it, as the forward wall outcharged the Browns all day." Lauder was wrong on two counts. First, Beck, in his third year with the Giants, was playing middle linebacker in Tom Landry's new 4-3-4 defensive scheme, and, second, he was hardly the key man in the Giants' defensive line. On this day at least, that would have been Robustelli.

What Lauder, along with the other New York writers who covered the game, failed to mention was that Beck's replacement, rookie Sam Huff, played very well, making about a half dozen tackles and was being ubiquitous on defense. Even Tom Landry was amazed at Huff's performance. As it would develop, Beck remained with the Giants through the 1957 season, but he never regained his middle linebacker position. Young Huff was just too good to keep off the field. He may have been too light to play on the defensive line and not fast enough for the offensive line, but somehow he turned out to be well-nigh perfect to play middle guard—or middle linebacker, as Landry called it. To excel at the position, as did Huff's contemporaries Bill George of the Bears and Ray Nitschke of the Packers, a linebacker has to be able to fend off a blocker and then make a tackle, break through the offensive line and sack the quarterback (a move that became known in the 1950s as a "blitz"), cut down a receiver going out for a pass over the middle, and cover a would-be receiver as part of the pass defense.

Huff reveled in all of those assignments. "At West Virginia, playing on the front line, I had to get into a three-point stance and mainly could only see what was right ahead of me," Huff was to say shortly after starting to play the position. "At middle linebacker, I could stand up as a play began and see everything unfold in front of me. I loved it." He also loved the contact. "I like hitting the other guy," he said. "If you don't like to hit and be hit, you don't belong in the NFL."

—

Even though the Browns were obviously not the same team without Otto Graham, the Giants were elated during their train ride back to New York. Cleveland still was the preseason favorite to win the Eastern Conference title again, and the victory not only was the Giants' first over the Browns since 1952, but it was also decisive. And now, riding high, the Giants were finally going to play their first home game of the season against the Pittsburgh Steelers. The World Series was over, with the Yankees having beaten the Dodgers in seven games, and Yankee Stadium, the Giants' new home, was now all theirs for the rest of 1956. The big question was how many people would care enough to show up on Sunday, October 21. After all, the Giants had played six preseason games and three regular-season games over a two-month span, all of them on the road. It wouldn't be hard to imagine that out of sight might also mean out of mind as far as New York–area sports fans were concerned.

7

From the Polo Grounds to "The House That Ruth Built"

Though the Giants had been out of sight in New York since the previous November, not having played a single game at home through the first quarter of the 1956 season, it turned out they had not been out of mind after all. Because of their upset victories on the road against the 49ers and the Browns, along with the bevy of fresh faces, the New York papers waxed optimistically about what the New York *Herald Tribune* called "this new Giants team" and their new playing field. Indeed, never before had the city's sports sections devoted so much space to the Giants in advance of an opening game at home.

Besides their playing at Yankee Stadium for the first time, the game against the Pittsburgh Steelers was notable as the first Giants home game to be televised. Under an agreement with the Columbia Broadcasting System, each NFL team could televise all of its home games, but with a blackout stretching for a radius of seventy-five miles from the home team's stadium. For the Giants, the nearest television station able to televise its home games was in Hartford, Connecticut, 110 miles away. Since the station's signal could not be picked up in the New York metropolitan area, Giants fans desirous of watching them play would have to drive at least seventy-five miles to the north and northeast to watch the games on television at motels, restaurants, and bars.

For Andy Robustelli, though, playing in a televised game was old hat. In what was the first nationally televised NFL game ever, NBC had telecast the championship game between the Los Angeles Rams and the Cleveland Browns in 1951, his rookie season. But for one of his teammates, the game meant a good deal indeed.

For twenty-five-year-old Dick Modzelewski, so wide at six feet and 260 pounds that he sometimes had to squeeze through doors sideways, the game provided him with extra motivation, since the Steelers had traded him after just one season. Pittsburgh, in a sense, was Modzelewski's hometown team, since he had grown up in the nearby coal-mining town of West Natrona, Pennsylvania, rooting for the Steelers.

Before their first game at Yankee Stadium, the Giants worked out at The House That Ruth Built several times. For most of the players, it was the first time they had been inside the stadium. Having grown up in nearby Stamford, Robustelli had gone to a number of baseball games at the stadium as a boy but still found the iconic ballpark a mystical sports venue. So did head coach Jim Lee Howell, who, following the team's first practice at the stadium, walked around the infield and outfield, somewhat in awe, as he later conceded.

"There was this great Yankee tradition," Howell was to say. "And they were the greatest team, and I felt that playing there was going to help us."

If the players and Howell were awestruck at practicing at the most famous of American stadiums, they were equally in awe at sharing lockers with players like Mickey Mantle, Yogi Berra, and Whitey Ford, and, before them, Babe Ruth, Joe DiMaggio, and Lou Gehrig. Perhaps in deference to his seniority with the Giants, Charlie Conerly was given—or took, it never was made clear—Mantle's locker, at least for the rest of the football season.

"I had been a Giants baseball fan, but it was still very special being in that locker room and on that field, especially the first time," Robustelli said.

But, as sports columnist Arthur Daley was to note in the following day's *New York Times*, there was a stark difference in that locker room when it was inhabited by the New York Yankees than by the new fall tenants. "The Yankees laugh and joke and engage in horseplay," Daley wrote. "The Giants look like men who are heading for a mass execution without any hope of a reprieve from the governor."

That collective serious mien that Arthur Daley observed could have been due to the fact that the game marked the Giants' debut at the hallowed ballpark. Or perhaps the players sensed that the ghosts of Ruth and Gehrig were hovering about, wondering, perhaps, why a team named the Giants was in *their* locker room. More likely it was because the team's two leaders, Conerly and Robustelli, wanted the locker room kept quiet so that everyone could focus on the game. Eventually it would become a lighthearted clubhouse.

From the moment the Giants ran onto the field shortly before the kickoff on a cloudy but warm day, old-time Giants like Conerly and Tunnell noticed the difference: The crowd—at 48,108, the largest ever to see a Giants home opener—cheered loudly. That was definitely something new. But soon after the game began, it was reminiscent of many other autumnal Sundays in the Polo Grounds, as thousands of fans began to vent their wrath at Conerly. They booed vigorously after he overthrew and underthrew several receivers and was sacked for an 11-yard loss shortly after replacing Don Heinrich late in the opening quarter with the Giants trailing, 3–0. But then, as Gene Ward wrote in the next day's New York *Daily News,* "Chucking Chuck," as Ward (but nobody else) called the veteran quarterback, turned the "jeers to cheers" when he threw two touchdown passes within a span of one minute twenty seconds early in the second period. The first, to right end Ken MacAfee, climaxed an 80-yard drive during which Conerly completed 5 of 8 passes. The second, to Alex Webster, came after Robustelli and Rosey Grier forced a fumble by Steelers quarterback Ted Marchibroda, which Bill Svoboda recovered at the Pittsburgh 29-yard line. In less than two minutes, the big crowd went from booing to cheering Conerly, and with an ensuing field goal by Ben Agajanian, the Giants took a 17–3 halftime lead. *New home field,* Conerly thought to himself, *but same old fickle fans.*

By the time Marchibroda threw a 4-yard touchdown pass midway through the final quarter, the Giants had scored 31 unanswered points, including 6 more on a third touchdown strike by Conerly, who finished with 14 completions (7 of which went to Gifford) on 23 passes for 208 yards in the Giants' 38–10 victory. An even more revealing statistic was the mere 91 yards the Steelers gained on the ground—as against 249 amassed by the Giants—and only 77 yards passing. That was a considerable accomplishment, and a testament to the much-improved Giants defense since the Steelers had won two of their first three games.

For the Giants, their successful home debut was cause for celebration, and for that the Conerlys were well prepared, hosting a cock-tail party in their apartment at the nearby Concourse Plaza Hotel. Later, about half of the thirty-three Giants, along with some wives and girlfriends, walked two blocks to an elevated subway station and boarded a train for a twenty-minute ride to the Fifty-Ninth Street station in mid-Manhattan. From there they walked or rode taxis to Toots Shor's restaurant, where they were greeted by the burly and Rabelaisian proprietor himself and cheered by several hundred pa-trons at the bar and inside the dining area. Like the cheering that the players had heard as they ran onto the field about seven hours ear-lier, this too had never happened before. Just maybe, Charlie Conerly thought, this was not only the beginning of a new era but the start of something big.

In his New York debut as a Giant, Robustelli clearly demon-strated to Giants fans why he had been named to the all-NFL team the last four seasons, taking part in about a half dozen tackles and consistently harassing Marchibroda. In addition to his wife, Jeanne, and other family members, there had been hundreds of friends and a number of former high school and college teammates in the stands cheering for the onetime Arnold end. The next day, though, it was as if that debut had been a dream. For football players, then as now, Monday is usually a day of rest, but for the new Giants right end, it was back to work—in his sporting goods store in the Cos Cob sec-tion of Greenwich. He spent the day stocking shelves with partner Ed Clark, waiting on customers, and, when someone brought it up, talking about the previous day's game. With a family of six and earn-ing only $10,000 playing football, Robustelli felt he had to be working in the store, both on practice days at Yankee Stadium, and even on the day after games, both home and away.

Not that he was complaining. Robustelli had come to realize that, although he was conflicted about it at first, his being traded from the Los Angeles Rams to the Giants had been a blessing in more ways than one. Most important, not only was he close to home, much of the time he *was* home with his growing family. Then, too, the current Giants team was better than the one he had been traded from three thousand miles away, which was no longer the Los Angeles Rams of the early 1950s. Playing for the Giants also had another benefit: Fairfield County, where Robustelli lived, was Giants country when it came to football. That, Robustelli was quick to realize, was very, very good for business. After all, not many customers could walk into a store in the 1950s, and most certainly not decades later, and be waited on by an All-Pro defensive end, even during the football season.

——

Perhaps it was because the Giants' victory put them at 3-1 in the NFL standings for only the second time in eleven years. Or maybe it was because of the record opening-day crowd, the New York debut of new standout players, or the Giants' first game at Yankee Stadium. Or maybe it was a combination of all of those factors. But all of the New York newspapers led their Monday sports sections with the win over Pittsburgh. All three tabloids—the *Daily News,* the *New York Daily Mirror,* and the *Post*—headlined the Giants' triumph on the back page, the lead page of the sports sections, and, like the other dailies, ran more than one story on the game. In the *New York Times,* which ran three stories on the game, Louis Effrat, who wrote the lead story, raved about the Giants' "superb defense," and, in a prescient observation, said that the record opening-day crowd "seemed convinced that the New Yorkers are headed for a 'big' year."

The surfeit of coverage could be attributed to the Giants having a sports monopoly of sorts in the city's sports sections the day after the home opener. After all, the baseball season was over, and neither of New York's other two big league teams, the hockey Rangers or the basketball Knickerbockers, was playing at home that Sunday. But that had been the case in the past, and still the Giants did not get the press attention they got on October 22, 1956.

The Conerlys, who still lived in their hometown of Clarksdale, Mississippi, were now back at their second home: at the Concourse Plaza Hotel, three blocks north of Yankee Stadium. The then-elegant hotel, adorned with brick towers and marble vases, was the centerpiece of the tree-lined and spacious Grand Concourse, a five-lane boulevard that was looked upon as the Park Avenue of the Bronx since it opened in October of 1923, six months after the Yankees had begun playing at their new stadium. In her book, *South Bronx Rising,* Jill Jonnes wrote that "the new hotel, aglow with lights in the crisp fall darkness, was every bit as elegant as the Waldorf-Astoria in downtown Manhattan."

The Conerlys had been staying at the hotel since Conerly's rookie year, and they weren't alone. By 1956 about a third of the team—

roughly a dozen Giants and their wives—along with about twenty children, were ensconced at the hotel for the season. "It worked out perfectly," Perian Conerly recalled. "The accommodations were very good, and it was close enough for Charlie and the rest of the players to walk to practice and to the home games. It was also just a short walk to the subway station near Yankee Stadium, where you could get a train and be in midtown Manhattan in about twenty minutes."

Among the players who stayed at the Concourse Plaza at one time or another—mostly with wives—were Tom Landry, Frank Gifford, Kyle Rote, Sam Huff, Dick Modzelewski, Pat Summerall, Don Heinrich, Jimmy Patton, Y. A. Tittle, and Del Shofner. "We were all very close," Perian said, "with the players walking to the stadium together and with some of the wives often playing bridge together, and also shopping, going into Manhattan to see shows, and, in the case of the couples with children, going to the park across the street from the hotel. We didn't have children, and it was nice to have so many of the players' children around, especially at Halloween, when they would go trick-or-treating from door to door in the hotel, and at Christmas-time during the years the Giants were in the playoffs."

And, of course, there were the traditional Conerly cocktail parties after Giants home games. With the Giants now playing so close to the Concourse Plaza, that made it even easier for players and wives who didn't stay there and other friends to get to the Conerly parties. Some of the players' wives who didn't live at the hotel would have their husbands drop them off at the Concourse Plaza so they could leave clothes they wanted to wear after the game and have lunch at the hotel. "We always had a lot of people stop by," Perian Conerly recollected. "For all we knew, some of them just walked in off the street. We never did check on who was there. It was sort of an open house."

One of the regulars was Toots Shor, to whose restaurant many of the partygoers, including the Conerlys, usually would repair after the cocktail party. "Toots, who was a big Giants fan, would bring along some famous people like David Niven, Don Ameche, and Gordon MacRae, and athletes like Stan Musial and Eddie Arcaro," Mrs. Conerly said in referring to the then–St. Louis Cardinals star and the Hall of Fame jockey.

The thought of recognizable star players such as Conerly, Gifford, and Huff, among others, riding a subway train for about one hundred blocks boggles one's mind years later, when unrecognizable professional athletes making millions of dollars a year ride around in limousines. Perian Conerly recalled the looks of disbelief on the faces of some subway riders sharing the same cars as the Giants party. "They'd talk to us and congratulate the players after we'd won," she said, "but no one would really ever bother us. I guess it was a different time."

Eventually Landry, Gifford, Summerall, Patton, Modzelewski, Tittle, and some of the other married players who stayed at the Concourse Plaza would move to the suburbs, mostly in Westchester County and Stamford, where about a dozen players lived by the late 1950s and the early 1960s. Huff and his wife, who had previously lived at the Excelsior Hotel near Central Park in Manhattan, took up residence in a Queens apartment. Understandably, most of the single players lived in apartments in Manhattan.

While so many players lived within walking distance of Yankee Stadium, Jim Katcavage commuted ninety miles to and from the stadium, both on practice and game days, from his hometown of Philadelphia. "The train ride took about an hour and a half, and then I rode the subway from Penn Station to Yankee Stadium for about twenty minutes," Katcavage said. "Em Tunnell, who was also from the Philly area, also did it for a long time, and so did Tom Scott after he got traded from the Eagles to the Giants [in 1959]. He used to commute with me. On game days, we'd be riding on the subway with fans going to the game. If the train was crowded, some of the fans would give us their seats. And they'd be talking to us all the way to the stadium. It was kind of neat."

Apparently coach Jim Lee Howell had no idea that Katcavage, Tunnell, and then Scott were long-distance commuters. Once the coaches got wind of the team's long-distance commuters, neither the night nor morning before a game would ever be the same for any of the Giants.

But even marriage, which came to Katcavage a few years after he joined the team, did not change his commutation routine—except on Saturday nights when the Giants were playing at home the next day. According to Dick Modzelewski, "We were at Toots Shor's having a few at the bar when I introduced Kat to a gal named Kathy, who worked at Toots's, and they got married a short time later. As I recall it, Kathy was from Philly too, and so after they got married, Kat kept on commuting from Philadelphia. I didn't realize it at the time, but I turned out to be a matchmaker for one of my teammates."

Modzelewski also became a commuter, albeit from a much shorter distance, living in Stamford during part of his stay with the Giants. "A lot of us would carpool from Stamford to the stadium, which took about forty-five minutes," Modzelewski said in relating another example of the team's close-knit relationship, "and we got along very well." That so many players wound up living in Stamford was due in large measure to Robustelli, who had sung the praises of his hometown, particularly if players had children. Given Robustelli's entrepreneurial nature, some players felt that perhaps he had a vested interest in having teammates live in Stamford. Although his friendships with several Stamford Realtors did help in finding houses or apartments for Giants teammates, he denied that he had personally benefited from their living there.

Those suspicions may have been justified. As a teenager, Robustelli would collect soda bottles for their deposit value. He often rode the train into Manhattan, where he would buy neckties for twenty-five cents apiece from sidewalk salesmen on Forty-second Street, then sell them to classmates at Stamford High School for a dollar each. And his entrepreneurial spirit carried into his days with the Giants. "Andy was a hustler, and he had so many things going for him that it was hard to keep track," Sam Huff said. "He had his sporting goods store and later got into the travel business, sports marketing, and a few other things, and was always looking for some other way to make money. One time he got almost everyone on the team to order cashmere sports jackets that he was getting from Hong Kong at a huge discount, or at least that's what he told us."

Modzelewski recalled that Robustelli asked him to use a measuring tape to figure out each player's size. "That was kind of a joke, since I didn't know anything about measuring people for clothes, especially for a sports jacket," Modzelewski said. When the jackets arrived, the players, who had paid for them up front, were in for a surprise: They were good-looking, to be sure, but almost all of the garments were too small. "The manufacturer apparently had never dealt with football players before and also didn't pay attention to Mo's instructions," Huff said. "I gave mine away, and I think most of the other guys did too."

Huff also recalled a time when Robustelli persuaded some of the defensive players to buy shirts from him. "By that time, Andy was in the shirt business too, and he convinced us to buy these striped shirts to wear during a documentary being done about me for CBS in 1960," Huff said in referring to a well-done and widely watched program entitled *The Violent World of Sam Huff*. "In the documentary, those of us wearing the shirts looked like a bunch of prisoners. But that was Andy, always looking to make a buck, and everyone wound up laughing about it all."

So long as Robustelli continued to harass quarterbacks, as he had done now in four straight games, and be an inspirational force both on and off the field, none of the Giants was about to complain about spending $25 on a cashmere sports jacket, ostensibly from Hong Kong, that they could not possibly fit into. "The Pope," as the deeply religious Robustelli soon became known by his teammates, seemingly could do no wrong.

8

The Grocery Boy from
the West Side

rigging. Or as Andy Robustelli would say, "friggin'." At any rate, it was the strongest word in Robustelli's vocabulary from the time he was a boy through his days as a professional football player.

"We came from a pretty tough part of Stamford—the West Side—where you heard some rough language, but the worst thing Andy ever said was 'frigging,'" said Tony Pia, a longtime friend and high school teammate. "And he didn't like to hear anyone else swearing. You could tell by the expression on his face."

Perhaps it was the fact that Robustelli had been an altar boy at the Sacred Heart Roman Catholic Church in his neighborhood, as he would be until he was eighteen years old and a high school senior. Whatever the reason, Robustelli never swore, in or out of mixed company.

Tony Pia hardly ever swore, either, as the boyhood friends walked about two miles each day to Stamford High School—Robustelli a lanky six-footer and Pia about five-foot-seven and around 140 pounds. By his senior year, Robustelli had distinguished himself as a forward in basketball and a catcher on the baseball team, while Pia had starred in returning kickoffs and punts on the football team. As they were about to begin their senior year, Pia, aware that Robustelli was a star on the Sacred Heart CYO football team—both as a fast and overpowering running back and a quick and agile lineman—suggested that Robustelli try out for the high school football team. "I knew we needed a couple of good linemen and that

Andy could help us," Pia said. "I also reminded him that it was his last chance to play football at Stamford High. But he said he really didn't want to, since he was working in a grocery store after school and on Saturdays and was happy playing with the CYO team. But I kept after him, and he finally agreed to come out for football in his senior year."

Robustelli—whose older brother, Lou, was then a lineman at Georgetown University—never forgot his friend's convincing him to come out for football as a senior in high school. "If Tony didn't talk me into it, who knows if I would have kept playing after high school," Robustelli said. "But he was very persistent."

The diminutive Pia had good reason to be glad that Robustelli listened to him. In the team's biggest game of the year, against archrival Norwalk High School in late November of 1942, Robustelli threw a key block as Pia ran back a punt 60 yards for the game's only touchdown. "It was nice having Andy on the field throwing blocks whenever I was running back a kickoff or a punt," said Pia, who a month later would be drafted into the army while still a senior at Stamford High. "I actually was drafted in early November, but Carl Nutter, the head of the history department at Stamford High, was also head of the Stamford draft board and a big fan of our team, and he gave me a deferment so I could play against Norwalk."

The low- to middle-income neighborhood where Pia and Robustelli grew up may have been tough, but it produced some of Stamford's best athletes, and was a place where boys could be seen all year round playing football or baseball at the Stevens Elementary School playground, in vacant lots, and at nearby Woodside Park, and then playing basketball in school gymnasiums. Though predominantly Italian, the West Side of Stamford also had a number of black families, including five that lived in the same six-family tenement in which the Robustellis lived on Spruce Street. "It was a great neighborhood to grow up in," Robustelli was to recall. "Hardly anyone ever got in any kind of trouble, and maybe it was because most of us were always playing baseball, football, or basketball. Also, we all had very strict parents who kept us in line, along with older brothers in some cases, who also made sure you stayed out of trouble."

What some of Robustelli's old friends remembered best about him as a teenage athlete was a supreme confidence and outstanding athletic ability. "Andy was not only a tough competitor but a rough one, too," said Tony Pia, "although he was never a dirty player and wouldn't tolerate anyone who was. And I don't think I ever saw anyone who hated to lose more than him. He didn't sulk about losing, but you could see it bothered him a lot."

Another former high school teammate who also grew up with Robustelli, Vito DeVito, said that while Robustelli was a good sandlot player in the pre–Pop Warner football era, none of his friends foresaw him as a professional football player. "Andy wasn't big for his age as a kid and even in high school," said DeVito, a lifelong friend who played baseball and basketball with Robustelli at Stamford High and also attended Arnold College with him. "I was surprised when he decided to go out for football in his senior year, and especially for the line, because he probably didn't weigh more than one hundred seventy pounds."

As an assistant baseball and football coach at Arnold, DeVito also got to watch Robustelli progress as a football player. "By then, after spending three years in the navy, Andy weighed over two hundred pounds and actually was better known for his pass-catching ability than for his defense, although he was good all around. Apart from his abilities, what stood out for Andy was that he was a very smart and crafty football player whose great speed, quickness, and intelligence made up for what he lacked in size."

As a boy, Robustelli was shy and unassuming, his boyhood friend said. "Although we're the same age, I was the leader and organizer of our baseball, football, and basketball teams as a kid, and as a rule Andy didn't say much, but he went all out in whatever sport he was playing."

DeVito recalled that he and Robustelli grew up in an era when most boyhood teams in Stamford did not have adult coaches. Instead they relied on one of their own teammates—in Robustelli's case, it was DeVito—to arrange games, make out lineups, and make sure everyone showed up for games, usually by bicycle or on foot. "Hardly any parents came to our games at Woodside or Cummings Park or at Mill River Park downtown," said DeVito, who, after an outstanding minor league baseball career, became a teacher and coach at Jonathan Law High School in Milford while also serving as an assistant freshman football coach and the freshman basketball coach at Yale University. "Andy's father didn't have any interest in

sports and never came to his games, but his mother sometimes did."
When she did, Kate Robustelli had to walk or take a bus, since the
Robustellis, like most people living on Stamford's West Side, did
not have a car.

That absence of attention to their children's games was not
unusual in a neighborhood where most parents were Italian immi-
grants and had little or no interest in American sports, although
Robustelli's father was born in the United States. "We did everything on our own, and hardly anyone was ever watching," DeVito
recalled. "But that didn't bother us, because that's how it was in
those days."

It was also a time when many children on Stamford's West Side
had serious work ethics instilled in them by their parents. In Robustelli's case, he bagged and delivered groceries and did other chores
at Sclafani's grocery store on West Main Street, not far from home,
contributing his weekly salary of a few dollars to his parents, who
in turn gave him money for occasional movies or whatever else he
needed. For someone whose needs were scant, that never amounted
to much. After selling neckties in high school for two or three times
what he had paid for them on Forty-Second Street in Manhattan,
his work ethic and entrepreneurial skills would only grow in college. While at Arnold, Robustelli spent the week before Christmas
carrying a mail bag loaded with Christmas cards and other mail
for the Stamford Post Office. "Andy always was looking to earn
money," Vito DeVito said. "During the football season, he would
buy a bunch of pins, buttons, and other Arnold souvenirs, and have
a teenager named Bob Griffin, who later became the football coach
at the University of Rhode Island, sell them at Arnold games, with
Andy paying Griffin and keeping the rest for himself."

Perhaps because of the modest circumstances Robustelli grew
up in, he was always frugal, both privately and in his business.
Though he went to college and received a monthly allowance under
the G.I. Bill, Robustelli usually hitchhiked to and from the Arnold
College campus from Stamford, a distance of about thirty miles.
"While we were freshmen, we'd go to an entrance to the Merritt
Parkway in Stamford or out on the Post Road on Monday morning and hitch rides to Milford," said Carmine Tosches, a longtime
friend and the quarterback of the Arnold football team while Robustelli was at the school. "Then we'd usually do the same thing on

Friday to go home. But then Andy got married after our first year and moved to Milford to be close to school."

Another boyhood friend and former teammate, Fred "Lefty" Giuliani, recalled how, at Robustelli's suggestion, he and his friend would hitchhike to the Polo Grounds in Manhattan, a distance of about forty miles, to watch Robustelli's beloved baseball Giants play when they were teenagers. "Andy was always looking to save money and also to make money," said Giuliani, who, like Vito DeVito, also played minor league baseball—in his case, as a pitcher—and later became a banking executive in Stamford.

Before joining the navy, Robustelli, along with Giuliani, accepted scholarships to attend LaSalle Military Academy on Long Island after graduating from Stamford High School in June of 1943. "The scholarship offers required us to play three sports—baseball, football, and basketball," Giuliani said, "and for Andy and I to both play end, both ways, as you did in those days, even though I hadn't played football in high school."

Attending LaSalle also meant that Robustelli and Giuliani had to wear gray uniforms. "When we went home—which was rare, since Stamford was more than fifty miles away—we looked as if we were West Point cadets," said Giuliani. At six-feet-three-inches tall, he was the big man on the 1942–43 Stamford High basketball team that went all the way to the state final, where Stamford lost to Warren Harding High of Bridgeport. While Giuliani remained at LaSalle for the entire academic year, Robustelli changed uniforms in January, when he joined the navy at the age of eighteen and served as a water tender, stoking the boilers of a destroyer escort in the South Pacific during World War II.

Not having played football while in the navy, and not having had extraordinarily successful seasons in the sport at Stamford High or LaSalle, Robustelli was not sought out by any college coaches when he returned home in April of 1946, about twenty-five pounds heavier than when he had gone into service. Aware that several former high school teammates were enrolling at Arnold College in the fall of 1947, Robustelli decided to join them and go out for football, with a view toward getting a degree in physical education and becoming a gym teacher and coach. But from his freshman season on, Robustelli was generally the best player on the field, a sure-handed pass receiver, a swift and nimble pass rusher, a deadly tackler, and an extraordinary blocker of punts.

"If Andy hadn't made it in the NFL, he might well have made it to the big leagues in baseball," said DeVito, who as an infielder progressed as high as Triple-A with the San Diego Padres of the Pacific Coast League in the early 1950s. "He was a very good catcher with a strong arm, and he was a very good hitter," DeVito said. "He also was very versatile, agreeing to play third base at Arnold because we had a few good catchers."

Indeed, upon graduating from Arnold, Robustelli, a lowly nineteenth-round draft pick by the Los Angeles Rams, felt that his best chance of making it as a professional athlete was in baseball. Thus his decision to accept an invitation, along with Arnold teammate Tosches, to a tryout with the baseball Giants at the Polo Grounds. During the daylong audition, Robustelli, working out at third base, impressed Giants coaches and scouts with his defensive skills and at bat, as he sprayed line drives to all fields and hit a number of balls into stands in both left and right fields. "They really liked Andy, and offered both him and me contracts to play in the Double-A Southern Association at Knoxville," recalled Tosches. "But by then, Andy was married, and I had a job offer with the FBI, and the four hundred dollars a month they offered each of us wasn't very much, so we turned it down."

Ironically, Robustelli would return to the Polo Grounds, but as a football player, going up against New York's other Giants—the ones who wore helmets and cleats and not caps and spikes.

9

The Original Fearsome Foursome

Although the Giants had played only four regular-season games in 1956, Robustelli already knew that he, Rosey Grier, Dick Modzelewski, Jim Katcavage, and Walt Yowarsky had melded into an extraordinarily cohesive defensive line. Yowarsky, who like Robustelli had been in the NFL since 1951, and Katcavage had been alternating at left end. And Sam Huff had surprised everyone with his maturity, quickness, and tackling ability at middle linebacker alongside veterans Bill Svoboda and Harland Svare in Tom Landry's new 4-3 defensive scheme. And even though Landry no longer was a cornerback, the secondary, comprised of Tunnell, Patton, Nolan, Rich, and Hughes, was as good a defensive backfield as there was in 1956.

Even before Robustelli reached Yankee Stadium for practice sessions during the week, he was learning more and more about the art of defensive football. "Tom Landry had rented a house from a friend of mine in Stamford, and we often drove to the stadium together," Robustelli said. "Tom spent almost all of the time talking about different defensive schemes he had come up with and was eager to implement." Robustelli, always quiet to begin with, was a rapt listener, interrupting only to ask questions about something Landry had just said. "Howard Cosell, who was a good friend of mine, occasionally rode in with Tom and me, and I'm sure Howard learned a lot about the game listening to Tom. I don't think anyone on the Giants got to know Tom and his creativity as a coach better than I did."

The blustering and verbose Cosell, who somehow managed to ingratiate himself with more famous athletes than perhaps any broadcaster of his time, went on to become the best-known and most controversial sports commentator in the United States. Though a quintessential New Yorker, Cosell for many years lived in bucolic Pound Ridge, New York, a Westchester County village that borders Stamford. He got to learn even more about football when he and his wife, Emmy, often joined the Robustellis and other Giants and their wives at dinner on Friday nights at Emily Shaw's, a charmingly rustic nineteenth-century restaurant on the Connecticut-New York border. Such was the case on Friday, October 26, two days before the Giants' second home game, this one against Philadelphia. The Eagles had fallen on hard times but had still managed to win two of their first four games despite a relatively weak offense. Through-out the week, New York sports columnists like the acerbically witty Dan Parker of the *New York Daily Mirror*, Jimmy Powers of the *Daily News*, Jimmy Cannon of the *Post*, and Frank Graham of the *Journal-American* waxed optimistically about these new New York Giants—in particular, the defense, which had allowed only two touchdowns in the last two games.

Given the conviviality among the players and their wives, no one seemed to be thinking about the Philadelphia Eagles—perhaps because New York was heavily favored—and the players were convinced they would win the game easily.

—

By Giants' standards, the crowd for the second home game again was big, but, at 40,960, was about 7,000 less than the previous Sunday. Though a 13-point favorite over Philadelphia, which had scored only one touchdown in losing to the Chicago Cardinals the week before, the Giants had to contend with former longtime head coach Steve Owen, who was now the Eagles' defensive coordinator and was all too familiar with New York's offensive patterns. That was particularly evident in the opening quarter, when the Giants, unable to get their running game untracked against the traditional six-man defensive line still employed by most NFL teams, had to settle for a 20-yard field goal by Ben Agajanian. But even then, the home team was only able to tie the score after Emlen Tunnell intercepted a pass by Eagles backup quarterback Adrian Burk at the Philadelphia 30-yard line late in the quarter.

Failing to make any progress with Don Heinrich, again the starting quarterback, Lombardi sent in Charlie Conerly at the start of the second period, and the move proved propitious. Conerly quickly led the Giants on two scoring drives that resulted in a second field goal by Agajanian and a 1-yard plunge by Alex Webster to give the home team a 13–3 halftime lead.

With the new Giants defense again proving nearly impregnable, Philadelphia failed to advance beyond midfield over the last three quarters while the Giants added a second touchdown in the third period on a 20-yard pass from Conerly to Frank Gifford en route to a 20–3 victory.

The win, highlighted by the defense on a day when the Giants twice fumbled the ball away and were intercepted twice, put the team at 4-1 and in a first-place tie in the Eastern Conference with the Chicago Cardinals, the only team to have beaten the Giants.

Playing against his hometown team, Katcavage showed why, in due time, he would no longer be sharing left end with Yowarsky but would become a fixture at the position. Repeatedly harassing both Burk and the regular one-eyed quarterback, Bobby Thomason, who entered the game in the last quarter, Katcavage elicited mixed emotions from the Eagles' first-year coach, Hugh Devore, who, while coaching Katcavage at the University of Dayton, had recommended him to the Giants. Following Devore's recommendation, Vince Lombardi had watched the six-foot-three 230-pound defensive end in several Dayton games and raved about him to Jim Lee Howell and Tom Landry.

"Katcavage is real fast with good moves and the kind of defensive end that a quarterback hates to know is coming his way," Lombardi told his fellow coaches. Ironically, Katcavage had wound up at Dayton, not renowned for football talent at the time, because of a basketball injury. "After I dislocated my shoulder in a basketball game while I was a senior at Roman Catholic High in Philadelphia and had to have it operated on, the schools that had been interested in me for football lost interest," Katcavage was to say. "But my high school football coach managed to get me a scholarship to Dayton, which depended on how well I did my first year. As it turned out, I did well enough to get a scholarship for all four years."

Even though Dayton was a small-time football school, Katcavage was invited to play in the annual College All-Star Game in Chicago in August of 1956 and also in the East-West All-Star Game, which, like the College All-Star Game, showcased most of the best seniors in the country. In 1956 that group included such All-Americans as Lenny Moore, Earl Morrall, Forrest Gregg, and Hopalong Cassady. Katcavage, relatively unknown to most coaches, sportswriters, and even his teammates in those postseason games, was outstanding, particularly as a pass rusher, and his performance convinced the Giants that he was worth drafting in the fourth round in 1956.

"Early in my rookie year, Vince Lombardi—who I had never heard of before he scouted me and then talked to me at Dayton—told me he was glad that he had scouted me in college," Katcavage recalled. "Then he told me that now that I was in the NFL, I could use some life insurance, which wasn't offered by NFL teams. Turns out he was selling life insurance on the side while coaching, and he convinced me to take out a policy!"

Whether he was pleased with the policy Lombardi sold him or not, Katcavage was happy with his new team. "Our defensive line worked very well right from the start," he said. "We had a great defensive coach in Tom Landry and were always working on new maneuvers. And you had to come up with new things back then, because there were so many great offensive linemen, all bigger than us on the defensive line, and much bigger than the guys I played against when I was at Dayton."

—

While most of the Giants slept late the day after the Eagles game and the traditional cocktail party at the Conerly apartment, followed by dinner in Manhattan, Andy Robustelli was behind the counter of his sporting goods store when the first customer of the day walked in at ten o'clock. "No matter what the weather was like or how tough the game had been the day before, Andy showed up for work on Mondays and after every practice day at Yankee Stadium," his partner, Ed Clark, said. "And if he wasn't in the store, he would be outside sweeping the sidewalk. That was Andy, always doing something. In the off-season, it wasn't unusual for him to be working from fourteen to sixteen hours a day."

Looking for an off-season job following his rookie season with the Los Angeles Rams, Robustelli went to see Clark at a downtown sporting goods store in Stamford that Clark managed. "But then I said to Andy, 'Hey, why don't we open our own sporting goods store?' " Clark recalled. "Andy liked the idea, and after looking around, we found space for a small store in the Cos Cob section of Greenwich that winter."

Having an All-Pro defensive end both as a part-owner and salesman in the store certainly helped business. So much so that in 1957, Clark and Robustelli opened a second store on the periphery of Robustelli's old West Side neighborhood in Stamford. As business increased, the two partners moved into bigger quarters in downtown Stamford. By then Robustelli and Clark, in a magnanimous gesture, had given the Greenwich store to a longtime employee.

"By that time, around 1960, Andy had made a lot of contacts with some major corporations like General Electric, U.S. Rubber, and Allied Chemical, and got those companies to buy a lot of stuff in our Stamford store," Clark said.

Enraptured with the business world and looking to expand his business horizons, in the early 1960s Robustelli took advantage of an offer to buy a branch of a travel business in downtown Stamford from a new friend, travel impresario Bill Fugazy. As it developed, the travel business was to become the centerpiece of a business conglomerate that would eventually include a speakers' bureau made up of athletes, mostly NFL players, that Robustelli had met and in some cases even tackled; a sports marketing unit; and a video production service. All were housed in a two-story building that Robustelli had built in 1973.

Given his love of the game and his intensity as a player, Robustelli's outside ventures never seemed to have had any adverse effect on his play, since whatever business he became involved in became eminently successful while being run by friends with good business acumen, and, in later years, by family members. In 1956, though, and for quite a few seasons beyond that, Robustelli's main consideration after his growing family was the New York Giants football team.

"I knew this team was something special when I joined the Giants at Winooski Park in Vermont in July," Robustelli said. "And I could feel that more and more as the season went on."

10

The Coal Miner's Son

*F*or Dick Modzelewski, the Giants' fifth game of the 1956 season, against the Pittsburgh Steelers, was a homecoming in two ways. First, "Little Mo" had spent the previous season playing for the Steelers. And second, Pittsburgh was only twenty-five miles east of his hometown of West Natrona, Pennsylvania. If you were an adult male from West Natrona, chances are you were Polish and worked in a coal mine, a steel mill, or one of the two chemical companies in the small, gritty town. "We had some black people in town, and even most of them could speak Polish too," Modzelewski said.

For more than thirty years, Modzelewski's father, Joseph, a Polish immigrant, worked in a coal mine, while during summer breaks from college, Dick and his brother Ed toiled at the Allegheny-Ludlum Steel Company, where one heard as much, if not more, Polish than English being spoken. "One summer, Ed also worked in the mine, but I wanted no part of that," Dick Modzelewski said. "Working in the steel mill was hard enough."

On the Saturday night before the game against the Steelers in November of 1956, Dick Modzelewski launched a tradition that would last for years whenever the Giants played in Pittsburgh. His sister's husband, Rich Nowicki, would pick him up at the Giants' hotel in Pittsburgh and drive him and the rest of the team's defensive line—Andy Robustelli, Jim Katcavage, and Rosey Grier—to the Modzelewski household in West Natrona, where his mother, Martha, had whipped up a Polish dinner of kielbasa, pierogi, stuffed cabbage, and duck soup. "Sometimes Rosey Brown came along too," Modzelewski said, referring to the team's All-Pro offensive tackle, who often filled in at defensive end on short-yardage situations near the Giants' goal line. "Then after dinner, my brother-in-law would drive us back to our hotel in Pittsburgh."

Since their high school days, Modzelewski had been called Little Mo and Ed, who was two years older, "Big Mo," because he had outweighed Dick by twenty pounds when they were in high school. That would change: By the time they got to the NFL, Dick, the same height as Ed, had grown to be more than thirty pounds heavier, but the nicknames remained. (An even younger brother, Gene, played guard at New Mexico State University and had a tryout with Cleveland in 1964. "He was called 'No Mo,' " Ed Modzelewski recalled, "because after he was born—the sixth child in our family—our mother said, 'No more,' which became No Mo, as in Big Mo and Little Mo.")

Little Mo had followed his older brother to the University of Maryland, where they played together for a year and were both All-Americans before Big Mo was drafted in the first round in 1952 by the Steelers. He remained there for only one season before being traded to Cleveland. A year later, Little Mo, drafted by the Redskins in the second round, was offered $3,500 by Washington owner George Preston Marshall. "I told him that my father was making six thousand dollars working in the mines and that Ed had gotten ten thousand as a rookie the year before with the Steelers," Modzelewski said. "He finally raised the offer to sixty-five hundred and then agreed to give me a thousand-dollar bonus. To get paid, every week you had to go to his office in a laundry he owned, and a secretary would give you an envelope with the money inside. That's how George Marshall operated."

After two years with the Redskins, Dick Modzelewski was traded to Pittsburgh, where he played in all twelve of the team's games in 1955 before being traded again, this time to the Giants. In later years, Modzelewski could take solace in having been traded by his "hometown" Steelers, since, during training camp his one season with Pittsburgh, a young quarterback out of the University of Louisville named John Unitas was cut without getting into a single preseason game. "None of us had heard of him, and he was a skinny, kind of funny-looking guy who wore old-fashioned high-top shoes

and had a funny way of walking. And from what I saw, he wasn't particularly impressive. But, then, he may have been nervous because
nobody seemed to pay much attention to him. Anyway, Walt Kies-
ling, the head coach, cut him, and we went with Jim Finks and Ted
Marchibroda at quarterback and finished dead last in the Eastern
Conference."

Tom Landry thought highly of Modzelewski, saying that he always played under control. Robustelli, Katcavage, and Grier—and
especially Grier—might take chances, but Little Mo played within
Landry's system. "Grier made strong moves with great speed, but
he often was overanxious and out of position, and Mo covered for
him," Landry was to say. "Though he was only about six feet tall,
Mo also had great strength and could control blockers. And he
could slide up and down the line very well."

Gregarious and fun loving, Modzelewski soon became the locker-
room cutup, regaling teammates with tales of his father's and other
relatives' coal-mining experiences and also singing Polish folk songs
that only he among the Giants could understand. Well liked by his
teammates, he was also a keen student of the game, often peppering
Robustelli with questions about strategy and tactics, which eventually
would lead to a long career as an assistant coach in the NFL.

Like most of the married Giants, Modzelewski lived in hotels
during his first few seasons with the Giants—first at the Excelsior
and then at the Concourse Plaza—before moving to Stamford with
his wife, where he would be closer to his best friend on the team,
Robustelli. "Everybody on the team respected Andy," Modzelewski
said. "He never raised his voice, but when he did talk, the guys paid
attention. I guess you might say he was a quiet leader. I think it was
Dick Lynch who gave him the name 'the Pope,' which is how we
used to refer to him when he wasn't around. Not that he probably
would have resented it. I guess the name fit, too, because he was
Italian and had been an altar boy right through high school.

"Once the team started to stay together at the Roosevelt Hotel
in Manhattan on the night before home games, Andy and I had a
regular routine," Modzelewski recollected. "We'd go to dinner at
Trader Vic's and then walk back to the hotel and watch *Gunsmoke*
on TV from ten to eleven o'clock, and then go to bed."

Maybe it was the big Polish feast the night before, but whatever the reason, the Giants came out flat against the Pittsburgh Steelers on Sunday, November 4 at Forbes Field, then also the home of the Pittsburgh Pirates. It was at Forbes Field where another Polish athlete, Bill Mazeroski, hit a dramatic home run over the left-field wall in the ninth inning of the seventh game of the 1960 World Series to beat the New York Yankees. Forbes Field also was where a forty-year-old Babe Ruth, playing for the Boston Braves and in his last major league season, hit his final home runs, three in all, in one afternoon during the summer of 1935. One of the Ruthian blasts carried over the right-field roof, something no one had ever done before.

Having routed the Steelers, 38–10, only two weeks earlier, the Giants were 10-point favorites. But they barely escaped with a 17–14 victory in a sloppy game in which each team lost the ball twice on fumbles and was forced to punt eight times. A field goal by Ben Agajanian in the second period, which gave the Giants a 10–0 lead, proved to be the margin of victory. Once again, though, the Giants' defense played a key role, blunting Pittsburgh offensive drives at the 12- and 6-yard lines, the first time on an interception by linebacker Bill Svoboda in the end zone.

The victory, the Giants' fifth in six games, left them tied for first place in the Eastern Conference with the Chicago Cardinals, the only team to have beaten the Giants. It also set up a showdown with the Cardinals the following Sunday at Yankee Stadium that drew a record crowd for a Giants home game: 62,110. Demonstrating clearly how the team had by now captured the imaginations of die-hard New York football fans, along with a remarkable number of casual sports followers, a game between the Giants and Cardinals thirteen months earlier at the Polo Grounds had drawn no more than 7,000 people. But, then, the Giants entered that game with a 2-6 record.

One aspect of Andy Robustelli's defensive talents that had attracted the attention of Rams scout Lou DeFilippo—his punt-blocking ability—set the tone for the game. Early in the first quarter, Robustelli spun around a former Los Angeles Rams teammate, left tackle Tom Dahms, and blocked a punt by Dave Mann at the Cardinals' 10-yard line, sending the ball bounding toward the end zone. Mann managed to pounce on it, but Dick Modzelewski immediately tackled Mann for a safety. With Don Heinrich still at quarterback—normally, Conerly would replace him early in the second quarter—the Giants scored their first touchdown midway through the second period when Heinrich faked handoffs to Alex Webster and Mel Triplett at the Chicago 6-yard line and then fired a pass to MacAfee in the end zone. The Cardinals finally got on the scoreboard late in the half when Pat Summerall, who had missed two field-goal attempts, nailed one from 30 yards out to make it 9–3 at halftime.

A 12-yard touchdown run by Webster and an 11-yard pass from Conerly to Gifford widened the Giants' lead to 23–3 before the Cardinals scored their lone touchdown late in the fourth quarter when backup quarterback Jim Root connected with Ollie Matson on a 12-yard pass.

Stymied by the Giants' defensive line, the perennial All-Pro running back Matson gained only 43 yards rushing, while the Cardinals' other outstanding runner, Johnny Olszewski, was limited to 46 yards. By contrast, Webster and Gifford accounted for 76 and 68 yards, respectively, in a 23–10 victory that gave the Giants sole possession of first place in the NFL's Eastern Conference. Not only that, but the Giants' defense had now given up only four touchdowns in the last five games, and suddenly New York sports fans were raving about these new Giants defenders. So much so that when the Cardinals reached the Giants' 10-yard line in the fourth quarter, several hundred fans in the center-field bleachers began a chant never heard before at an NFL game—"*Dee*-fense! *Dee*-fense!"—which spread throughout the stadium. Over the next eight years, it would become a rallying cry to the Giants' defense whenever an opponent neared their goal line. And the bulk of the credit went to the defensive line. In the following years it would also be heard at other football games, and basketball games, too. Before long, something else unique would happen at Giants home games: The defensive team would be introduced, sometimes ahead of the offense, which, traditionally, always was introduced. Under Landry's 4–3 scheme, the middle linebacker was the key player, and generally was credited with the majority of the team's tackles. Then the chant of "Huff! Huff!" often resounded through Yankee Stadium.

"I know I got credit for a lot of the tackles," Huff was to concede, "but quite often one or more of the guys up front already would have slowed down the runner, and it was easy for me to put him away. Here I was a rookie, who for a while thought I might not even make the team, and I was playing behind one of the best front fours of all time. Maybe even the best one ever."

Suddenly the Giants were the toast of the town, with as many of the defensive players as those from the offense readily recognized out in public. When about fifteen players and their wives walked into Toots Shor's on Sunday night after the Cardinals game, most of the patrons stood up and cheered. Same thing happened a few hours later when some of the group entered Mike Manuche's steak house a few blocks away, and then again later that night when the group stopped off at P. J. Clarke's to close out the night's partying.

With all of the Giants' games now being televised by CBS, albeit with a blackout within a seventy-five-mile radius of New York City, the team's fan base was expanding considerably. Football fans who had never seen the Giants play and had no intention of driving to New York to see a game now found themselves rooting for the Giants. And as crowds at Yankee Stadium grew increasingly larger, more and more fans from the New York metropolitan area drove to motels and restaurants—particularly in Connecticut—on Sundays to watch Giants home games on television. Suddenly, too, Gifford, Conerly, Rote, Robustelli, and Huff, among others, became some of the biggest celebrities in a city of celebrities. And now that CBS was televising NFL games, more and more TV executives, along with advertising agency honchos with television ties, got caught up in the growing tide of support for the Giants. Frank Gifford, who had been doing some television commercials since joining the team in 1952, now found himself so much in demand that he had to hire an agent to handle his nonfootball affairs. Around the same time, Conerly was portraying the Marlboro Man in cigarette ads, and a number of Giants who had taken to rubbing elbows with advertising and network TV executives would find themselves being asked to do commercials and, in a few cases, sports commentary on radio and television.

Not that New York was the only city to afford NFL players such opportunities. It also was happening, although on a much more limited basis, in Chicago, Los Angeles, and some other NFL towns. But New York was where CBS had its world headquarters, as did the other two major broadcasting networks at the time. It was also where most major advertising agencies and news agencies were based, and where the New York football Giants not only had perhaps the game's most glamorous player in Frank Gifford, but were the hottest team in the National Football League.

"Can't Anybody Out There Block?"

$\mathcal{I}$f the Giants were the hottest team in the NFL in mid-November of 1956, the Washington Redskins were sizzling too. After losing their first three games, the Redskins had won three straight while having to use their backup quarterback. Al Dorow, who had thrown only a dozen passes the previous season, would start against the Giants at Griffith Stadium in Washington, since the Redskins' starting quarterback, little Eddie LeBaron, was still hurt.

Though LeBaron was the NFL's smallest quarterback at five-foot-seven and 165 pounds, and had trouble seeing over the huge members of his offensive line, he had been the Redskins' starter since his rookie year of 1952, succeeding the great Sammy Baugh. Alluding to LeBaron's size, one of his receivers once said, "You run a pass pattern and look back, and there's nobody there to throw the ball. Or at least you can't see him behind the line of scrimmage. And then suddenly the ball is coming your way, as if from out of nowhere." Extremely agile, with an arm that belied his small stature, and a good runner and punter, LeBaron had developed into one of the league's best quarterbacks. Dorow, by contrast, was a journeyman who in 1960 would become the first starting quarterback for the New York Titans of the new American Football League. But on this day in Washington, Dorow shone.

Favored by a touchdown, the Giants, inept on offense and surprisingly porous on defense, were stunned by an early Washington attack that gave the Redskins a 24–0 halftime lead before a crowd of 26,261. A roughing-the-kicker penalty by the Giants on the

Redskins' first drive and a fumble by fullback Mel Triplett deep inside Giants territory set up the first two Washington touchdowns, after which Redskins halfback Billy Wells recovered a Dorow fumble in the end zone for a third touchdown.

After Sam Baker kicked his second field goal to make it 27–0, the Giants recorded their only score when Charlie Conerly completed 7 passes during an 85-yard drive late in the third period, the last one a 12-yarder to end Bob Schnelker. Though Dorow was intercepted three times, he outplayed Conerly, completing 10 of 18 passes for 160 yards, while Conerly made good on 12 of 27 for 151 yards. Don Heinrich and seldom-used Bob Clatterbuck, making his first appearance of the season, connected on 2 of 5 passes for 24 yards between the two of them.

The loss startled the Giants. Afterward most of them stared into the darkness outside the Pennsylvania Railroad train that carried the team back to New York or quietly played cards. Vince Lombardi, as he was wont to do when things went wrong, spent the five-hour return trip in a funk, reading a newspaper and not uttering a word.

Most startling of all the statistics were the 231 yards the Redskins gained on the ground against what had begun to look like the best defense in the NFL. "Tackling was not a strong point for New York," Lou Effrat understated, in his story for the *New York Times*. "Too often the Redskins were allowed to pick up additional yardage after they apparently had been stopped."

Startling, too, were the paltry 13 yards that Alex Webster and Mel Triplett combined for out of the Giants' backfield. On the offensive side, only Frank Gifford had a reasonably good day, gaining 61 of the 74 yards the Giants amassed on the ground.

If there was any consolation, it came in the form of a victory by the Pittsburgh Steelers over the Chicago Cardinals, which enabled the Giants to maintain their one-game lead in the Eastern Conference. But that was small balm for such a one-sided loss to a team that had been beaten by three teams—the Steelers, the Eagles, and the Cardinals—that the Giants had defeated in the previous three weeks. Looming ahead the following Sunday were the Chicago Bears, who not only had won seven straight games but were averaging 35 points per contest. Typifying their turnaround, the Bears had avenged their lone defeat at Baltimore by crushing the Colts three weeks later, 58–27.

Meeting at Yankee Stadium on Monday morning, Jim Lee How-ell, Tom Landry, Vince Lombardi, Ed Kolman, and assistant coach Ken Kavanaugh repeatedly went over films of the game, stopping the projector time and again when blatant flaws, particularly in the Giants' defense, were spotted. Landry, as usual, said little but seethed inside at the Giants' poor tackling and weak play in the secondary. Lombardi bellowed aloud at several junctures. "Jesus Christ! Hold on to the god-*dam* ball!" he shouted when the film showed Triplett fumbling the football. Similar rants were voiced by the old Fordham Block of Granite when Giants blockers failed to open up holes for Webster, Triplett, and Gifford.

"Can't anybody out there block?" he yelled at another point when Alex Webster was hit by two Redskins defenders and thrown for a 7-yard loss. Howell, apart from a few exclamations directed at the defense, remained quiet during most of the session, but he would not remain silent as the film, exposing the numerous mistakes of omission and commission, rolled in front of the entire team on Tuesday morning. Lombardi, to no one's surprise, continued to scowl and harangue the offense during the grueling practice session that followed. Apart from Conerly and Gifford, practically no one was spared his wrath. Landry, by contrast, dressed down the defensive unit collectively. "You can do better," he said sternly, "if for no other reason than you can hardly do worse."

It would be a film and practice session that the Giants players would not forget for the rest of the 1956 season.

━━━

In meeting the Bears on Sunday, November 25, at Yankee Stadium, the Giants would be confronting a team with running back Rick Casares (the 1956 NFL leader in touchdowns and yards gained), two solid quarterbacks in Ed Brown and George Blanda, an outstanding receiver in Harlon Hill, and a strong defense. In Blanda, the Bears also had the league's most accurate placekicker. A month earlier, he had missed his first extra point after converting 156 in a row, a streak that began during his rookie year in 1951. Blanda's streak broke the NFL record of 105, set by another eventual Hall of Famer, Lou Groza, the Cleveland two-way tackle who also handled his team's placekicking. This was an era when most teams, with a maximum roster of thirty-three, did not have the luxury of affording players who did nothing but kick extra points and field goals.*

Though Blanda would make 45 of 47 extra points and 12 of 28 field-goal attempts for 81 points in 1956, he would be outscored by another eventual Hall of Fame quarterback, Bobby Layne of the Detroit Lions. The colorful and feisty Layne, renowned almost as much for his carousing as his all-around excellence on the football field, would connect on the same number of field goals—12—and all 33 extra-point attempts. He also would score five touchdowns for a grand total of 99 points, which would lead the NFL in scoring.

Missing from the sidelines during the game—but watching from the press box—was the Bears' founder and owner, George Halas, who stepped aside as coach following the 1955 season after having coached the team since its start in 1922 (though he would return in 1958 for another ten years). In his place was Paddy Driscoll, a longtime Bears assistant coach and former Bears and Chicago Cardinals player who, like Halas, could trace his pro football roots to 1920 and the formation of the American Professional Football Association, the predecessor of the NFL. For long-term associations with professional football, no one went further back than Halas, a founder, coach, and player with the Decatur Staleys, and Driscoll, an eventual Pro Football Hall of Famer, who coached and played for the Chicago Cardinals from 1920 through 1929, then joined the Bears as an assistant coach. Though Driscoll had played and coached in an era when players wore leather helmets, the football was a good deal more round, and the dropkick— which he excelled at—was still popular, both for field goals and extra points, he was hardly old-fashioned, as he was to demonstrate against the Giants.

Despite temperatures in the 20s and the lopsided loss to Washington the week before, a crowd of around fifty-five thousand turned out for the game. Fired up after a series of stern lectures by Landry during the week, the defensive line in particular was outstanding, holding the high-scoring Bears without a touchdown for the first three quarters and limiting Casares to only 18 yards in 13 carries and the Bears to 12 yards net overall on the ground.

*Blanda's record eventually would be broken by Jason Elam of the Denver Broncos, a contemporary-type placekicker who, unlike Blanda, Layne, and Groza, was not a position player, and kicked 371 consecutive extra points. The seemingly indestructible Blanda, though, would wind up with an NFL record of 943 extra points in 959 tries for a 98.3 percentage. And 4 of his 16 misses were in his last year of 1975, when he was forty-eight years old.

Meanwhile, the Giants would take a 17–0 lead on a field goal by Ben Agajanian and a 17-yard touchdown pass from Don Heinrich to Kyle Rote in the first half, and a 2-yard burst by Alex Webster early in the third period after Modzelewski recovered a fumble by Blanda at the Chicago 18-yard line.

Given the outstanding defensive play by the Giants, there was no cause for alarm when midway through the third quarter the Bears finally scored on Blanda's 22-yard field goal. The 17–3 score would last into the final period. Then Harlon Hill, a strapping third-year end who had played college ball in obscurity at tiny Florence Teachers College, and had been recommended to Halas by the legendary coach and T-formation innovator Clark Shaughnessy, made two catches that stunned both the Yankee Stadium crowd and the Giants. On the first one, quarterback Ed Brown faked a handoff to Casares at the Bears' 21-yard line, then handed the ball to Bill McColl, an end who was lined up as a halfback. McColl, while running to his right, then fired a perfect 50-yard pass to Hill, who had beaten safeties Emlen Tunnell and Jimmy Patton on the right side and ran 29 yards for a touchdown. Blanda's extra point drew the Bears to within a touchdown.

With slightly over a minute to play, the Bears struck again on a long pass play, again involving the six-foot-three Hill. On this one, he sprinted down the middle, then cut again to his right. Patton appeared to have Hill well covered as Brown unloaded a pass that hit Hill's outstretched hands just as he was tackled by Patton, jarring the ball loose. Somehow, though, while falling to the ground in the end zone under Patton's grasp, Hill managed to grab the ball for a spectacular touchdown. Blanda's ensuing extra point gave the Bears a 17–17 tie and touched off a spate of boos for the first time during what had become a glorious Giants season.

The Giants defensive unit walked off the field stunned. With less than a minute to play, the Giants still had time, but were unable to get within field-goal range before the game ended. After having taken the 17–0 lead, New York had played conservatively, seemingly content to sit on the lead. Later, Lombardi blamed himself for allowing the Bears to tie the score, conceding that he had told Charlie Conerly—who, much to his chagrin, had sat out the first three quarters—not to take any chances and to stay on the ground when he entered the game. "I learned a lesson," Lombardi said. "From then on, no matter what the score was, I coached as if it was nothing–nothing."

Suddenly, in a week's span, the Giants seemed to have lost their momentum, despite still maintaining a half-game lead in the Eastern Conference.

Never one to gloat, "Papa Bear" George Halas, sitting alongside Driscoll after the game, could not help but admit he was pleased with the outcome. "I've got to be happy with a tie after the poor game we played today," the Bears' patriarch said with a smile. "Those were two great plays we made at the end." As a result of Harlon Hill's heroics, the Bears, at 7-1-1, took a half-game lead in the Western Conference over Layne's Lions, which had won their first six games before losing to Washington by 1 point and to Green Bay by 4 points to fall to 7-2, with three games left in the regular season.

As usual, Charlie and Perian Conerly hosted a postgame cocktail party in their suite at the Concourse Plaza Hotel, but what laughter occurred was subdued, as was the case later at Toots Shor's, where even the ebullient proprietor could not extricate the Giants from the gloom that had enveloped the team in the game's final moments. Still, the Giants were in a position to control their own destiny and win the Eastern Conference title, with the next two games at home, against Washington and Cleveland, and the final one in Philadelphia. The problem, as Howell, Landry, and Lombardi realized, was that the team, so strong on both offense and defense at the start of the season, had turned out to be inconsistent at the worst possible time.

―

Jimmy Patton, Emlen Tunnell, Dick Nolan, Ed Hughes, and Henry Moore all looked on incredulously Tuesday morning as Tom Landry played what for the Giants' secondary was a horror film: the final minutes of the tie with the Bears. Landry, patient as always, pointed out mistakes by the Giants' defenders while at the same time conceding that Harlon Hill had twice been outstanding, both in running his routes and in making difficult catches. Meanwhile, Lombardi, again "Mr. Low," scowled at his offensive charges, particularly while watching the Giants fail to score over the last twenty-five minutes. "Scoring one touchdown in a half isn't going to do it, even when your defensive line is playing a helluva great game," he said loudly at one point. "You guys had better wake up for Washington next Sunday, or it's going to be over; you all know what they did to us last time." The Giants didn't have to be reminded; they remembered that 33–7 thrashing nine days earlier all too well.

12

The Complete Football Player

*G*oing to work at his sporting goods store the day after the one-sided loss to Washington the week before had been bad enough, but for Andy Robustelli, having to wait on customers and stock shelves after the tie with Chicago was worse. The Bears were definitely better than the Redskins, yet the Giants had outplayed them through three quarters. But the tie was particularly disturbing because the Giants seemingly had the game won, then let victory slip away. As usual, everyone coming into the store who knew Robustelli played with the Giants—and most customers did, even in tony Greenwich—wanted to talk about the game, which was the last thing Robustelli wanted to do. But he knew he had to do it, and, painful though it was, he did.

"I never liked to talk football while I was in the store working, or, later, when I started my company," Robustelli said years later. "But I found myself in situations where I could not avoid it."

Robustelli knew what the questions would be before they were asked. More than a few people would ask, "What happened to the Giants' offense in the second half?" Always gracious, Robustelli probably would answer it by praising the Bears' defense. Inevitably, too, he'd be asked, "What happened on those two long touchdown passes by the Bears?" Again, he probably would praise the execution of both touchdown plays and note—as he would in subsequent interviews—that Harlon Hill's catch on the second touchdown was "one of the greatest catches I ever saw."

The questions would keep coming, even from friends, after Robustelli had stopped for gas on the way home and then during phone calls, when, again, he would do his best to answer them, often in a circuitous manner—a rhetorical style he had already mastered—that left one wondering what he really had said. But, hey, if this was part of the price of being a successful football player—and then, he hoped, a successful businessman—answering such questions was well worth it.

On Tuesday at Yankee Stadium, two days after the Bears game, Robustelli and the rest of the Giants' defensive unit listened intently as Landry dissected the two touchdown passes to Hill. Landry was not one to cast blame easily, and in the case of both passes, no one in the Giants' secondary or on the pass rush was to blame. Hill, Landry pointed out, had run perfect routes, and both passes were perfectly thrown. And the Bears' blocking on both plays was excellent. Lombardi—"Mr. High-Low"—might not talk to his offense for a few days because of their second-half flameout, but Landry, in cases where he felt no one was to blame, would not bear a grudge toward his players. And he did not during the film session and practice that Tuesday.

"Tom was never moody like Vince," Robustelli said. "When mistakes were made, he'd say, 'Okay, you know what went wrong, now it's up to you to fix it.' " But in the case of the two touchdown passes to Harlon Hill, Landry felt that nothing went wrong; it was just a matter of everything going right for the Bears on both plays.

If the Giants had good reason to bounce back from the one-sided loss to the Redskins and the blown 17–0 lead against the Bears, Washington had much to gain too. After losing their first three games, the Redskins had now won seven in a row and were within striking distance of first place in the Eastern Conference with three games to play.

With that in mind, almost five thousand Redskins fans, along with the one-hundred-member Redskins marching band, were among a crowd of almost forty-seven thousand at Yankee Stadium on December 2. Charlie Conerly, always quiet to begin with, was to recall later that the Giants' locker room in the hours before the game was the quietest he could recall in the nine years he had been with the team. Jim Katcavage, as would become his trademark, was the first player to arrive, shortly before ten o'clock in the morning—more than three hours before the opening kickoff. "Mr. First," as some players came to call him, had a fetish about being first, whether it was for practice, a game, or to board a team bus. "I don't know why, but I always had to be first," Katcavage said. "It had nothing to do with ego; I just had to be the first guy to have his ankles taped, the first one in a restaurant, the first at practice, and so on. And as the first one on the bus, I always sat right up front. Sometimes, if I was running late, the guys would wait until I arrived so I could be the first one on the bus. I don't know why, but that's the way it was."

In contrast to the first game between the two teams two weeks earlier, the Giants struck for two touchdowns early in the first quarter. Then they added touchdowns in the third and fourth quarters to beat the Redskins, 28–14. For Frank Gifford, enjoying his best season yet since joining the Giants in 1952, it was a memorable afternoon as he figured in all four Giants touchdowns—twice on runs, once as a pass receiver, and the fourth time when he threw a touchdown pass. In all, Gifford gained 108 yards on 19 carries for an average of better than 5 yards a carry; caught six passes for 53 yards, including a 14-yard touchdown pass from Charlie Conerly (who completed 10 of 16 passes after relieving Don Heinrich in the second period); and threw a 29-yard touchdown pass to Ken MacAfee for the Giants' first touchdown.

Responding to the repeated chants of "*Dee*-fense! *Dee*-fense!" the Giants forced three fumbles by the Redskins and picked off four Al Dorow passes—two by Sam Huff, who seemingly was all over the field in his best game yet as a Giant; and the others by safety Emlen Tunnell and cornerback Jimmy Patton. Tunnell's interception came in the end zone, averting a possible Redskins touchdown in the second quarter.

Redskins coach Joe Kuharich, paid high tribute to Gifford. "He's one of the finest backs around today," Kuharich said. "He does so many things well. I thought my club played harder than usual, but there was nothing we could do. No question, the Giants have all the attributes of a championship team."

They certainly did on this cold early-December afternoon. The big question was, would the Giants once again suffer a letdown in their remaining two games against Cleveland at home and Philadelphia on the road? If they did, not only would there be no championship for the Giants, there would be no championship game.

But for now, after having lost some of their allure over the previous two weeks, the Giants had reinstated themselves as the toast of the town. They may have been largely ignored while playing at the Polo Grounds, but now with a team that included such charismatic players as Gifford, Huff, and, in his quiet way, the Marlboro Man himself, the Giants had seemingly overtaken the Yankees in popularity. After all, the Yankees were *supposed* to win every year, and usually did. But the Giants? This collection of players, cohesive and friendly with one another and with their fans in public, was something new and something special, and everyone, from network and advertising executives to sports fans who had paid scant attention to the NFL in the past, had jumped on the Giants' bandwagon.

No one reveled more in the attention and adulation of Giants fans, and the public in general, than Frank Gifford. Movie-star handsome and articulate, though somewhat shy (although certainly not with women), Gifford was a real-life Hollywood version of a football star—a perfectly proportioned six-foot-one, 195-pound halfback, who, Vince Lombardi said, "could burst through a line faster than any player I've ever seen." Besides being fast, with a graceful style of running, Gifford had uncanny instincts on how to avoid a tackler or, on an option play, whether to throw the ball or keep on running. In the Giants' backfield, he was the antithesis of Alex Webster and Mel Triplett, both of whom relied to a considerable extent on brute force and power. Gifford, the elusive open-field runner, complemented his two backfield colleagues perfectly.

Moreover, no one on the team was more versatile than Gifford, the only Giant named to the Pro Bowl game at the end of the season as both an offensive and defensive player. During his first two years with the Giants, Gifford played in the defensive secondary, punted, kicked off, and returned punts and kickoffs. Though no longer asked to assume those duties, he was the team's best receiver, a very good passer, a good blocker, and on occasion was still called on to kick field goals and extra points. Indeed, with two games left in the regular season, he was among the top five NFL players in yards gained rushing and receiving.

Off the field, Gifford, often in the company of Conerly and Kyle Rote, or his wife, Maxine, appeared as comfortable at Toots Shor's, Downey's, P. J. Clarke's, the Copacabana nightclub, and other popular and fashionable restaurants and nightspots as he did at Yankee Stadium. And by 1956, Gifford was a well-established star, respected by both his teammates and Giants fans in general. It had not always been that way. Over the years, Gifford has said that, in addition to Steve Owen and Jim Lee Howell, some of the old-school Giants coaches and some Giants veterans resented him when he first joined the team in 1952. At times Gifford suspected that, at Owen's instructions, the offensive line would not block for him during practice scrimmages, and he would get hit hard by several players. "During practices, I'd get a thumb in the eye here, an elbow in the ribs there," he wrote in his biography, *The Whole Ten Yards.* "Or if I missed a block, I'd hear 'You dumb f——!' They also had their little cliques, and I didn't belong to any of them." Gifford went on to say that he understood their attitude—that they had perceived him from the time he arrived at training camp as a glamour boy, "all glitz and no substance."

Gifford, of course, had proven them wrong. There may have been an aura of glamour about the handsome halfback, and even some glitz, but there was definitely substance, both on and off the field. Still, some of the Giants never entirely came around to liking him, in part, no doubt, because of his movie making and endorsements.

"Frank was an opportunist who was always looking for a connection," said Don Smith, who first covered Gifford as a sportswriter and was the Giants' public relations director during the latter part of Gifford's career. "If he was introduced to two people in a restaurant and found out that one was, say, an advertising or broadcasting executive, Frank would spend all of his time talking with the executive, who he realized might be able to help him, and totally ignore the other guy. But that was Frank."

But even though there occasionally was tension between the Giants' offense and defense—to the point where some writers maintained that there were, in fact, two Giants teams, the offensive team and the defensive one—it is clear that most of the Giants had tremendous respect for Gifford on the playing field. He was at his best in big games and in pressure situations. And he rarely missed a game, often playing while he was hurt, as did many of the Giants of the era. Gifford was tough, immensely talented, extremely resilient, a very good team player, and the best all-around player in Giants history. He was indeed the complete football player.

—

On paper, at least, the Browns would seem to have had little chance of beating the Giants in their second meeting on Sunday, December 15, at Yankee Stadium. At 4-6 with two games to go, the Browns' streak of winning Eastern Conference titles all six years they had been in the NFL was nearing an end. The only incentive the Browns had was to try to avoid a losing season. And that seemed unlikely, since they had been beaten by the Giants, 21–9, in the third game of the season and would have to play the Chicago Cardinals, who had also already beaten the Browns. For the Giants, meanwhile, there was ample motivation, since a loss to the Browns would mean they would have to beat or tie the Philadelphia Eagles in their final game of the season to win the Eastern Conference title. Still, the Browns had won three of their last five games and had regained the services of several offensive linemen who had missed the first game against the Giants. And Tommy O'Connell, the third quarterback the Browns had used following season-ending injuries to George Ratterman and Babe Parilli, had been impressive in the four games he had started.

To the astonishment of a small crowd of 27,707, the Browns, 10½-point underdogs, outplayed the Giants in a game played in rain and snow on a cold December afternoon. Unlike the first game, the Cleveland offensive line kept the vaunted Giants' front four at bay, blocking superbly. Lou Groza, the Browns' outstanding left tackle, had been overpowered by Robustelli in the first game, allowing Robustelli to sack Ratterman six times. But in the rematch, Groza marginalized Robustelli, preventing him from spinning him around and getting to the quarterback as he had in Cleveland. Dick Modzelewski, also outstanding in that first game, was kept in check by Herschel Forester, while Sam Huff was contained by the fierce Cleveland blocking during most of the game.

Chuck Heaton wrote in the next day's *Cleveland Plain Dealer*, "Particularly hard hit by Groza and company were Robustelli and Huff, the rookie linebacker, who had been the villains" in the first game between the two teams.

After the Browns took advantage of a fumble by Mel Triplett on the Giants' 19-yard line to score their first touchdown in the opening quarter, the Giants tied it at 7–7 in the second quarter when

Charlie Conerly led New York on a 63-yard drive that ended with a 16-yard pass to Frank Gifford in the end zone.

Remarkably, the Giants would not score again in the mud, rain, and snow on a day when they could have ended their first season at Yankee Stadium by winning the Eastern Conference title. They would now have to beat the lowly Philadelphia Eagles in Philadelphia six days later if they were to earn a berth in the NFL championship game for the first time since 1946.

Slightly more than two minutes after the Giants' lone touchdown, Groza booted a 41-yard field goal that gave the Browns a 10–7 lead. The Giants went nowhere on their next possession, then the Browns drove 74 yards in 13 plays for their second touchdown, which came on a 6-yard pass from quarterback Tommy O'Connell to fullback Fred Morrison—the only pass thrown during the drive.

Cleveland's defense remained unremitting in the second half, holding the Giants scoreless. Many in the chilled crowd began to boo Conerly, who made good on only 10 of 24 passes for 103 yards. The Browns, meanwhile, tacked on a third touchdown early in the third quarter when O'Connell capped an 81-yard march by sneaking over from the 1-yard line as he had for the visitors' first score. By then, the crowd had switched from its intimidating chant of "*Dee*-fense!" into a chorus of boos.

O'Connell surprised the Giants with his play in the 24–7 victory. A journeyman at best, he had been a backup quarterback with the Bears during his rookie year of 1953 but then served the next two years in the army during the Korean War. When he returned in 1956, he was cut by the Bears' owner and coach on the grounds that, at five-feet-ten, O'Connell was too short to play quarterback. Apparently Papa Bear Halas got the impression that O'Connell had mysteriously shrunk during his military service, since he was still the same height as when he had played with the Bears in 1953. He was signed by the Browns after George Ratterman suffered a career-ending knee injury in the fifth game of the season, and backup Babe Parilli also had been hurt. With Paul Brown focusing on a ground game, whose trap and draw plays flummoxed the Giants time and again, O'Connell threw only 11 passes, completing 7.

"He was amazing," Paul Brown said of O'Connell. "He was calm and poised throughout the game. We've won three of four games he's started, and should have won the fourth too. Just think of what we could have done if he had been here since preseason training."

If the Giants had trouble stopping O'Connell, they had an even worse time with the Browns' runners, especially Morrison. Time and again, Morrison, who gained 116 yards on the ground—8 more yards than the Giants netted rushing—caught the Giants off guard and out of position on draw plays. By comparison, Frank Gifford, the Giants' primary running threat, was stymied by both the soggy field and the stalwart Browns defense, managing only 16 yards on six carries, although he did catch six passes for 56 yards.

Jim Lee Howell's brief summation of the game spoke volumes. "We couldn't stop them," the head coach said. "We just weren't sharp. We took too long getting the ball, and when we did, we did nothing with it. And their blockers took us out of there."

None of the Giants was about to argue with Howell's succinct critique of a game that seemingly everyone had expected the Giants to win. Despite the defeat, the Giants remained atop the Eastern Conference and needed only a win or a tie in their final game the following Saturday in Philadelphia. Nevertheless, the loss would linger in the minds of most of the Giants players and would mark the beginning of one of the NFL's biggest rivalries.

Fortunately for the Giants, their final regular-season game was against an injury-depleted Philadelphia Eagles team that had won only one of its last seven games and had not scored more than two touchdowns in any of those games. The lack of interest in the Eagles and their disappointing 3-7-1 record was reflected in the small crowd of 16,562 that turned out on Saturday, December 15, at Connie Mack Stadium, home of the baseball Philadelphia Phillies.

Playing for pride and not much more, the Eagles forced the Giants to punt on their first two possessions and held the visitors scoreless in the opening quarter. But thereafter Gifford, Webster, and Triplett became virtually impossible to stop en route to amassing a total of 291 yards on the ground. Meanwhile, the Giants' defensive line, so surprisingly porous the Sunday before, held the Eagles to only 71 yards rushing and more resembled the unit that had become the first front four in NFL history to be called the "Fearsome Foursome"—a name subsequently given to a host of other defensive lines over the years.

For the first time all season, Don Heinrich went the distance at quarterback. Once the Giants got rolling in the second quarter, scoring twice, with Gifford figuring in both touchdowns, and totally dominating the Eagles, both Howell and Lombardi felt there was no reason to replace Heinrich with Conerly and risk injury to the thirty-five-year-old veteran. At that, Heinrich, on instructions from Howell and Lombardi, primarily handed the ball off to Gifford, Webster, and Triplett. Heinrich threw only 11 passes, completing 4 of them for 41 yards and one interception.

On the first touchdown, which climaxed a 65-yard drive, Gifford took a pitchout from Heinrich and, running to his left, threw a 6-yard pass to Kyle Rote in the end zone. Shortly thereafter, the Giants scored again when Gifford burst through right tackle from 10 yards out to take a 14–0 halftime lead.

The lead increased to 21–0 in the third quarter when Emlen Tunnell intercepted a pass by Eagles quarterback Adrian Burk deep in Philadelphia territory, and Webster eventually barreled through the left side for the Giants' third touchdown. By then, the Eagles still had not crossed the 50-yard line and had demonstrated they were no match for the Giants' running game or its revitalized defense. Philadelphia finally scored its lone touchdown with less than two minutes to play when Burk connected with Bobby Walston in the end zone.

Even though the Giants had advanced to the NFL championship game with the 21–7 win, the team's celebration was muted, apparently because of the failure to have done so the previous Sunday and also because they had squandered a 17–0 lead over the Chicago Bears, also at the stadium, the week before that. As it developed, in the championship game on December 30, they would get an opportunity to avenge the deflating tie to the Bears; Chicago beat the second-place Detroit Lions in a game that decided the Western Conference championship the day after the Giants had won the East. Since winning their last NFL title in 1938, the Giants had been beaten four straight times in a championship game—twice by the Green Bay Packers and twice by the Bears. Jim Lee Howell had started at right end for the Giants in four of those five games, missing only the one in 1944 when he was in the marines. But, then, in none of those four losses did the Giants have a defensive line to compare with their current one, or an offense with players like Frank Gifford, Charlie Conerly, Kyle Rote, and Alex Webster, and assistant coaches like Tom Landry and Vince Lombardi.

13

Ed and Andy's Sports Store
to the Rescue

*A*s with most NFL teams, Tuesday was traditionally the day the Giants began preparation for a game the following Sunday. But in the week before the championship game against the Bears on December 30, Tuesday was Christmas Day, so Jim Lee Howell instead had the team practice on Monday morning, Christmas Eve, at Yankee Stadium. A cold, blustery day, it would serve as an omen for the following Sunday.

Of the thirty-three Giants, only Andy Robustelli, Alex Webster, and cornerback Dick Nolan were able to spend the holiday at home, since they all lived less than an hour's drive from the stadium. For the Robustelli family, it was a very special day, since it was the first Christmas for five-month-old Andra. Surrounded by his large family, including his three older children, his parents, his brother, and five sisters at the home of his in-laws, the Giants' All-Pro defensive end could hardly have been happier. Though his wife and three children had been with him on Christmas the previous year in Los Angeles, the Rams had spent a good part of the day practicing for their NFL title game on Monday, December 26, against the Cleveland Browns.

More than half of the rest of the Giants lived too far away to spend Christmas at home. Most of them were married, almost all to women they had met in high school or college. They were treated to a full-course dinner by the Mara family in the dining room at the Concourse Plaza Hotel. For a number of years, Tim Mara had invited the players and their families to dinner at the hotel on Thanksgiving. Now, with the season having extended beyond Christmas for the Giants for the first time ever, he had begun another holiday tradition that would extend for years.

Unlike the media hype and the hoopla in the two weeks leading up to latter-day Super Bowl games, the Giants-Bears title game in 1956, like other NFL championship games of the era, was a low-key affair. "The Giants treated it as if it were just another game," said Robert Daley, the team's public relations director at the time. Indeed, the Bears did not arrive until the day before the game and did not even hold a press conference following their one and only workout at Yankee Stadium. Also, media interest—so overwhelming starting in the 1970s—was minimal. Apart from writers from Chicago and New York, few newspapers sent sportswriters to New York to write advance stories or even to cover the game, and game day was a far cry from "Super Sunday," which in large measure because of a collective media excess and high-powered publicity by the league and the broadcasting networks, the day of the NFL championship game eventually evolved into a national holiday of sorts. Nor at halftime of NFL title games in the 1950s were there flyovers of Air Force jets nor fireworks displays, both of which became staples of the extravagant Super Bowl festivities following the first half and which drew as many spectators as the games themselves.

"The Maras weren't about to spend any money for entertainment because there wasn't much money in the budget as it was," Daley said. Veteran broadcaster Bob Wolff said the notoriously parsimonious Redskins owner George Marshall did not offer halftime entertainment for another reason, possibly shared by some other NFL owners. "Marshall felt that if you gave the fans entertainment at halftime they wouldn't go to the concessions and buy hotdogs, hamburgers and other stuff," Wolff said, "and the team would lose out on a lot of money."

Ironically, though, the Redskins were one of the first NFL teams to organize their own band, which became immensely popular both at home games and when the team played on the road. Rather than follow suit, the Giants eventually brought in high school bands from the metropolitan area to entertain at home games at Yankee Stadium.

As the week wore on, the weather turned colder, and by Friday, with a forecast of temperatures in the single digits on game day, the Yankee Stadium turf was rock hard and in danger of freezing over. Suddenly Wellington Mara's memory flashed back twenty-two years. Though he was only fifteen years old at the time, Mara vividly recalled how the Giants had slipped and slid across the frozen turf at the Polo Grounds during the first half of a championship game against the Bears on December 9, 1934, before switching from cleats to basketball sneakers.

Taking note of the frozen field before that game at the Polo Grounds, Ray Flaherty, a Giants end, had suggested to coach Steve Owen that the Giants wear sneakers. "When I was playing for Gonzaga U., we did that once on a frozen field, borrowing them from the basketball team, and beat a team a lot better than us," Flaherty had told Owen. The coach promptly dispatched Abe Cohen to Manhattan College, about a fifteen-minute ride away where Cohen, a tailor and a general factotum of sorts for the Giants, was also connected with the college football team and knew his way around the equipment room. Cohen had immediately hailed a taxi and ridden to Manhattan College, in the Riverdale section of the Bronx, asking the cabdriver to wait outside while he grabbed about thirty pairs of basketball shoes and returned to the Polo Grounds.

Cohen's timing could not have been better. The Giants had only been able to score a field goal and trailed the Bears, 13–3, when Cohen arrived back in the third quarter. "Some of the players didn't want to put them on, but those who did had so much success that eventually most of our players put them on," Wellington Mara recalled. "In the second half, we began to move the ball, and one of the Bears players went over to the sideline and told George Halas that we were wearing sneakers. 'Step on their toes!' Halas shouted to his players."

The sneaker caper paid off, big. The Giants exploded for 27 points to win the game and the NFL title, 30–13. It prompted poetic praise from a New York *American* sportswriter, who wrote, "To the heroes of antiquity, to the Greek who raced across the Marathon plain, and to Paul Revere, now add the name of Abe Cohen."

So it was that two days before the 1956 championship game, Jim Lee Howell, at Mara's suggestion, had halfback Gene Filipski run around the field in a pair of basketball shoes while defensive back Ed Hughes did so with cleats. It was obvious that Filipski got far better traction. Aware that Robustelli was the co-owner of a sporting goods store, Mara asked him if he could put through a rush order of rubber-soled basketball shoes. "Later that day, I called Frank Yohan, who was a district manager for the U.S. Rubber Company and lived in Greenwich, where our store was, and asked if he could bring in four dozen pairs of a new sneaker called Big League, which we already were stocking, by Saturday morning," Robustelli said, "and he said he would." Sunday morning, the day of the game, Robustelli's partner, Ed Clark, drove to Yankee Stadium with four dozen pairs of the rubber-soled Big League sneakers, sizes 9 through 16, which Howell hoped would be as effective as were the Manhattan College basketball shoes twenty-two years before.

—

As had been forecast, Sunday, December 30, dawned sunny but windy and bitter cold in New York, with the temperature around 10 degrees at eight o'clock and rising to only about 12 degrees by the time the Giants and Bears took the field at Yankee Stadium at one o'clock. By then, Andy Robustelli and his wife, Jeanne, had gone to an early-morning Mass at St. Benedict's Roman Catholic Church, not far from her parents' house in the Cove section of Stamford. Afterward he had a breakfast of steak, toast, and tea, and then left for the stadium around ten. As usual, even with four very young children, Robustelli had slept soundly for about eight hours. Nothing, it seemed—even playing in an NFL championship game thirty-five miles from his hometown—could rile or unnerve Andy Robustelli. Perhaps spending two years in the South Pacific during World War II and then having four children were more than enough to leave Robustelli relaxed, even before a big football game.

But if Robustelli was relaxed, Howell, Landry, and Lombardi were not. Driving to Yankee Stadium from his home in Fair Haven, New Jersey, with his son, Vincent Jr., then fourteen, Lombardi never said a word during the hourlong trip. "During the regular season, he might critique my play in a high school game that he had seen me play the day before," Vince Lombardi Jr. said. "But as I recall, he didn't say anything on the way to the championship game."

Despite the frigid weather and a wind-chill factor of about 20 below 0, a raucous crowd of nearly sixty thousand was in the grandstand and the outfield bleachers well before the two o'clock kickoff.

Tens of thousands and perhaps even millions more saw the game televised across the country by NBC, which paid the NFL $75,000 for television rights. Not much, certainly, but, in the opinion of Bert Bell and the NFL club owners, a good deal, since it helped publicize the NFL, which was still overshadowed in most of the country by big-time college football. DuMont, a major network in television's nascent days, also had televised the first coast-to-coast NFL game: the championship contest between the Los Angeles Rams and the Cleveland Browns in 1951. Andy Robustelli was a rookie end for the Rams that year; thus, he had the distinction of having played in the first two nationally televised NFL championship games.

In the locker room before the game, the Giants seemed remarkably loose and relaxed, bantering with one another and, not surprisingly, talking about the weather. Ed Modzelewski, who had driven to New York from Pittsburgh to see the game and then to drive his brother Dick and his wife and son home, couldn't believe the horseplay in the locker room. "They were laughing and clowning around and loose as can be," Big Mo said. "Paul Brown never would have put up with that stuff before a game. I finally told Dick that 'you guys are going to get the shit kicked out of you because you're not taking the game seriously.' "

The jovial mood also did not suit Jim Lee Howell well, although he didn't say anything about it to the players. "I always thought players should be pretty quiet and alone before a big game," the old Giant end said. "At least, that's the way we always were when I played."

It had been cold for both the previous game against the Bears and the one with Cleveland a week later, but this was far worse: blustery and bone chilling, with a strong northwesterly wind blowing in from over the bleachers behind one goal line.

Even though the Giants had outplayed the Bears five weeks earlier at the stadium before blowing a 17-point lead, Chicago was a 3-point favorite, perhaps because it had scored a league-leading 363 points compared with New York's 264 points, which was good enough to lead the Eastern Conference. But, then, as some Giants bettors had noticed, the Bears had yielded 246 points, for an average of 20.5 a game, as against the 197 points that the Giants had given up, for an average of 16.4 points a game, the third lowest in the NFL.

More than an hour before the kickoff, Gene Filipski and guard Jack Stroud went out to check the field conditions, Filipski in sneakers again, courtesy of Ed's and Andy's sporting goods store, and Stroud in conventional football cleats. Running back and forth between the goal line and the 20-yard line on the home-plate side of the stadium, Stroud slipped and fell several times, while Filipski sprinted and zigzagged without losing his footing. After both players told Howell what had happened, the coach bellowed, "Sneakers all around!"

The five-foot-ten, 180-pound Filipski was delighted. As a kickoff-return man, he knew he'd have much better traction with Robustelli's Big League sneakers and, hopefully, gain more yardage on runbacks. Though he had averaged 6.5 yards in 13 carries while scoring one touchdown during the regular season, Filipski had been kept on the squad solely to return kickoffs, and he had done it well. In all, he had run back 19 kickoffs for 390 yards, an average of 20.5 yards. But now, in the biggest game of his life, the twenty-five-year-old rookie from Sacramento, California, was jittery, although being kidded about his role as the designated sneaker tester had settled him down a bit.

Standing in the end zone after the Giants won the toss and elected to receive, Filipski also found himself in awe. After all, he'd been expelled from West Point after an early 1950s cribbing scandal and was then rejected by the Cleveland Browns, who, after drafting him in the third round, had traded him to the Giants for a seventh-round draft pick. Now here Filipski was, on national television, along with Jimmy Patton, awaiting the opening kickoff by George Blanda in the biggest football game of the year.

Appropriately enough, the first player to touch the ball in the game would be the first one to have tried out Robustelli's Big League sneakers on the frozen stadium turf. End over end, the ball sailed into Filipski's hands at the 7-yard line. He immediately picked up a covey of three blockers and headed straight upfield, never wavering, except for an occasional cut to either side. At the 25-yard line, Filipski eluded one would-be tackler who had broken through the phalanx of blockers, then cut to his right before picking up his blockers again. With one Bear after another being cut down by the superb Giants blocking, Filipski found that he had only three players to beat once he got past midfield. He was finally brought down with a crushing tackle by 255-pound rookie John Mellekas at the Bears' 39-yard line.

Relatively unknown Gene Filipski had run back the opening kickoff 54 yards, eliciting the biggest roar he had ever heard. On the Giants' sideline, Vince Lombardi beamed. It had been on Lombardi's recommendation during training camp that the Giants had given up a low draft pick for Filipski, who Lombardi had coached at West Point and who he was convinced could help the Giants. "That run by Gene gave the team its opening spark," Lombardi was to say later. Indeed, not only had Filipski just made the biggest run of his life, he had also set the tone of what was to come.

After two running plays gained only 2 yards, Don Heinrich, again the starting quarterback, connected with Frank Gifford on a 21-yard pass play that put the ball at the Bears' 17-yard line. Expecting another pass, the Bears put seven men up front, whereupon Heinrich, who had called another pass play, checked off at the line of scrimmage, calling an audible that sent Mel Triplett through a gaping hole in the middle and into the end zone after flattening referee Sam Wilson and taking two Bears defenders with him.

Less than two minutes later, Rick Casares, on the Bears' second play from scrimmage, was hit by Andy Robustelli and fumbled, with Robustelli pouncing on the ball at the Bears' 15. Not only was Robustelli one of the league's best pass rushers and punt blockers, he also shone at recovering fumbles. In his six years in the NFL, he had already recovered about 10, and by the time he was done, he would have recovered 21, an astonishingly high number. Ben Agajanian, who had added the extra point after the Giants' touchdown, eventually kicked a 17-yard field goal to make it 10–0 less than five minutes into the game.

Another turnover on the Bears' next possession led to another Agajanian field goal, this one from 43 yards out, his longest of the season. It was set up when Jimmy Patton intercepted a pass by Ed Brown and returned it 26 yards to the Chicago 37-yard line. That gave the Giants a 13–0 lead with three minutes left in the opening period.

Determined to break the Giants' momentum, Bears coach Paddy Driscoll decided to go for it on a 4th-and-1 situation at the Bears' 44-yard line after the ensuing kickoff. With the chilled crowd again chanting "*Dee*-fense!" Robustelli turned to his fellow linemen and called out, "Hold 'em! Hold 'em!" After faking a handoff to Casares, Brown handed the ball to J. C. Caroline. He spotted a hole on the right side and hit it—only to run head-on into cornerback and perennial All-Pro Emlen Tunnell, who stopped Caroline for a 2-yard loss.

By then it was obvious that the Bears runners were having trouble gaining traction because of the rock-hard and slippery turf.* And on the few occasions when Casares and Caroline got past the Giants' Fearsome Foursome, they usually ran into Sam Huff, who made almost a dozen tackles, and the other two linebackers, Bill Svoboda and Harland Svare.

"Those linebackers were terrific," said the Bears' All-Pro end Harlon Hill, who had caught two long touchdown passes in the fourth quarter to enable Chicago to tie the Giants, 17–17, only five weeks before. "No matter which way I turned, there was a linebacker on me."

With Conerly in at quarterback in the second quarter—wearing full-hand golf gloves during his first two series—the Giants drove 58 yards for their second touchdown, a 3-yard run by Alex Webster, who had caught a 25-yard pass from Conerly on the previous play. That made it 20–0 only three minutes into the second quarter.

Still unable to move on offense, Chicago punted again on its next possession. But Tunnell, the league's best punt returner, fumbled, and the Bears recovered at the Giants' 25-yard line. Five plays later, Casares bolted through the right side from 9 yards out to narrow the gap to 20–7. With more than thirty-eight minutes left in the game, the high-scoring Bears, even more accustomed to the cold than the Giants, were still not out of it.

But by halftime, they had dropped behind by two more touchdowns. The first one came only three minutes after Casares's run, when Webster capped a 71-yard drive by plunging in from a yard out. Then after the ensuing kickoff, the Bears failed to move at all, and Ed Brown was forced to punt from the end zone. But his kick was blocked by—who else?—Robustelli, and recovered by Henry Moore in the end zone for a touchdown. It was the lone moment of glory in 1956 for Moore, the Giants' first-round draft pick, who

---

*There were no electric heaters beneath the field's surface as there were when the 2007 Giants upset the Packers to win the National Football Conference title on a below-zero night at Lambeau Field in Green Bay on Sunday, January 20, 2008.

had seen little action because of an injury and would be traded to Baltimore the following year. That score in particular, which, following Agajanian's fourth conversion, made it 34–7, sent the crowd into a frenzy. It also sent about half the numb and shivering spectators home three and a half minutes later when the first half ended. Among those who stayed, a small group of fans in the right-field bleachers tried to warm up by starting a small fire. The flames were soon doused by security officers, to the chagrin of cheering spectators nearby who had hoped to avail themselves of the fire's warmth.

The 34 points were the most the Giants had scored in a half all season and 14 more than the Bears defense had yielded on average in a game during the regular season.

Seemingly demoralized because of their inability to penetrate the Giants' defense, at its very best on this frigid Sunday, the Bears never did score again. Meanwhile, the Giants added two more touchdowns in the second half on touchdown passes from Charlie Conerly to Kyle Rote and Frank Gifford en route to a stunning 47–7 victory and their third NFL title. (The first two were won in 1934 and 1938.) As Tex Maule, the highly respected football writer for *Sports Illustrated*, was to write, "The Giant lines—both offensive and defensive—administered a thorough cuffing to the opposing Bear units, and the Giant secondary defense, which had given away two late and tying touchdowns in a regular-season game between these teams, leaked not at all with the world championship in the balance."

For Conerly, especially, it was a redeeming experience after having endured so much approbation during his first few years with the Giants. Near perfect in his execution, Conerly completed 7 of 10 passes for 195 yards and two touchdowns, for which he was given a standing ovation when he left to make way for third-string quarterback Bobby Clatterbuck. Even the great Sid Luckman, the Bears' quarterback during their dynastic years of the 1940s and now a Bears assistant coach, had to appreciate Conerly's performance.

Winning the NFL title also was, in a way, redemption for Jim Lee Howell, whose selection as the successor to Steve Owen had been met with considerable opposition, both among fans and the media. However, he endeared himself by delegating virtually full authority to Vince Lombardi on offense and Tom Landry on defense. More specifically for Howell, the title also capped a marvelous week during which his wife gave birth to their second child two days before the championship game.

If there was any criticism of the forty-two-year-old Howell, it was over his system of starting Don Heinrich at quarterback and then inserting the putative starter, Charlie Conerly. Indeed, Howell had said the day before the game that he might stay with Heinrich all the way if the Giants got off to a good start. They did, but the coach still switched to the thirty-five-year-old Conerly. Asked why, the former Giants end, who as a player had endured losses to the Bears in the 1941 and 1946 championship games, said, "We had them set up for passing when Heinrich got them rolling. Not that Heinrich isn't a good passer, but Conerly is just a bit better, and it was the spot for him to ensure things." What Howell did not point out, of course, were Conerly's experience and leadership. Then, too, Howell no doubt felt that Conerly, after all the abuse that had been heaped on him during his early years with the Giants, deserved to play in the biggest game of his nine years in New York.

Whatever good or bad moves Howell made, even he was surprised at how easily the Giants beat the Bears. "I didn't think any team could handle them like that," Howell said.

Paddy Driscoll, the Bears' coach, conceded that his team was powerless to cope with the Giants. "When you run up against some fellows playing like that, there's just nothing you can do," Driscoll said.

Could the sneakers the Giants wore have made a difference in the outcome? Driscoll thought so. As it turned out, some of the Bears wore rubber-soled shoes with small cleats in the first half and then switched to flat-soled shoes in the second half, but it hardly seemed to have helped. "I don't know where they got theirs," Driscoll said of the Robustelli-provided sneakers, "but those sneakers were better than ours. The soles were thicker than the soles of our shoes, and I think this helped their footing greatly."

For their victory, each Giants player received $3,779.19, a new high for an NFL championship game. By contrast, Jim Lee Howell and his teammates on the last Giants team to win an NFL title, in 1938, had each received $504.45.

The following day, a banner front-page headline in the *Chicago Tribune* read, somewhat perplexingly, "Bears Crushed and Why." In the sports section, the Bears' star running back, Rick Casares, seemed to sum up the answer to the headline when he said, "They smashed us from start to finish. We were outplayed, terrifically out-played."

As usual following a home game, Perian and Charlie Conerly hosted a cocktail party in their suite at the Concourse Plaza Hotel, still gaily decorated for Christmas. Joyous as the party was in light of the championship game victory, there was an element of sadness for the Conerlys, who would leave the next day for their Missis-sippi home and not be around to savor the afterglow of the Giants' victory. Then, in keeping with tradition, many of the Giants and their wives or girlfriends rode the subway to Toots Shor's, where they were greeted by a standing ovation as they walked into the bar area. Then it was on to Mike Manuche's steak house and another ovation, followed by the usual last stop at P. J. Clarke's restaurant and yet more applause and cheering. There would be no victory parade, but for the Giants, celebrating at their favorite Manhattan haunts was as good as it got, especially after winning the team's first championship in eighteen years.

14

This Is the Army, Mr. Grier

*T*he Giants' victory was front page news in some of New York's dozen dailies the next day, New Year's Eve, but restricted to the sports pages of the city's two most influential papers, the *New York Times* and the New York *Herald Tribune*. In the lexicon of the era's sportswriting, Arthur Daley, the sports columnist for the *Times* (only one person held that exalted title at the time), wrote that the Giants "peeled the pelts off the Monsters"—the Bears were known as the Monsters of the Midway—"and jammed the remains down Chicago throats with such savage disdain that 56,836 awed customers at the world championship play-off had to forget their discomfort."

In addition to winning the NFL title, the Giants were showered with other tributes. Frank Gifford was voted the league's most valuable player and was named to the All-Pro team along with offensive tackle Rosey Brown and defensive players Andy Robustelli (who had been voted the most valuable player in the championship game), Rosey Grier, and Emlen Tunnell, while Sam Huff was named Rookie of the Year. In a remarkable achievement, Gifford was fifth in the league in rushing, with 819 yards, first in the league with an average 5.2 yards per carry, and third in receiving, with 51 catches for 603 yards. No player had ever finished in the top five in all three categories before. And all of this with a total payroll of $260,000, less than an NFL rookie was making in 2008.

By Tuesday, New Year's Day, most of the Giants had left New York for home and off-season jobs. Only Robustelli, Webster, and defensive back Dick Nolan, who was from nearby White Plains in Westchester County, remained in the area, as did Lombardi, who would spend the winter selling insurance. Gifford and Landry also would sell insurance in California and Texas, respectively. As for Sam Huff, he and his wife returned to their hometown of Farmington, West Virginia, where Huff went back to his old job of bagging groceries in a local supermarket.

Somewhat overlooked during the championship game weekend was a most momentous event at the Waldorf-Astoria Hotel in Manhattan. On Saturday, with little fanfare and practically no publicity, ten players representing ten of the twelve teams in the NFL had gathered with Milwaukee lawyer Creighton Miller—a former Notre Dame halfback and the first general manager of the Cleveland Browns—to form a players' association. Even though Kyle Rote was to play in the championship game the next day, the Giants' receiver was at the meeting; he had to be, since he'd been a key figure in conversations leading up to the December 29 meeting. Earlier that year, some team captains and other players had met in Cleveland and then Philadelphia to protest a decree by NFL Commissioner Bert Bell that, starting with the 1956 season, players' face masks would be limited to one bar rather than the two bars that were being used. Bell eventually rescinded his decree, but the meetings led to the December gathering in New York.

Only the Bears and the Pittsburgh Steelers did not send representatives to the meeting. Lynn Chandnois, a halfback for the Steelers, was scheduled to attend but was unable to make it. As for the Bears, they declined to send anyone after George Halas reportedly told his players that if they formed a union, the Bears organization would recognize it but would eliminate some benefits that the team provided, such as spending money on road trips. Most of the Bears also were believed to be getting more than the minimum wage of $5,000 that the new union was going to demand. Another veteran owner, George Preston Marshall of the Redskins, always a hard-liner, whose players averaged a league-low of less than $8,000 a year, was reported to have said that if any of his players joined the union, they would be traded. No doubt that was why Redskins quarterback Eddie LeBaron attended but refused to be photographed with the other representatives at the milestone meeting.

In addition to a minimum wage, the new union, the National Football League Players Association (NFLPA), sought training camp expenses, which many teams did not provide; $50 for exhibition games; a pension plan; payment for all players' equipment; and continued payment to injured players.

Representatives at the meeting included two of the league's best quarterbacks: Y. A. Tittle of the San Francisco 49ers and Norm Van Brocklin of the Los Angeles Rams. Van Brocklin was considered a conservative in labor-management matters; his participation in the formation of the union may have been a factor in his trade to the Philadelphia Eagles following the 1957 season. The ten players and Miller, far from being adamant about their requests, were circumspect and diplomatic. As Miller put it, the players merely wanted to have "some control over their own destiny."

Hardly any football fans paid attention to newspaper stories, all of them brief, about the meeting. The relative mildness of the new union's demands, all of which were eventually met, reflected the one-sided relationship between the players and management in the mid-1950s. With only twelve teams and fewer than four hundred players, club owners held a firm upper hand. If the players didn't like what they were getting, they could go drive a truck, tend bar, or sell insurance year-round. After all, as the owners knew all too well, there were hundreds of talented football players out there dying to play in the NFL.

Led by Marshall, the last owner to sign a black player, the owners initially refused to recognize the union even though Commissioner Bert Bell told a Congressional hearing the following August that he would recognize the players' association. Furious, Marshall said, "He doesn't have the power to recognize them. Bell works for us." Apparently Marshall had forgotten that, as the NFL commissioner, Bert Bell was the chief executive of the entire league, both the owners and players alike. The league, which had assumed that it, like major league baseball, was not subject to antitrust laws, finally bent when in February 1957 the United States Supreme Court ruled in favor of a former NFL lineman, Bill Radovich, who a dozen years earlier had sued the league for an antitrust violation. Threatened now by an antitrust suit by the new players' association, the owners quietly gave in during 1958 and granted most of the association's demands. Late in the year, when the association threatened to sue again under the antitrust law, the owners went even further and agreed on a plan that would provide hospitalization, life insurance, retirement, and some other benefits. In subsequent years, as the league expanded and its membership grew exponentially, the players' association eventually became one of the most influential and powerful unions in the country.

———

During the winter months following the championship game, Andy Robustelli lost track of how many banquets he attended in New York, New Jersey, and Connecticut. "I seemed to be going to a couple a week," he was to recall. As to speakers' fees, there were none. "I never asked for anything or got anything," said Robustelli, whose sporting goods store in Greenwich was doing better than ever in the aftermath of the Giants' championship victory. "I just felt I was helping to build up the NFL."

For Alex Webster, the situation was similar. "If I accepted all the invitations, I would have been out every night, but I couldn't do it because I had a job with a printing company during the day and wanted to be with my family at least some nights," Webster said. "You did it both because you enjoyed it and to publicize the NFL."

Of the Giants' coaches, only Lombardi remained in the New York area, but, as he explained in talks to Boys Clubs, YMCAs, and a number of adult organizations—for which he did not get paid— his insurance business, family matters, and his almost daily trips to the Giants' offices in Manhattan kept him much too busy to go out at night and make speeches. Except for Kyle Rote, Lombardi was probably the Giants' best speaker—albeit more fiery and impassioned than the much gentler Rote—and no doubt could have commanded a fairly large fee to speak before business groups, but Lombardi's excuse was legitimate: He just didn't have the time.

Looking ahead to 1957, the Giants' management team of Howell, Landry, Lombardi, and President Jack Mara did not see the point of making any changes, except to welcome back former backfield coach Allie Sherman as a part-time coach. Sherman had spent three seasons coaching the Winnipeg Blue Bombers of the Canadian Football League, reaching the play-offs all three years. Every member of the championship team except for Henry Moore, who was traded to Baltimore, and Rosey Grier, who was drafted into the army for at least a year, was expected back. To fill Grier's slot at right tackle, Jim Katcavage would move over from left end; he had split time there with Walt Yowarsky, who would now have the position all to himself. As for Charlie Conerly, who had been threatening to retire for seven years, he soon let it be known that he definitely would be back. With most of the players under thirty—only Conerly, at thirty-six and Robustelli at thirty-one were older—the Maras felt that with the younger players such as Huff and Katcavage now more experienced, the team should be better than ever. And who could disagree? The only question seemed to be whether the army would be able to find a uniform big enough to fit the six-foot-five, 285-pound Rosey Grier.

In 1957, team rosters were expanded from thirty-three to thirty-five players, then would be enlarged to thirty-six in 1959. Among the new players were the top draft choices: halfback Jon Arnett (Los Angeles); Jim Brown, a running back and star lacrosse player from Syracuse who had grown up in Manhasset, Long Island; Paul Hornung, a quarterback from Notre Dame who would be converted into a halfback at Green Bay; quarterbacks Len Dawson (Pittsburgh), John Brodie (San Francisco), Milt Plum (Cleveland), Sonny Jurgensen (Philadelphia), and Jack Kemp (Detroit); tackles Jim Parker (Baltimore) and Henry Jordan (Cleveland); end Ron Kramer (Green Bay); and linebacker Jack Pardee (Los Angeles). Of those twelve, six would end up in the Pro Football Hall of Fame: Brown, Hornung, Dawson, Jurgensen, Parker, and Jordan. Ironically, the only ones not to make it to the Pro Football shrine in Canton, Ohio, were the first two players drafted, Arnett and Brodie, and Plum, who was the sixteenth choice.

The first-round choices in order were Arnett, Brodie, Kramer, Dawson, Brown, Clarence Peaks, and Parker.

As it developed, Cleveland and Green Bay seemed to benefit most from the draft in 1957, even though, in retrospect, more than a few fans would wonder how four players could possibly have been picked ahead of Jim Brown.

The Giants did not have a pick in the first round, having traded it to the Rams in exchange for Andy Robustelli. Ironically, the Rams' choice, selected tenth overall, was end Del Shofner, who eventually would wind up with the Giants. Of the twenty-nine players drafted by the Giants, only two would make the team: Don Maynard, an end from Texas El Paso, who would spend only the 1958 season with the Giants before launching a brilliant career with the New York Titans (later the Jets) of the new American Football League in 1960; and defensive back Johnny Bookman, who would last only one season, during which his only action would be to return four kickoffs for 102 yards. Everyone else on the thirty-five man squad was a holdover from the 1956 world championship team.

—

With Katcavage replacing Rosey Grier at right tackle, the team was losing something. Katcavage was at his best as a pass-rushing end like Robustelli—and the coaches knew that Grier's absence would be felt. He may have ballooned to over 300 pounds during the 1956 season, but even so was remarkably fast and nimble.

"Rosey was probably as fast as any lineman who ever played the game," Sam Huff said. "He could run down and catch a fast runner coming out of the backfield, and when he set his mind to getting the quarterback, not many linemen could stop him."

At the time, however, Grier, not always in the best of shape, tended to let up to conserve energy or to regain his breath. "I could have been a better football player, but I just didn't play hard on every play," Grier conceded some years later after he had become an entertainer, actor, author, and then a political and social activist and minister in Los Angeles. "Andy Robustelli used to get on me a lot to play harder, but I just didn't like to do too much running out there." But even without going all out all the time, Grier was still one of the best defensive linemen in the NFL and good enough to be named an All-Pro three times.

Not surprisingly, when Grier reported for active duty at Fort Dix in New Jersey in January of 1957 after playing in the Pro Bowl game in Los Angeles, the army quartermaster in charge of supplies could not find a uniform to fit him. "Consequently, I stayed in civilian clothes a bit longer than the other inductees I was with," said Grier, who was named a platoon sergeant in charge of a barracks at the New Jersey army base. Army life was hardly difficult for Grier, who spent all of his eighteen months in service at the base, which was less than an hour's drive from his home. He played on the base football team, which went undefeated in 1957 and subsequently played in the interservice bowl game in Cocoa Beach, Florida, in

December of 1957.

Grier would be missed during the 1957 season, not only for his quickness, agility, and strength at left tackle, but for his good humor and even his guitar strumming and singing in the Giants' locker room (which he would eventually parlay into a brief career as an entertainer). "Everybody loved Rosey," Huff said. "Off the field, he was a gentle man." So much so that almost none of the Giants were surprised when Rosey—who was named for President Franklin Delano Roosevelt—took up needlepointing and polished his skills at it in the locker room and at times even on the sidelines during a game.

But with or without Grier, before long it was time to get back to work. While training at Saint Michael's College in Vermont again, the Giants took a brief break to play in the College All-Star Game in Chicago on August 9—an honor bestowed upon the defending NFL champion. It was a rewarding experience insofar as it gave the Giants their first close-up glance at Jimmy Brown and Paul Hornung, among a banner crop of recent college players who had signed to play in the NFL. As usually happened in the all-star game, the NFL team won—in this case, 22–12—and also showed the recent collegians what pro football was all about. Forty-five years later, Len Dawson, an eventual Hall of Famer who played in the game, said, "I can still feel it from having been hit a few times by Andy Robustelli."

After splitting their ensuing four preseason games, the Giants were particularly impressive in their last one, inflicting a 17–0 shutout against the Detroit Lions, who had finished a half game behind the Bears in 1956. Ironically, in a move that shocked the NFL, Buddy Parker, who had coached the team to league titles in 1952 and 1953, announced a few weeks before the beginning of the 1957 season that he was resigning, ostensibly because of interference by several of the team's dozen owners.

Both the Lions and their fans in working-class, blue-collar Detroit were stunned and saddened by the decision of the fifty-three-year-old Parker, whose fiery persona was a perfect fit for a team that included such lovable—to Detroit fans—players as eventual Hall of Famers Bobby Layne, Ernie Stautner, and Yale Lary. Fellow Texans, Layne and Parker were raucous hard drinkers but brilliant in what they did on the field and on the sidelines. They were largely responsible for increasing the Lions' attendance by slightly over one hundred thousand in 1951, Parker's first season as head coach, when Layne led the NFL in passing while throwing a career-high 26 touchdowns. Everyone knew that Parker, an innovator who developed what became known as the "two-minute drill" would coach again, and he did, taking over at Pittsburgh a few weeks after announcing he was leaving the Lions.

Layne, one of the NFL's most colorful personalities, but deadly serious on the field, was a notorious carouser, infamous for staying out all night before a game and then, often hungover, performing brilliantly the following afternoon.

"I remember once when Andy Robustelli and I were walking along Fifth Avenue, heading back to the Roosevelt Hotel about half past nine the night before a game against the Steelers," Dick Modzelewski said. "And there comes Bobby Layne walking along with a girl on each arm, looking a little tipsy, and obviously not about to call it a night as we were. Then the next day he throws a couple of touchdown passes against us." That was on November 15, 1959, when Layne, who had been traded to the Pittsburgh Steelers the year before, was among those who closed up P. J. Clarke's popular East Side restaurant at four in the morning and then, as Modzelewski recalled, threw two touchdown passes against the Giants that afternoon.

Don Smith, the former Giants public relations director, recalled a situation where Layne, ignoring the team's curfew the night before a game, went to a formal party in a tuxedo, drank a lot, and then boarded a streetcar to return to the team's hotel. "Bobby apparently stretched out on the backseats during what was the streetcar driver's last run and fell asleep," Smith said. "Not knowing that Bobby is still in the car, the driver takes it back to the car barn and locks it up for the night. When Bobby wakes up, he finds he's locked in and has to wait until morning before someone lets him out. Then, still in his tux, he takes a cab to the stadium, takes a nap, and then goes out and throws for three touchdowns. That was Bobby Layne."

Fellow quarterback Y. A. Tittle recalled spending part of a summer on the University of Texas campus in Austin rooming with Layne while both were taking classes before freshman year began. "I was being recruited by Texas, and even though we roomed together, I hardly saw Bobby, who was a legendary high school quarterback in Texas. The girls all loved him, and even though the fall

semester hadn't even started, Bobby, who was going to be a freshman, already was a big man on campus. And when I saw how good
he was on the football field, I took advantage of an opportunity to go
to LSU [Louisiana State] and left Austin. I knew Bobby was going
to be the starter, not me." Frank Gifford, who became friendly with
Layne when they played in NFL Pro Bowl games, also recalled
Layne's free-spirited ways and how, whenever they met, Layne's
first words inevitably were, "Frank, let's go drink some whiskey."

Despite his penchant for the night life, Layne, a fiery but highly
respected competitor, spent fifteen years in the NFL. Blond and
ruggedly handsome, Layne often would lash out at a teammate who
had missed a block. One time, after being sacked, he screamed at
Steelers center Ed Beatty, "Once, just once, take out your man, and
we'll declare a national holiday!" Threatening, cajoling, implor-
ing—they were all characteristic of Layne. But rather than resent
him for it, his teammates reveled in his gung-ho leadership qualities
and refusal to accept defeat.

"Bobby never lost a game in his life," said Hall of Fame halfback Doak Walker, who, in an unusual trifecta, played with Layne
in high school, college, and with the Lions. "Time just ran out on
him."

Lou Creekmur, the perennial All-Pro guard for Detroit in
the 1950s, remembered Layne's somewhat aggressive leadership.
"He'd call you out of the huddle and stand there, raving at you and
shaking a finger in your face, and you wanted to punch him," said
Creekmur, who followed Layne and Walker into the Hall of Fame.
"A couple of times, we had to grab people to keep them from hitting
Bobby. But off the field, there was nothing he wouldn't do for you.
We would have killed for him."

Reflecting his independent spirit, Layne shunned protective
equipment like pads for his knees, ribs, thighs, and hips, claiming
they hindered his mobility, and wore only a helmet and a light pair
of shoulder pads. He also was the last player to play without a face
mask, and quite possibly the first quarterback to call audibles at the
line of scrimmage, where he changed plays at the last minute.

"Bobby was a helluva leader," said Yale Lary, the Hall of Fame
safety and punter, who played with Layne in Detroit. "When
Bobby said 'block,' you blocked. And when Bobby said, 'drink,' you
drank."

Sadly, life in the high-voltage fast lane caught up to Layne, who died at fifty-nine. But during his career, from 1948 through 1961, Layne threw 196 touchdown passes and led the Lions to three Western Conference championships and one NFL title, in 1953, when he led Detroit on an 80-yard touchdown drive in the last two minutes to beat Cleveland by 1 point.

—

The Giants' preseason victory over the Lions, predicated primarily by New York's hallmark defense, seemed to portend another outstanding season, with the Giants and Cleveland Browns regarded as the leading contenders for the Eastern Conference title. It was also the last time the Giants would see Layne in a Lions uniform. When they saw him again, on October 16, 1958, he would be a Pittsburgh Steeler. Appropriately enough, the Giants and Browns opened the 1957 season against each other before a crowd of 58,095 at Cleveland Municipal Stadium in a game that marked the NFL debut of heralded rookie fullback Jim Brown. A perfect physical specimen at six-foot-two and 230 pounds, Brown was a combination of speed and power. Paul Brown knew from day one in training camp that there was no need to nurse along the rookie from Syracuse University; he could fly past or run over anybody. At Syracuse, Brown had set records in both football and lacrosse, and had been an All-American in both sports, the first athlete to have done so, while also lettering in basketball and track. (At Manhasset High School on Long Island, Brown had won letters in baseball and water polo in addition to those four sports—six in all.) When he was inducted into the Lacrosse Hall of Fame, officials at the Hall said Brown "was widely considered to be the greatest lacrosse player ever."

Brown's backfield mate was Lew Carpenter, who had been obtained in a trade from Detroit, where he'd spent three seasons. In a bizarre twist, Carpenter replaced his younger brother, Preston, who along with fullback Ed Modzelewski had been the Browns' primary runners during the 1956 season. Indeed, Preston would carry the ball only three times for the Browns in 1957 while being used primarily as a receiver. Modzelewski's playing time also would be drastically reduced, as he would be called on to run only ten times.

"As soon as I saw Jim blow past me when we were running the forty"—a 40-yard sprint—"I knew I was in trouble," Modzelewski said. "And then when I saw him in a scrimmage, I knew I wouldn't be the starting fullback anymore. But Jim actually prolonged my career because Paul Brown began to use me on special teams."

Jim Brown was not only good; he knew he was good. Though not boastful, and respectful toward Cleveland veterans, Brown was both cocky and confident, convinced that no one defensive player could stop him. In that first NFL game against the Giants, Brown carried the ball 21 times—thereafter he would often carry it more than 30 times—and gained 89 yards for an average of more than 4 yards a carry. During his nine years in the NFL, Brown would average an astonishing 5.2 yards per carry.

The game between New York and Cleveland would turn out to be a defensive struggle devoid of touchdowns and won with twenty seconds left on a second field goal by Lou Groza from 47 yards out to give the Browns a 6–3 victory.

With broad shoulders and a muscular torso that included a thirty-two-inch waist, Brown was an amalgam of a powerful and punishing fullback like Marion Motley and a slithery and swift open-field runner with moves akin to that of a Hugh McElhenny, who it was almost impossible to stop with only one man. Indeed, as the season went on, Brown often would be tackled by as many as three defenders, but was strong enough to shed all of them as he broke free.

The Giants bounced back with three straight victories: over Philadelphia and Washington on the road and Pittsburgh at home before an adoring crowd of 52,589. Once again the Giants' defense played brilliantly, holding the Steelers scoreless in a 35–0 rout. And again, the crowd included a large number of Johnny-come-lately Giants fans from the advertising, broadcasting, and public relations worlds, an influential assemblage who had become smitten with this team. In fact, fan interest ran so high by the start of the 1957 season that the Giants had sold more than thirty thousand season tickets, about twenty-five thousand more than the team had averaged at the Polo Grounds. With the seventy-five-mile television blackout still in effect, thousands of Giants fans would drive up to two hours to motels and bars in Connecticut to watch Giants games after tailgating in parking lots far from Yankee Stadium.

A week later at home, the cheers were less frequent, as the Giants, for the second year in a row, were stunned by a relatively weak Washington team, 31–14. But then, once again, the Giants rebounded to win four games in a row, including another shutout, over the Eagles, at Yankee Stadium, to stand at 7–2 and stay within a half game of Cleveland in the Eastern Conference with three games to play. Then the bottom fell out, and the Giants lost to San Francisco at home and to Pittsburgh at Forbes Field to fall out of the race.

When the 49ers came to Yankee Stadium, Giants fans were introduced to the "alley-oop" pass, which had been perfected by San Francisco's Y. A. Tittle and rookie flanker R. C. Owens. On the play, Tittle would lob the ball high into the air in Owens's direction, and, invariably, the six-foot-three former basketball star would outjump a defender or two and make the catch. In that same game, the fans also got to see one of the season's most memorable tackles. Hall of Fame halfback Hugh McElhenny took a screen pass from Tittle and took off behind blockers Bruce Bosley and Lou Palatella, who between the two of them weighed about 475 pounds. Going after McElhenny, Huff, with his head down, plowed into both Bosley and Palatella almost simultaneously, splitting them and enabling him to tackle the somewhat startled McElhenny. "It was the only way I was going to get to McElhenny," Huff said, "and what made it even better, it happened right in front of the 49ers' bench."

Six days later, the slide continued as the Giants lost to the Steelers, who had lost three games in a row while scoring only 16 points, and who, like the Giants, were going nowhere.

Though the Giants' next, and last, game of the season, against the Browns at home, was meaningless, since Cleveland already had won the conference title, it drew the biggest crowd of the year to Yankee Stadium—54,294, of which 50,511 had been sold in advance. Since coming into the NFL in 1950, the Browns had become the Giants' chief rivals. And the rivalry had grown each year, reaching a zenith now that Jimmy Brown had established himself as the NFL's best runner in his rookie year. Brown's presence helped bring in the gate receipts for the game, since hundreds of fans from Long Island, where he had played high school football, were on hand to root for the former Manhasset High School star. Brown did not disappoint his Long Island fans, carrying 15 times for 78 yards, which included a 20-yard touchdown run after he had taken a pitchout from another rookie, quarterback Milt Plum, a New Jersey native who had starred at Penn State.

In an effort to stop Brown, who through eleven games had averaged almost 5 yards a carry, Landry decided to have Huff key on Brown on plays where he lined up behind the quarterback, indicating that he was going to carry the ball. Over the years, a myth grew that Huff, acting on Landry's instructions, had focused on Brown on every play. Andy Robustelli said that was not the case. "If Sam did that, even following him when he didn't have the ball, the Browns would have 'cross-keyed' us and tricked us into thinking he was going to carry the ball on certain plays when he wasn't," Robustelli said. "That would have opened up room for their other running backs."

Huff agreed. "Tom Landry would tell me that Jim Brown was my first responsibility and to shut him down. But even if he wasn't the ball carrier, I had to watch him if he came out of the backfield, because he was a good pass receiver. I also had to watch the other back, especially Bobby Mitchell, because if I just committed to Jim Brown, and he wasn't involved in the play, I could get burned." As it was, in the eyes of many fans, a rivalry developed between Huff and Brown—a rivalry within a rivalry, as it were.

Huff said, though, that it was a respectful rivalry. "We never said a mean word to each other in the years we went head-to-head," said Huff. "He'd try hard to psych me out. After I tackled him, he'd get up slowly, pat me on a shoulder pad, and say, 'Nice tackle, Big Sam.' "

In the second game against the Browns, the Giants' defense gave up 298 yards on the ground, including 68 yards that Plum gained running in addition to completing 11 of 16 passes for 190 yards and one touchdown. Plum, in his first start, was playing in place of Tommy O'Connell, who had sprained an ankle the week before.

From the opening kickoff, it was obvious that, because of the rivalry, both teams would go all out in a contest that had no bearing on the standings. And during much of the game, the crowd was in an uproar, chanting "*Dee*-fense!" when the Browns threatened, and "Go! Go! Go!" when the home team began to launch a drive. The drama and excitement lasted to the very end when the Giants ran out of time at the Browns' 26-yard line after Cleveland halfback Lew Carpenter, who ran for a game-high 117 yards, scored from 2 yards out to cap an 80-yard drive with a little over six minutes left in the final quarter. That made it 34–28, the final score. Earlier, Carpenter's brother, Preston, on his only carry of the day, had sprinted 35 yards for a touchdown. Once again, though, Lou Groza had made the difference by kicking two field goals.

To the crowd, it seemed to matter not at all that the Giants had lost their previous two games and would not repeat as NFL champions. Even in defeat, they were beloved, all the more so against the archrival Browns, and particularly when—in what was becoming a hallmark of the Giants' defense—Cleveland was unable to score from the 1-yard line.

After the game, Paul Brown said that the Browns had been "playing for fun"—a comment that evoked looks of incredulity from the assembled media. Howell, meanwhile, paid tribute to what he said was the "best team" in the league, even though it didn't look that way a week later when the Detroit Lions routed the Browns, 59–14, in the NFL championship game.

Meanwhile, NFL officials and club owners reveled in the size of the crowd at the Browns-Giants game and the excitement and interest it had generated. It was yet another sign that the NFL had solidified itself in the media and financial capital of the United States, not to mention the phenomenon the Giants had inspired among football fans in the New York area and throughout much of New England, and thus given the league another boost in popularity.

———

The season had been dominated by the exploits of Jim Brown, who led the league in rushing with 942 yards and a 4.7 average, was named the most valuable player, rookie of the year, and was the leading vote getter for the all-NFL team. Teammate Tommy O'Connell, Cleveland's journeyman quarterback, was the leading passer with a 57.3 percentage and was picked as the team's most valuable player by his teammates. Though he would fully recover from his ankle injury by the following season, O'Connell was cut by the Browns, as he had been by the Chicago Bears the year before without even getting into a game. That made O'Connell the first MVP of an NFL team to be cut before the start of the following season. An obviously disillusioned O'Connell would then serve as an assistant coach at his alma mater, the University of Illinois, for two years before making a comeback with the Buffalo Bills in the inaugural year of the American Football League in 1960. There he once again would be a starter, if only for one season, before playing in only one game in 1961 and retiring, this time for good.

For the Giants, it was a depressing finish. After winning seven of their first nine games to stay apace with the Browns, they lost their last three—and in so doing, had given up a total of 82 points. That had even prompted Howell to complain, which rankled Tom Landry, who might have noted that the offense had scored only 55 points during those three games. Still, the late-season fadeout led some Giants fans to wonder if the championship season of 1956 had been an aberration.

Nevertheless, there were considerable postseason honors. Andy Robustelli, Frank Gifford, and Rosey Brown were named to the all-NFL team, and those three, along with Emlen Tunnell, Jack Stroud, and Ray Wietecha, were selected to play in the Pro Bowl. Once again Gifford led the Giants in both rushing and receiving, while finishing fifth in the NFL in the latter category for the second year in a row. Conerly, at thirty-six, had another good season, throwing 11 touchdown passes and completing 55.2 percent of his passes for 1,712 yards while sitting out much of the first half of each game. And Don Chandler, the second-year punter who almost left training camp during his rookie year, led the NFL in punting with a 44.6 average, a new Giants record. Moreover, the Giants set a new home attendance record, drawing almost three hundred thousand fans for an average of about fifty thousand for each of six games.

Still, overall, it was a disappointing season. Were the Giants suddenly getting older, or were other teams getting better? With Jimmy Brown, Milt Plum, and a veteran team behind them, the Browns most definitely were. Then there were the vastly improved Baltimore Colts, led by their young and daring quarterback Johnny Unitas, who had finished third among the league's top passers and seemed certain to eventually be ranked among his era's outstanding assemblage of quarterbacks: Sammy Baugh, Sid Luckman, Otto Graham, Charlie Conerly, Y. A. Tittle, Bobby Layne, Norm Van Brocklin, Bart Starr, Ed Brown, and little Eddie LeBaron—a group so good that O'Connell, the league's leading passer in 1957, would be out of a job the next season.

15

The Kicker with the
Wrong-Way Foot

*U*nlike in 1957, the Giants did not stand still with their roster in 1958. Losing their last three games taught both the coaches and Wellington Mara that the team needed help. And they got it by obtaining defensive back Lindon Crow and placekicker and end George Allen "Pat" Summerall from the Chicago Cardinals for Dick Nolan, rookie wide receiver Bobby Joe Conrad, and a number one draft pick; another defensive back, Carl Karilivacz, from Detroit; and Al Barry, an offensive guard, from Green Bay.

The Giants also did well in the draft, picking up running back Phil King and offensive linemen Frank Youso and Bob Mischak. Jim Lee Howell would later call the trade for Crow and Summerall one of the best the Giants ever made. What made it even better was that Nolan, whom Howell and Landry liked, would return to the Giants in another trade a year later.

Those acquisitions seemed, at least on paper, to strengthen an otherwise veteran team whose only players over thirty were Charlie Conerly and Andy Robustelli. Gone were defensive end Walt Yowarsky, who had been traded to San Francisco; thirty-nine-year-old placekicker Ben Agajanian, who had retired but would return to the NFL in 1960 and play for four more years; Gene Filipski, who had served the Giants well for two years running back kickoffs and had gone off to the Canadian Football League; and defensive back Johnny Bookman, who had played sparingly as a rookie in 1957. Yowarsky became expendable because of the return from military duty of Rosey

Grier, who showed up in camp reasonably fit and trim and immediately lit up the locker room at Willamette University with his good humor and, to a lesser extent, with his guitar, which he obviously had polished up on during his spare time at Fort Dix.

Most of the Giants thought that the loss of Agajanian would hurt the most. Long one of the NFL's leading placekickers, he was a rarity in that he had made most of his field-goal attempts—46 out of 84—and extra points—157 out of 159—during his five seasons with the Giants. Summerall, over a similar period of time, had connected on only 41 of 100 field-goal tries and 121 of 127 extra-point attempts for the Cardinals. Granted, Summerall was more versatile; he could play tight end and on the defensive line, but rarely did so with the Cardinals or with the Giants, who had obtained him solely to placekick.

That Summerall was in effect making his living with his right foot was somewhat remarkable. He had been born in the tiny northern Florida town of Lake City on May 10, 1931, with his right foot facing backward. "The toes were where the heel was supposed to be, and the heel was in the front," he said. "My mother asked the doctor, Harry Bates, a general practitioner, what could be done, and he told them the only thing he could think of was to break the leg and turn it around and hope for the best."

Since there apparently was no alternative at the time, Mrs. Summerall, who was separated from her husband and subsequently divorced, decided to let Dr. Bates do just that. "Dr. Bates broke the leg at Lake Shore Hospital in Lake City when I was two weeks old," Summerall said. "Then he turned the foot around, reset the bones, and put the foot in a cast for six weeks."

The prognosis was not good.

"Dr. Bates told my mother that I might not be able to walk, let alone run, and if I did, I'd walk with a limp, and that my right leg would always be shorter than the left one," added Summerall. As the product of a broken home, he was brought up by his mother until he was three years old, then by his mother's sister and her husband, and finally by his grandmother through his grade school and high school years. "Dr. Bates also said I certainly wouldn't be able to keep up with the other kids when we were playing," Summerall added.

Fortunately for Summerall, the good doctor was wrong. Not only did Summerall manage to keep up with his friends, but at Lake City High School, he played football, baseball, basketball, and ran the 440-yard dash and threw the discus on the track team. During the summer, besides baseball, Summerall also played tennis, and was so good that when he was fifteen he hitchhiked 350 miles to Fort Lauderdale to play in the Florida sixteen-and-under boys' tennis tournament. Using the only racket he had, Summerall went all the way to the final amid strong competition and beat Herbie Flamm, who went on to become a top-twenty player on the international circuit. "Then I hitchhiked home," Summerall vividly recalled. "But I was happy because I had won."

Ironically, the doctor for the Lake City High School sports teams was none other than Dr. Harry Bates. "Dr. Bates used to marvel at what I could do," said Summerall, who went on to play football and some basketball at the University of Arkansas while majoring in Russian history. "He told me he didn't think I'd even be able to run."

While at Arkansas, Summerall spent the summer after his sophomore year playing first base for a St. Louis Cardinals farm team in Lawton, Oklahoma, in the Class C Sooner State League. "I had trouble hitting a good curve ball, which convinced me that I wasn't going anywhere in baseball," he said. Later, during the NFL's off-season, Summerall taught English and history as a substitute at a junior high school in Lake City and worked as a truck farmer while he was with the Chicago Cardinals and, for a while, with the Giants.

Coming to the Giants from what he called the "low-rent" Cardinals, who were not only parsimonious but overshadowed by the Bears, Summerall said, "was like becoming part of royalty."

"It was a very intelligent group of players and a first-class operation," he recollected years later, "and in Vince Lombardi and Tom Landry, we had two incredible assistant coaches. And almost everywhere you went in Manhattan, people recognized you. As a matter of fact, I hardly ever had to pay for a meal."

Summerall's only problem at first was finding a holder, someone who would take the snap from center and then put the ball down for him to kick. "Not many players want to hold, because you're kneeling down and are a sitting duck after the kick," he said. "And it takes a lot of skill. Charlie Conerly had been the holder for Agajanian, and he was one of the best, but at first he didn't want to hold for me. So Don Heinrich, the backup quarterback, did for a while. I think I had to prove myself before Charlie would hold for me. But I must have done all right because he agreed to hold early during my first season."

Summerall agreed that he also benefited from center Ray Wietecha. "Kicking field goals requires perfect timing and a good snap from the center and then a good hold, and, of course, a good kick. What helped was that Ray may have been the only center who could snap the ball without looking," Summerall said. "That way he was looking up when he snapped the ball and was ready to block. Other centers are focused on the holder, and by the time they snap it, the charge is on, and they can't be of much help. And Charlie has such quick hands that as soon as he gets the snap he spins the ball so that the laces are facing forward and not toward me. In my time with the Giants, I never once saw the laces."

Many years later, Summerall was still convinced that his performance as a placekicker improved dramatically when he came to the Giants, in large measure because of Wietecha, Conerly, and Landry, who also was the kicking coach. "Tom Landry was a perfectionist in every area of defense," Summerall said. "He had been a very good punter in college and with the Giants, and picked up on things I was doing or wasn't doing that made me a better kicker."

———

While losing Agajanian and Yowarsky, the Giants also almost lost Lombardi. Now forty-four years old and growing increasingly frustrated, he finally got an offer to coach an NFL team. Unfortunately, it was from the Philadelphia Eagles, who had gone into a tailspin and suffered through three straight losing seasons. The offer was made after the Eagles fired Hugh Devore, who had been an assistant coach at Fordham when Lombardi was one of the Seven Blocks of Granite. Even Bert Bell, the NFL commissioner who once had owned the Eagles, tried to convince Lombardi to take the job. Getting wind of the offer, Wellington Mara called Lombardi and urged him—for his own good, Mara said—not to take it, because the Eagles' ownership was in total disarray and the owners would always be looking over his shoulder, something that Mara knew Lombardi would never tolerate.

Still, Lombardi found the offer tempting, if for no other reason than no else had come calling. They may have fallen on hard times, but Lombardi knew the Eagles had some quality players, including former Rams quarterback Norm Van Brocklin, a future Hall of Famer, who had been traded to Philadelphia after the 1957 season. Other solid players they had included flanker Tommy McDonald, running back Clarence Peaks, and linemen Tom Brookshier and Chuck Bednarik. *What I could do with that team with those guys as a nucleus,* Lombardi thought. But then the more Lombardi thought, the more he felt that he would be the logical one to replace Jim Lee Howell as the Giants' head coach, although the Maras had never told him so. Jim Lee, though still young at forty-two, had indicated a number of times that he might not stay around much longer, since he and his wife were anxious to remain year-round at their cotton farm in Arkansas. But who knew when that might be? Finally, Lombardi made a decision: He would stay with the Giants, hoping that eventually he would become the head coach. So, once again, the old Block of Granite would spend the winter selling life insurance and watching film of the past season's games and puffing away on one cigarette after another in his den at the Lombardi home in Fair Haven, New Jersey.

—

After two summers of preseason training at Saint Michael's College in Vermont, the Giants returned to Willamette University in Oregon, where they had trained in 1954 and 1955. The coaching staff remained the same, with Howell beginning his fifth year as the head coach, and with Landry and Lombardi as his chief assistants. Once again, Lombardi had brought along his son, Vince, now sixteen and a starting halfback at Red Bank High School in New Jersey. Young Vince again would spend about five weeks as the team's ball boy while picking up pointers from Alex Webster, his favorite player, and some of the other Giants, all of whom had taken a liking to the offensive coach's polite and eager-to-please son. But then that could have been because, once in camp, Vince Sr., totally absorbed with football, had little time to spend with young Vince, who saw more of the other coaches and staff than he did his dad.

Why the Giants had once again gone so far afield for preseason training was never explained. However, the Maras, always looking to hold down expenses, might again have realized that since their first two exhibition games were on the West Coast, it made economic sense to establish a base nearby. The move, though, appeared to backfire early on, as the Giants, after beating the 49ers, 19–10, in the first preseason game in San Francisco, lost their last five exhibitions, never scoring more than 21 points. The last loss, a week before opening day, was by far the worst, as Unitas's Colts routed the Giants,

42–21, in Louisville, Kentucky, where the unprepossessing Unitas had starred for the University of Louisville. Those losses left Lombardi baffled and wondering whether he had made a mistake in not taking the head-coaching job in Philadelphia. At any rate, the preseason appeared to be a bad omen, especially since the team's first three regular-season games were to be played on the road once again.

"This may be my weakest team," Howell said after the loss to the Colts, perhaps more to motivate his players than with any deep belief, given that practically all of the Giants were in or approaching their prime as football players.

The first regular-season game actually was more of a "home" game to the Giants than it was to their opponent, the Chicago Cardinals, since it was played in City Stadium in Buffalo. The game had been scheduled to be played at Comiskey Park in Chicago, but the Cardinals had to give way to the baseball White Sox, who owned the South Side ballpark, since they were playing at home on the last day of the baseball season. Such scheduling changes were not unusual at a time when every NFL team except the Los Angeles Rams and the San Francisco 49ers shared a stadium with a baseball team that owned the facility and thus had first shot at it when there was a scheduling conflict.

Though the weather was warm and sunny, not many people in the Buffalo area seemed to care about the game. Only slightly over twenty thousand showed up for the game in a city that had hosted several NFL franchises during the 1920s and had hosted about a dozen exhibition games in the past.*

After losing five exhibitions in a row, the Cardinals, who had won only three of twelve games the previous season to finish last in the Eastern Conference, were just what the Giants needed. Taking advantage of a porous defense, the Giants led 37–0 on three touchdowns by Frank Gifford and two by Alex Webster, and a field goal and four extra points by Pat Summerall before Chicago was able to score in the last quarter. Able to virtually run at will against the Cardinals, the Giants threw only 10 times, with Charlie Conerly completing 4 for 43 yards, while Chicago, unable to move much

---

*Two years hence, though, when the Buffalo Bills would become charter members of the American Football League, the city would become a rabid football town.

against the Giants' stout defense, threw 35 passes for 207 yards, 84 yards more than they gained on the ground.

The game would be notable in that Howell and Lombardi appeared to have abandoned the system wherein, for the last two years, Don Heinrich had started almost every game at quarterback, with Conerly coming on in relief. Heinrich, however, would not play a single down in the Giants' first two games—the second one, a 27–24 loss at Philadelphia (which no doubt gave Lombardi second thoughts again about not becoming the Eagles' coach). Lombardi's second thoughts would wear off, though, as the Eagles would win only one more game in 1958 to finish dead last again at 2-9-1.

Heinrich started the following week in Washington, and he did well, throwing a touchdown pass in the first quarter that gave the Giants a 14–0 lead before the Redskins responded with two touchdowns in the second period to tie. But then in the fourth quarter, Conerly, on in relief of Heinrich once again, was being pursued by three defenders when he managed to throw a wobbly 10-yard pass to Ken MacAfee in the end zone for the game-winning touchdown. That put the Giants at 2-1 as they prepared for their home opener against the Chicago Cardinals. The Cardinals had improved since week one, though, beating Washington and then losing, 35–28, to the unbeaten Browns in Cleveland.

A crowd of 52,684 greeted the Giants on Sunday, October 19, at Yankee Stadium, giving loud ovations to both the offensive and defensive units. Thereafter, though, the fans had little to cheer about as the Cardinals opened up a 6–0 halftime lead, withstood a 1-yard touchdown plunge by Mel Triplett in the third period, and then scored 17 unanswered points in the last quarter to win, 23–6. Summerall missed the extra point against his former team, his second miss in four games, which made Howell wonder if trading for him had been a good idea. As it would turn out, the missed conversion was the last extra point he would miss as a Giant.

Against the Cardinals, the Giants already were handicapped by injuries to Rosey Grier and Jack Stroud, which kept them on the sidelines. But in the second quarter, they suffered an even more serious loss when Frank Gifford tore ligaments in his right knee. The prognosis was that the Giants' star halfback would be out for at least two weeks, meaning he most likely would miss what could be a showdown in Cleveland.

And though they had routed the Cardinals in the season opener, the Giants were unable to generate any offense in the rematch. Conerly had another bad day, as did Heinrich. The home team gained only 97 yards rushing and 118 yards passing compared with 215 and 156 by the Cardinals, whose first-year coach, Frank "Pop" Ivy, had obviously learned well from the one-sided loss to the Giants in Buffalo.

A subheadline over the game story in the *New York Times* summed up the Giants' performance: "Giants Miss Blocks, Tackles, and Passes Against the Cards." The defeat left the Giants at 2-2, while Cleveland stood at 4-0. Most certainly, the Giants, after a poor preseason showing and two losses in their first four games of the regular season, did not look like contenders for the Eastern Conference title, especially after the blazing start Jimmy Brown had made.

Back at Yankee Stadium the following Sunday, the Giants were confronted by Bobby Layne, who had been traded to Pittsburgh after the second game of the season following ten years with the Detroit Lions, before a crowd held down to twenty-five thousand because of a driving rain. Layne's trade reunited him with his former coach and close friend with the Lions, Buddy Parker, who after quitting in Detroit was determined to get the thirty-one-year-old Layne. But on this day, Layne would fall short.

Because of the Steelers runners' inability to breach the Giants' defensive line, Layne threw more often than usual, firing off 34 passes with a wet football and completing only 14 for 194 yards, not bad given the weather conditions. Never a pure passer, Layne completed many, if not most, of his passes with sheer determination rather than with skill. "I don't care how they get there as long as they do," the fiery Layne once said of his passing. Making matters worse, the Steelers' two best runners, Tom Tracy and Tank Younger, Andy Robustelli's former teammate with the Rams and now in his final NFL season, were held in check as Pittsburgh gained only 32 yards on the ground. Tracy was particularly culpable, fumbling away the ball three times, with one fumble resulting in a 23-yard touchdown run by Giants cornerback Carl Karilivacz. As it was, the only scores by the Steelers in the 17–6 Giants victory came on two field goals by Tom Miner, playing his one and only season with Pittsburgh, during which he led the NFL by making 14 of 18 field-goal attempts.

With rookie Phil King starting in place of the injured Gifford, the Giants reeled off 146 yards rushing, while Don Heinrich, going all the way for the first time at quarterback, threw only 10 passes, completing 2 for 33 yards. Once again the Giants' Fearsome Foursome thrilled fans by stopping two Pittsburgh drives inside the 10-yard line, which had a significant impact on the outcome.

Despite the victory, the Giants did not gain any ground on Cleveland, which beat the Chicago Cardinals for its fifth straight victory, meaning the Browns would be unbeaten in five games when they met the Giants, now 3-2, in Cleveland the following Sunday. In those five games, Jimmy Brown, carrying the ball more than 50 percent of the time, had scored an astonishing 14 touchdowns while averaging 7 yards per carry and 164 yards a game for a grand total of 815 yards. So far as was known, no running back in NFL history had ever gotten off to such a dazzling start. While the Giants were beating the Steelers, Brown was scoring 4 touchdowns and gaining 180 yards as the Browns were defeating the Cardinals—who had beaten the Giants the week before—in Cleveland, 38–24.

Brown had not only delighted Cleveland fans with his running and pass catching—he caught 16 passes in his rookie year and would match that number in 1958—but had also earned the respect of his teammates. "From the time we first saw him in a scrimmage, we knew he was something special," said Walt Michaels, a former Browns linebacker who later coached the New York Jets. "Then when we saw him break a long run in a preseason game in Akron, we looked at each other and said, 'My God, where did he come from?' He was also a good guy, and we all got along fine with Jim."

Another Browns linebacker, Vince Costello, remembered Brown as "a complicated guy" with no weaknesses as a football player. Costello, who also was a rookie when Brown joined the team in 1957, said Brown had a strong work ethic. "I covered him a lot in practices and found that he was a good practice player. In my opinion, he was the greatest runner ever."

Even though Brown's running ability cost Ed Modzelewski his job at fullback, Modzelewski said that he knew from the beginning that Brown was going to give Cleveland a big boost. "At the beginning, some of the guys hit Jim harder than they'd usually hit a teammate in a scrimmage, but he'd still break away from them. But I don't think that ever dawned on Jim. And if it did, he never said anything."

As for me, playing behind Jim was like being the guy who played behind Babe Ruth."

—

The largest crowd ever to see the Giants play at that point, 78,404, turned out at Cleveland Municipal Stadium for the game on November 2. With Don Heinrich sidelined by an ankle injury, Charlie Conerly started at quarterback after having been kept on the bench the week before. The Giants' cause, it seemed, also would be hurt by the absence of the injured Frank Gifford. But all was not lost. Conerly, in his best game of the season, was brilliant, directing the offense flawlessly and throwing three touchdown passes. The defense was equally brilliant, holding the Browns—who had come into the game averaging 35 points—to 17 points, as the Giants upset the conference leaders, 21–17, to draw to within a game of Cleveland in the standings.

The Giants' defense set the tone on the first running play of the game when Robustelli and Dick Modzelewski, aided by Huff, stopped Brown for a 2-yard loss. Brown bounced back to gain 113 yards, including a 58-yard touchdown run in the second quarter when he broke free from three would-be tacklers. That score, along with defensive back Ken Konz's interception of a Conerly pass and his subsequent 46-yard run, gave the Browns a 17–7 halftime lead. But then Conerly threw touchdown passes in both the third and fourth quarters while the Giants' defense held Cleveland scoreless to win the game.

Now that the Giants had beaten the previously undefeated Browns, they were confronted with the Baltimore Colts, who had won all six games and were averaging even more points than Cleveland, in large measure because of the passing wizardry of Johnny Unitas, now in his third year. The game drew a standing-room-only crowd of 71,163 to Yankee Stadium, the largest ever to see a football game in New York, proving unequivocally that pro football had made its mark in the city. That same day, demonstrating clearly how the NFL had also taken hold elsewhere, a crowd of 75,363 turned out at Cleveland Municipal Stadium to see the Browns suffer their second loss, to Detroit, 30–10, while a game between archrivals the Los Angeles Rams and the San Francisco 49ers attracted 95,082 to the Los Angeles Coliseum.

Against the Colts, Frank Gifford was back sooner than expected, but Unitas was out because of cracked ribs sustained in a rout over Green Bay the week before, and the quarterbacking fell to twenty-five-year-old George Shaw. That hardly hurt the Colts, as Shaw threw for 238 yards and three touchdown passes. The Colts battled the Giants on even terms until Pat Summerall kicked a 28-yard field goal with just under three minutes to play to give the Giants a 24–21 victory after touchdowns by Gifford, Webster, and Kyle Rote, who caught a 25-yard pass from Charlie Conerly in the end zone. Along the way, the Giants' front four, by now fully acknowledged as the best in the NFL, staged another patented goal-line stand, this one at the 1-yard line in the opening quarter, preventing a Baltimore touchdown.

Remarkably, the Giants had now inflicted defeats on two previously unbeaten teams and, with a record of 5-2, had tied the Cleveland Browns. The tie, though, would be short-lived.

The following weekend, with the Giants playing at Pittsburgh, Dick Modzelewski again hosted a dinner party on Friday night in his hometown outside of the city, with his mother preparing a Polish dinner for her son, the rest of the Giants' front four, and Rosey Brown. Two days later, however, what joviality lingered from the dinner party at the Modzelewski family homestead vanished when the Giants were drubbed, 34–10, by the Steelers. Bobby Layne and Tom Tracy led the way along with a defense that held Gifford, Webster, and Triplett to 88 yards and limited Conerly to 103 yards passing. With four games to go, the Giants fell to 5-3 and back into second place. Fortunately for New York, the next three games were against teams with losing records before the last game of the season against the Browns. Assuming Cleveland was to win its next three games—which seemed likely, since two of them were against the hapless last-place Eagles and the third against the almost equally inept Redskins—the Giants would have to win all four to tie the Browns and force a play-off.

The Giants, saving some of their best football for last, did just that. First they crushed the Redskins, 30–0, then avenged the inexplicable early-season loss to the Eagles by beating them, 24–17, on a bitterly cold day during which Alex Webster was honored by his hometown fans from Kearny, New Jersey, along with thousands of others who had come to revere the rugged and personable fullback from just across the Hudson River.

Webster's acquisition in 1955 turned out to be one of the best the team ever made. The 225-pound Webster had been drafted, and then cut, by Washington Redskins coach Curly Lambeau, the former Packers coach, in the summer of 1953 after having been used solely as a defensive back even though his strength at North Carolina State had been as an outstanding running back. Back home in Kearny with a pregnant wife, Webster, at the suggestion of a sports editor from New Jersey, sent a telegram to Peahead Walker, the coach of the Montreal Alouettes of the Canadian Football League, saying that he was available. Walker, who had coached against North Carolina State while he was the head coach at Wake Forest University, and thus knew quite a bit about Webster, called to say he was interested as long as Webster reported immediately. He did, the very next day. For the next two seasons, Webster established himself as the best running back in the CFL and was named the league's most valuable player in 1954.

No one in the NFL seemed to have noticed, except for the Detroit Lions, who, Webster was to say years later, showed some mild interest but offered even less than the $3,000 he was receiving from the Alouettes. Indeed, in 1954 the Giants, forever looking for a replacement for Charlie Conerly, who was perennially threatening to retire, dispatched former tackle Al DeRogatis to check out Sam Etcheverry, the Alouettes' quarterback. Etcheverry eventually made it to the NFL in 1960 with the St. Louis Cardinals, but it was Webster, not the Montreal quarterback, who attracted DeRogatis's attention. "When I came back, I told the Giants that Webster was the big man they had been looking for," DeRogatis was to say.

And he was. Making an immediate impact in a backfield that included Frank Gifford and Mel Triplett, Webster, although he lacked the speed of many NFL running backs, was quick and a punishing, slashing runner with superb moves in the open field, able to run through and over defenders. He was also an excellent receiver and a good blocker. Webster averaged a team-high 5 yards per carry on 128 attempts and caught 22 passes while scoring six touchdowns in 1955, his first year with the Giants.

"It was an ideal situation," Webster recalled fifty-two years later at his home in Hobe Sound, Florida. "I was married with two children and was able to commute home to New Jersey in less than an hour. And, later, after Dick Lynch joined us, we drove to Yankee

Stadium together both for practice and for games. What made it even better is we always had good teams."

If Webster—who became known as "Big Red"—was happy, the Giants were ecstatic, even though, at times, he admitted, he had to be prodded by Vince Lombardi during his first few years with the Giants. "Vince would yell at me, and I must say I was scared of him," Webster recalled with a smile. "But, then, I know I was lazy at times, and Lombardi knew what he was doing. He was a great coach—the best I ever had—and I owe a lot to him. As it turned out, since we both lived in New Jersey, we became friendly and would get together for dinner with our wives, but only in the off-season." As the years went on, Webster became a Giants perennial, playing for ten years, averaging almost 4 yards a carry, catching 240 passes, 19 of them for touchdowns, and running for 39 TDs. One of the most popular Giants of all time, both with his teammates and with fans, Webster invariably would get the call in short-yardage situations and would almost always make the first down. Never forgetting his roots, he remained a familiar figure in Riley's and other bars and restaurants in Kearny, enjoying the good life with lifelong friends while raising a son and daughter, and, eventually, having four grandchildren and one great-grandchild. If Webster had a weakness, it was his heavy smoking. So much so that on occasion during a game, he would pull his hooded jacket over his head—even on warm days—so that coaches would not notice him sneaking a cigarette and then blowing the smoke into the helmet he held in his hands. "Yes, I did it, but looking back, I guess I shouldn't have," the Giants' quintessential power runner said.

Webster's toughness became legendary. Growing up poor in gritty Kearny, Webster got into more than his share of fights. Indeed, Gino Marchetti, the Hall of Fame defensive end for the Baltimore Colts and one of the best players to play the position, once said that if he were outnumbered in a bar fight and could have only one man on his side, it would be Webster, whom he called the toughest man he had ever known. That was quite a tribute, since it came from a player who was regarded by his peers as one of the toughest, if indeed not the toughest, players in the NFL.

Another very tough player, Sam Huff, no great fan of the Giants' offense, since he thought it got more attention than it deserved, once said that Webster "was a wild son of a bitch who should have played with us on defense." And Jim Lee Howell said there was no one more reliable in a third-and-short-yardage situation than Webster. "He fought hard for extra yardage on every play, even when he knew he might get hurt," Howell said. "He was one tough bastard."

In more than one instance, Webster's fighting instincts were noble and made him a hero in his hometown. One night Webster was in his favorite haunt, Riley's, with some friends and the bar owner, who, despite being blind, dispensed drinks with ease and, when it came to collecting, trusted his patrons, most of whom, like Webster, were regulars. One night two strangers came into the bar, and, after ordering several drinks and noticing that the barkeep was blind, gave him one-dollar bills while telling him they were twenties. "Eddie, trusting the guys, gave them change for twenties," Webster recalled years later. Witnessing this duplicitous act, Webster grabbed one of the men and head-butted him, sending him flying across the barroom floor and rendering him unconscious. He then dispatched the second man with a punch to the jaw. Webster and his friends then retrieved the ill-gotten change the two men had extracted from Eddie the bar owner and returned it to him before throwing both strangers out the front door. Such episodes, along with his determination to eke out every possible extra yard in a game made Webster a local legend and an extraordinarily popular player.

———

In the rematch against the Eagles, Don Heinrich again went the distance, since Charlie Conerly was sidelined with a kidney injury suffered against Detroit. Proving again that at best he was an adequate backup to Conerly, even though he continued to start almost every game, Heinrich made good on only 9 of 23 passes and was intercepted three times. With two games left, the Giants could only hope that their thirty-seven-year-old rock of ages quarterback would recover soon.

Conerly did, suiting up and playing most of the last two games. In the first, at Detroit against the defending NFL champion Lions, a safety made the difference. It occurred when Lions halfback Gene Gedman was tackled in the end zone by Jim Katcavage in the first quarter. But a bizarre call by the Lions' coach, George Wilson, in the fourth quarter was just as decisive—if far more inexplicable. Leading 17–12, the Lions were, understandably, in punt formation on a 4th-and-22 situation at their own 42-yard line. However, instead of kicking, Yale Lary, one of the NFL's most versatile players, who was both the league's best punter and also ran back punts, took off to his right and was forced out of bounds by Jim Katcavage, Rosey Grier, and Bill Svoboda after gaining only 2 yards. Wilson, defending his strange call, said that had the Lions' right end been farther outside and made the block he was expected to make, the play "might have worked." But it did not, and Detroit fans were left wondering why it was called. Lary had taken off on fake punts three times since joining the Lions in 1952 and gained 63 yards, so he definitely was a threat to run, but it seemed to make no sense to run instead of kick, especially with the Lions leading by 5 points late in the final quarter.

So now here were the Giants on the Lions' 43-yard line with four minutes to play. After a 34-yard pass from Conerly to Bob Schnelker and three running plays, the Giants found themselves at fourth down and inches to go on the 1-yard line, from where Frank Gifford burst through right tackle for the winning touchdown. As it was, the Lions still had a chance to win, driving to the Giants' 18-yard line after the ensuing kickoff and setting up for a 25-yard field-goal attempt. However, Andy Robustelli and linebacker Harland Svare, who played directly behind him, came up with a plan. At Svare's suggestion, Robustelli brushed aside six-foot-five, 237-pound offensive tackle Gerry Perry, allowing Svare to break through a gap in the line of scrimmage and block Jim Martin's kick with eight seconds left in the game.

Meanwhile, the Baltimore Colts lost their second game of the season, 30–28, to the Los Angeles Rams before a crowd of more than one hundred thousand at the Los Angeles Coliseum. But no matter; the Colts had already clinched the Western Conference title the week before when they overcame a 27–7 halftime deficit to the San Francisco 49ers in Baltimore by scoring four unanswered touchdowns to win, 35–27. Now all the Giants had to do to play the Colts in the championship game was to beat the Cleveland Browns two Sundays in a row. As expected, the Browns had won their last three games to maintain a one-game lead over New York. But now the Giants had to beat Cleveland in the final game of the regular season on December 14 at Yankee Stadium, and if they did, then defeat the Browns again in a play-off the following Sunday, also at Yankee Stadium—a tall order indeed against the team regarded as the best in the Eastern Conference. But having given up only 27 points in their last three games and beaten the Browns in Cleveland, coach Howell and his assistants were convinced that was indeed very possible.

16

"How About That Summerville?"

*J*n the week leading up to the final game of the regular season against the archrival Browns on Sunday, December 14, the main concern of Howell, Lombardi, and Landry was whether Pat Summerall would be able to play. Summerall had become a potent weapon for the Giants, having made 10 of 20 field-goal attempts, including one that proved decisive in the victory over the Baltimore Colts, and his last 17 extra points. In addition, he could play occasionally at tight end and on special teams, something the team's previous placekicker, Ben Agajanian, did not. But he had been hit after kicking a conversion the previous Sunday against Detroit and had a severely bruised right thigh. As a result, Summerall did not practice at all as the Giants prepared to play the Browns. That made it necessary for Don Chandler, the team's punter, who had been called on to kick only 3 extra points and no field goals since joining the Giants in 1956, to spend part of every practice working on placekicks in addition to punting. To help him, the Giants brought in one of their most legendary players, fifty-two-year-old Ken Strong, who had been a triple-threat halfback, placekicker, and defensive back with New York from 1933 through 1939, then returned during World War II to kick extra points and field goals from 1944 through 1947. The other option was Frank Gifford, who, like Strong years ago, had become a Giants jack-of-all-trades and occasionally had kicked both extra points and field goals early in his career with New York. But Gifford's toe hadn't met a football in a game since 1956, when he made 5 of 6 attempted field goals.

A very slender
Andy Robustelli at
the age of sixteen ready
to unload a pass to a
friend in the backyard
of his Stamford,
Connecticut, home
in the early 1940s.
ROBUSTELLI
FAMILY PHOTO

Robustelli (left) and
a shipmate aboard
the destroyer es–
cort *William C.
Cole* in the Pacific
shortly after the end
of World War II.
ROBUSTELLI
FAMILY PHOTO

Robustelli (far right) chatting with the other three members of the Giants' great Front Four of the late 1950s and early 1960s (from left to right: Rosey Grier, Dick Modzelewski, and Jim Katcavage), outside of Yankee Stadium following a practice in the late 1950s.
NEW YORK DAILY NEWS

The original Fearsome Foursome—Robustelli, Modzelewski, Katcavage, and Grier—coming off the field after another patented goal-line stand for the Giants.
DIAMOND IMAGES

Giants defensive coach Tom Landry, head coach Jim Lee Howell, and offensive coach Vince Lombardi. AP IMAGES

Future Giants quarterback
Charlie Conerly while at Ole Miss.
COURTESY OF PERIAN CONERLY

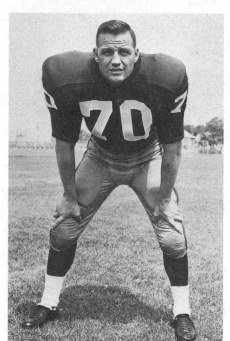

New York Giants Hall of Fame
middle linebacker Sam Huff,
the key player in the novel four-
three-four defensive scheme that
assistant coach Tom Landry
instituted in 1956. AP IMAGES

Giants fullback Alex Webster is tackled by Green Bay Packers defensive back Jesse Whittenton during the 1961 NFL championship game in Green Bay, which the Packers won 37–0. Others in the photo are Packers Hall of Fame defensive end Willie Davis (#87) and Giants offensive linemen Darrell Dess (#62) and Ray Wietecha (#55). VERNON J. BIEVER SPORTS PHOTOGRAPHY

One of the NFL's all-time great safeties, the Giants' Emlen Tunnell, the first black player inducted into the Pro Football Hall of Fame. AP IMAGES

Pat Summerall kicking the longest field goal of his career—about fifty yards—during a snowstorm that gave the Giants a memorable 13–10 victory over the Cleveland Browns at Yankee Stadium on December 14, 1958, which put them within one more victory of the 1958 NFL championship game. AP IMAGES

The notorious Hardy Brown, the most danger-ous man in the NFL. CLEVELAND BROWNS

The great
Jimmy Brown
breaking loose
against the
Giants in 1958.
CLEVELAND
BROWNS

Quarterback Bobby Layne,
whose love of nightlife
did not inhibit him on
the field during his
Hall of Fame career.
GETTY IMAGES

Johnny Unitas: from a six-dollar-a-game semipro quarterback to a great career with the Baltimore Colts and enshrinement in the Pro Football Hall of Fame. INDIANAPOLIS COLTS

Robustelli brings down Unitas. AP IMAGES

Raymond Berry, the Hall of Fame receiver for the Baltimore Colts, making one of three consecutive catches during a dramatic drive by the Baltimore Colts that led to their overtime victory against the New York Giants in the 1958 championship game. AP IMAGES

Berry kept sharp in unique fashion: Here he is catching a pass thrown by his petite wife, Sally, during an offseason practice session. *BALTIMORE SUN*

Pro football Hall of Famer Gino Marchetti of the Baltimore Colts, one of the best defensive ends in the history of the NFL. INDIANAPOLIS COLTS

Art Donovan, the Falstaffian defensive tackle for the Baltimore Colts, who like his 1958 teammates Unitas, Berry, Marchetti, and Lenny Moore was voted into the Pro Football Hall of Fame. INDIANAPOLIS COLTS

Baltimore Colts fullback Alan Ameche scoring the game-winning touchdown against the Giants in overtime in the classic 1958 NFL championship game at Yankee Stadium. AP IMAGES

Charlie Conerly and his wife, Perian, on Charlie Conerly Day at Yankee
Stadium on November 29, 1959. COURTESY OF PERIAN CONERLY

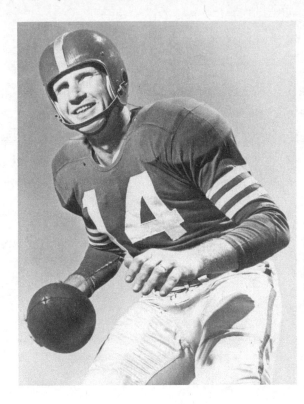

Y. A. Tittle in 1960,
his last season with the
San Francisco 49ers
before being traded
to the Giants.
SAN FRANCISCO 49ERS

Al Sherman

Allie Sherman as the 160-pound backup quarterback for the Philadelphia Eagles in the early 1940s. PHILADELPHIA EAGLES

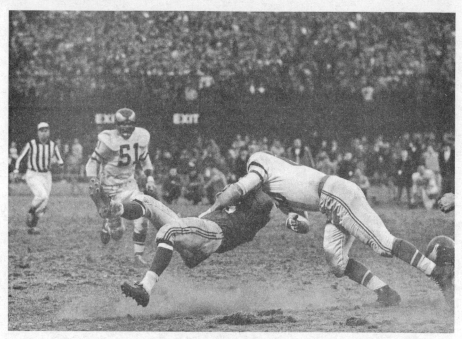

Chuck Bednarik of the Philadelphia Eagles makes a devastating tackle of Frank Gifford on November 20, 1959, at Yankee Stadium that sends Gifford to the hospital and keeps him out of football during the 1960 season. DIAMOND IMAGES

Y. A. Tittle, in his last year as a Giant in 1964, bleeding and with several cracked ribs after being tackled by two-hundred-eighty-pound John Baker of the Pittsburgh Steelers in Pittsburgh on September 20, 1964.
AP IMAGES

Frank Gifford, as a sportscaster for CBS, interviewing his former offensive coach with the New York Giants, Vince Lombardi, then the head coach of the Washington Redskins in 1969. VERNON J. BIEVER SPORTS PHOTOGRAPHY

Former Giants Andy Robustelli and Y. A. Tittle (bottom row, left and center) being inducted into the Pro Football Hall of Fame in Canton, Ohio, in 1971, alongside Norm Van Brocklin (bottom right). Second row, left to right: Vince Lombardi Jr. representing his deceased father, Vince Lombardi; Frank "Bruiser" Kinard; Mary Ellen Cocozza representing her late father, Bill Hewitt; and Jimmy Brown. GETTY IMAGES

Aware that the Giants had a chance to make it to the NFL championship game for the second time in three years, fans bought up all available tickets by midweek even though the outlook for Sunday was bitterly cold and windy. Because of the television blackout, thousands more again planned to drive anywhere from fifty to a hundred miles to motels and bars in Connecticut to watch the game on Hartford's WTIC-TV. By now, some of the motels, bars, and restaurants to which the growing number of Giants faithful flocked on Sundays, such as the Stratford Motor Inn just east of Bridgeport, had taken on the aura of a college football stadium, inviting high school bands to play before games and at halftime in motel and restaurant parking lots, where the fans tended to congregate at tailgate parties much like spectators going to games at the nearby Yale Bowl in New Haven.

Both the college and professional basketball seasons, along with the National Hockey League season, were well under way, but most of the talk on radio and television sports segments and at workplaces, bars, and restaurants dealt with the Giants-Browns game. By now, names like Gifford, Huff, and Robustelli were as common to New York–area sports fans as Mantle, Berra, and Ford. However, readers of New York's nine daily newspapers were left high and dry because of a strike by newspaper deliverers that began on Monday, December 8. Their picket lines were being observed by editorial employees, including sportswriters and sports columnists. To satisfy the needs of those not able to live without a daily paper, newspapers from as near as Newark, New Jersey, and Philadelphia were shipped into the city to be sold at outdoor newsstands, Grand Central Terminal, Pennsylvania Station, and at some other locations. Red Smith might not be available in the New York *Herald Tribune,* but, to the delight of his fans, Smith's column was in the *Philadelphia Daily News,* and he was at his customary seat in the press box on game day.

As usual before Giants home games, most of the players' wives gathered before the final regular season game to have lunch at the Concourse Plaza Hotel, then walked the three blocks to Yankee Stadium. By then snow, which had not been forecast, had begun to fall, making the sidewalks along the Grand Concourse slippery. The newspaper strike, coming as it did at the start of the Christmas season, was already having a serious effect on holiday shopping because of the absence of advertising; on funerals, which were going unpublished; on Broadway shows; and on some sports events—but not on the Giants-Browns game. Despite the strike, the snow, and the bitter cold, a near-capacity crowd of almost sixty-five thousand turned out, many with flasks containing beverages that they hoped would help get them through the gelid and snowy afternoon. Even though the Giants had beaten the Browns by 4 points in Cleveland six weeks earlier, the game was pegged as a toss-up by oddsmakers. That could have been because of Pat Summerall's uncertain status. During the pregame practice, Summerall found himself wincing as he tried kicking from varying distances, especially from beyond the 30-yard line. At one point, he turned to Chandler and said, "You better warm up. I don't think I'm going to be able to kick." Yet, strangely, the more he tested his right leg, the better he kicked, and finally decided that he could play.

"How's the leg, Pat?" Howell asked as his placekicker and fellow Arkansas alumnus walked off the field.

"It hurt a little, Jim, but I think I can do it," Summerall replied.

Howell was delighted to hear that, for he felt that in a game featuring two of the best defenses in the NFL, it could all come down to a field goal.

Light snow was falling on the already frozen field when the Giants, after having lost the coin toss, kicked off to Cleveland. On the first play from scrimmage, at the Browns' 35-yard-line, quarterback Milt Plum faked a pitchout to Preston Carpenter and handed off to Jim Brown, who bolted through a hole at left tackle. Sam Huff, partially blocked, managed to get his hands on Brown, but Brown shook him off and, slipping and sliding but maintaining his remarkable balance, outraced the four members of the Giants' secondary 65 yards across the frozen field for a touchdown, eliciting a roar from the approximately five thousand Browns fans in the stands. Groza's conversion made it 7–0 a minute and a half into the game.

Thwarted in the first half by the Browns' strong defense that included future NFL coaches Chuck Noll and Walt Michaels, the Giants could muster only a 46-yard field goal by Summerall, which was very long considering the condition of the field and the frigid weather. Groza also booted a 3-pointer for Cleveland to give the Browns a 10–3 halftime lead.

The Browns appeared to be on the way to building their lead when they drove to the Giants' 20-yard-line in the third quarter. On fourth down, as expected, Groza came in, ostensibly to attempt what for him would normally be an easy field goal. But when holder Bobby Freeman received the snap, he jumped up, ran left, and set to pass. As he did, Harland Svare, courtesy of a block by Robustelli, broke through and tackled Freeman for a loss. It was a call that Paul Brown would regret. "I wanted seven points and not three, so we'd be ahead by two touchdowns," Brown would say later. "In the first game against them this year, I went for a field goal instead, and we got beat by a touchdown."

Still, it looked like a very questionable decision, since a field goal would have put the Browns ahead by more than a touchdown.

Both teams went scoreless in the third quarter in what turned into a punishing defensive struggle, with Brown marginalized by Huff and the Giants' front four, and with Gifford, Webster, and Triplett unable to gain much yardage. In the fourth quarter, the Giants turned to Gifford's arm to tie the score. A misplayed handoff from Plum to Preston Carpenter resulted in a fumble recovery by Robustelli at the Cleveland 45-yard line. On the next play, Gifford took a handoff from Conerly and sprinted to his right, drawing in the Browns' defense as Rote raced down the left sideline. Just before reaching the line of scrimmage, Gifford, still on the run, fired a diagonal 25-yard pass to wide open Rote, who ran to the 6-yard line before he was tackled by Paul. Two plays later, Gifford, in what appeared to be a repeat of the same play, ran right after another handoff while Rote cut into the left corner of the end zone. This time, though, Gifford fired another difficult across-the-field pass to end Bob Schnelker for a touchdown. Summerall added the extra point, and the game was tied at 10–10.

But a tie would do the Giants no good. On their next possession, as the snow intensified, they again got to the Cleveland 31-yard line, setting up a 38-yard field-goal attempt with four and a half minutes left in the game. But Summerall's kick, on the snow-covered field, curled wide. "After that, I would have liked to have gone anywhere but back to the bench," Summerall said. "Knowing how I felt, the guys were great, with a couple of the defense players telling me not to worry because they were going to get the ball back, and that I'd get another chance. But I wasn't convinced that it would happen."

But it did with just two minutes left, thanks to that very Giants defense, which once again stopped Cleveland on three plays and forced a punt. Fortunately for New York, Dick Deschaine, under heavy pressure from Robustelli, shanked the punt, which went out of bounds around the Browns' 44-yard line, giving the Giants good field position. Unfortunately, the snow and wind had created blizzard-like conditions and obscured the line markers on the field; the Yankee Stadium lights had been turned on as darkness had set in as early as four o'clock in the afternoon. On the sideline, a hooded and cold Summerall stood alongside Giants defensive and special-teams players. He hoped that the offense could get the ball to at least the 30-yard line, which would call for a field goal from about where he had missed a short while before. But the field was now in even worse shape than it was then.

Because of the worsening field conditions, Howell and Lombardi decided to eschew the run and have Conerly throw on three straight downs. After Conerly overthrew Don Maynard on first down, Alex Webster, a good receiver coming out of the backfield, who had already caught 23 passes, six of them for touchdowns, in 1958, told the veteran quarterback that he could get past the left cornerback on a fly pattern. "The guys in the huddle looked at me like I was crazy," Webster said. "They all knew I wasn't very fast and that the snow would slow me down even more. But Charlie decided to go for it. Sure enough, I took off down the left sideline, with the cornerback on me. Then I gave him a move to the inside, and he went for it, and I blew right past him, and Charlie laid a pass in perfectly on about the 10-yard line. I saw it coming, but then, at the last second, I lost it in the snow and couldn't get a handle on it. If I had caught it, it would have been a touchdown."

But Webster didn't, and it wasn't. On third down, Conerly flipped a short pass to Gifford, also coming out of the backfield. Gifford appeared to have made the catch, but dropped the ball when he was hit by linebacker Galen Fiss. Walt Michaels, another Cleveland linebacker, scooped up the ball and ran 10 yards before he was tackled. But head linesman Charlie Berry signaled that it had been an incomplete pass. Incredulous, Paul Brown screamed at Berry as the Giants' defensive unit and the Browns' offense, both of which had already started to run out onto the field, turned and returned to the sidelines.

"That was the big play of the game," Brown was to say later. "I'm sure it was a fumble and a recovery."

At any rate, it was now 4th-and-10 with the Giants still at the Browns' 44-yard line. At that point, Howell told Lombardi he was going to send Summerall out to attempt a field goal. Lombardi objected strenuously, citing the poor field conditions, the blinding snow, and the wind as reasons to have Conerly try another pass instead. Howell, though, remained steadfast with his decision, walked over to Summerall, and barked out, "Field goal!" Summerall, who was not expecting a call to kick and thus hadn't warmed up for one, was in a state of disbelief. "It looked to me as if I'd have to kick it from midfield, and I hadn't kicked one that far all season, if ever," he said. "But I ran out to the huddle, and as I got there, Conerly turned to me and said, 'What the fuck are you doing here?' And I said, 'I'm going to try to kick a field goal.' It was obvious he didn't think much of the idea and had expected to pass again on fourth down."

Sitting in the press box, Wellington Mara turned to assistant coaches Ken Kavanaugh and Walt Yowarsky and, obviously referring to Howell, asked, "What's he doing? He knows that Pat can't kick it that far." Practically all of the Giants felt the same. Knowledgeable fans in the crowd felt the same way. With the snow coming down even harder, Conerly got down on one knee to receive the snap from Ray Wietecha 7 yards away and cleared out a small spot that Summerall had selected for the ball. Exactly where the ball would be put down no one knew because the snow had obliterated the yard lines. Kyle Rote was to say later that he was standing on the sidelines near midfield and that the ball was about 2 yards farther out, meaning the attempt would be about 52 yards. Summerall agreed. "Before the snap, I told myself I had to hit the ball dead center and drive it straight, hoping that it wouldn't hook to the left or go to the right because of the wind," he said.

The snap from Wietecha was perfect, and Conerly quickly put the ball down, laces facing the goalpost as always. Meanwhile, the offensive line held against the onrushing Browns defense. Summerall, about 5 yards behind Conerly at the snap, strode forward and, kicking as hard as he could, sent the ball soaring end over end toward the goalpost near the left centerfield bleachers. The huge crowd grew deadly silent. "I knew it was far enough, and I watched it for about forty yards, but then lost it in the snow," Summerall said. "Then I heard a roar from the crowd in the distance, and only then did I know I had made it." For a moment or two, it looked like it might not. Soaring dead-solid perfect, the ball suddenly began to fade to the right, but then drifted left and between the uprights.

As an exultant Summerall trotted back to the Giants' sideline, he passed Lombardi, in his camel-hair topcoat and snap-brim fedora. "You know you can't kick it that far, you son of a bitch, don't you?" Lombardi said with a derisory smile. Summerall smiled back, then was engulfed by his teammates.

It was, at the time, the most dramatic scoring play in the team's history, since it gave the Giants a 10–7 victory and forced a play-off against the same Browns the following Sunday, also at Yankee Stadium. It was also the Giants' fourth straight victory over a stretch in which their defense gave up only 37 points, an average of fewer than 9 points a game.

For Jim Brown, it had been another outstanding performance, and amid treacherous conditions at that. Brown carried 18 times for 152 yards, far more than the 72 yards gained on the ground by the Giants. That gave Brown a season total of 1,527 yards, breaking, by a remarkable 381 yards, the record set by former Philadelphia Eagles running back Steve Van Buren in 1949. His touchdown also tied Van Buren's record of 18 in a single season, and his rushing average of 5.9 yards led the NFL.

In the raucous Giants locker room after the game, Tim Mara, the patriarch of the Mara clan, raved about Summerall's kick. "How about that Summerville?" said Mara, a rare visitor to the clubhouse who never made it a point to get to know all of the players' names. "But what the hell, I'm paying him good money, and he doesn't even play. All he does is kick. That was the least he could do to earn his money."

The old bookmaker smiled when he said that to make certain everyone knew he was joking. As for Summerall's "good money," he was earning about $15,000 for the 1958 season.

Webster said that Summerall could thank him for becoming the game's hero. "If I'd caught that pass during that drive and scored the touchdown, nobody would have remembered you from the game because you wouldn't have had to try for a field goal," Webster would say for years thereafter whenever Summerall's dramatic kick was mentioned in their presence.

So dramatic was Summerall's kick that some sportswriters compared it to New York's most spectacular sports feat of derring-do, Bobby Thomson's walk-off home run against the Brooklyn Dodgers at the Polo Grounds that won the National League pennant for the

New York baseball Giants seven years before. That may have been a reach, but the game itself, a fierce defensive struggle waged in abominable conditions, came in for high praise. Writing in the *Cleveland Press* the following day, sports columnist Frank Gibbons said, "In many ways this game must be classified as one of the greatest football games in history."

Now all the Giants had to do, a week later, was to beat the Cleveland Browns for the third time in a row.

17

Where Have You Gone, Otto Graham?

*S*adly for avid newspaper-reading sports fans, unless they were able to buy an out-of-town newspaper on Monday, December 15, 1958, they could not read about the most dramatic victory the New York Giants football team had ever achieved.

Many heard about it on the radio. As for New York sportswriters who covered the Giants on a regular basis, it's easy to imagine them having mixed emotions about the game's outcome; most were probably happy that the Giants had won but saddened that they weren't able to cover the epic game and write about it. At least some of the city's syndicated columnists, such as Red Smith, had been able to. But to read Smith, whose New York outlet was the strikebound New York *Herald Tribune*, you had to buy the *Philadelphia Daily News*, which was available at some newsstands in New York.

In Cleveland, sports columnists and sportscasters were still criticizing head linesman Charlie Berry for not ruling that Frank Gifford had caught a third-down pass on the Giants' final possession before Pat Summerall's game-winning field goal and then fumbled the ball away. Some writers also second-guessed Paul Brown for not going for a field goal from the 20-yard line in the third quarter and instead having holder Bobby Freeman try to run with the ball. Such criticism, albeit mild, was almost heretical in Cleveland, where Paul Brown was the city's most revered sports figure.

Addressing the Cleveland Touchdown Club on Monday, a day off for the Browns, as would be Tuesday, Brown was uncharacteristically apologetic. "Maybe we should have gambled more when we were ahead," he said in response to a question as to whether the Browns had played too conservatively in the second half, apart from the fake field-goal attempt. Brown was also diplomatic when another member of the Touchdown Club asked him why the Browns allowed Robustelli "to swarm all over" Milt Plum throughout the game. Instead of criticizing his offensive line, Brown paid tribute to Robustelli's pass-rushing abilities.

On the same day in New York, Jim Lee Howell said he was convinced that Gifford had not fumbled the ball away after catching the pass from Conerly, as Brown suggested. "Frank turned to catch the ball and never had full control of it, so it wasn't a fumble," Howell said. Gifford, of course, agreed.

By Tuesday, all box seats, at $8 apiece, and reserved seats, which went for $7.50, were sold out for the play-off game. Bleacher seats, at $4, were going fast, and so too were standing-room tickets, at $5. Having beaten the Browns twice, in Cleveland and at home, logic would have seemed to dictate that the Giants would be favored. But the betting line was even money, or, in gambling parlance, eleven-to-ten, meaning that you had to wager $11 to win $10, regardless of which team you bet on. Apparently the feeling of the oddsmakers was that, perhaps, but just perhaps, the Browns were overdue to beat the Giants, especially since the first two games had been decided by 4 and 3 points, respectively.

Despite the continued newspaper strike, the play-off game was the talk of the town. When Pat Summerall and a few other Giants walked into Toots Shor's one night during the week, the crowd at the bar cheered, whistled, and applauded. Toots Shor himself conceded that not even Joe DiMaggio or Mickey Mantle had ever received such a welcome. The same thing happened a half hour later when the Giants' players strolled into the dining room for dinner.

By late 1958, they were true New York celebrities, even more so than in 1956, when the Giants won their first NFL title in eighteen years. Army, Fordham, and New York University had drawn big crowds to both Yankee Stadium and the Polo Grounds in the 1930s and 1940s, but before 1956, the Giants had not consistently drawn well. Likewise, the football New York Yankees, who had played, first, in the All-America Football Conference, and then, in 1950 and 1951, in the NFL, drew poorly at Yankee Stadium, averaging fewer then ten thousand spectators. As far as pro football went, New York, up until 1956, was a far cry from Cleveland, Chicago, and Los Angeles, where far more fans turned out for NFL games. But now the Giants were spun gold, and along with Jimmy Brown and his Cleveland Browns and Johnny Unitas and the Baltimore Colts, they were the biggest attractions in the league.

—

Surprisingly, on game day at Yankee Stadium, the crowd, at 61,174, was about 2,000 less than the previous week, even though the weather was far better: cloudy with the temperature in the mid-40s. Again there was a large Cleveland contingent, even larger than the approximately 5,000 who had attended the game the week before. And, again, the Cleveland sportswriting corps outnumbered the New York writers because of the newspaper strike.

If the weather was fairly good for late December, the field was not; it was frozen and thus rock hard, meaning that when a running back hit the ground, it was going to be akin to landing on a living room rug, most likely with a 250-pound defensive end or tackle on top. Nor would it be much better for a pass catcher being tackled in the secondary by a defensive back while in full flight until he collided with the frozen turf, especially on the infield dirt.

The game started ominously for the Giants when Jim Brown ran back the opening kickoff by Don Chandler 42 yards, which evoked a roar from the large Cleveland contingent, Ohio expatriates, and the hundreds of Jim Brown fans from Long Island, many of whom were Giants rooters except when the opponent was the Browns. But on the next play, after Brown caught a swing pass from quarterback Milt Plum, he was hit hard by Katcavage and fumbled, with Rosey Grier pouncing on the ball at the New York 38-yard-line. A short while later, Cleveland got to the Giants' 19-yard-line only to have Plum throw an interception.

The Giants scored shortly thereafter with Charlie Conerly, a Southerner inured to cold weather after eleven seasons in New York, playing a key role on every play. After the Giants reached the Browns' 19-yard-line on three Conerly passes, the thirty-seven-year-old quarterback decided it was time for some trickery. Conerly whirled and handed off to right halfback Alex Webster, who ran about 5 yards to his left, whereupon he gave the ball to Frank Gifford going the other way. Aware of Gifford's passing ability, the Browns sensed a pass as Gifford headed around right end. But Gifford kept running, reaching the 10-yard line. Just as he was confronted by linebacker Galen Fiss, he lateraled to Conerly trailing along on the right. With his close friend Gifford blocking for him, Conerly ran toward the goal line. There he was tackled by Fiss but managed to plunge into the end zone for a touchdown, only his tenth since joining the Giants, when, as a single-wing halfback, he had scored half of those touchdowns. As Conerly arose from the frozen turf and was mobbed by teammates, Lombardi broke into a rare game-day smile. For what he had just seen was exactly the type of play that Conerly, Gifford, and some other Giant veterans had ridiculed him for when he tried to put it in the team's playbook when he came aboard as the offensive coordinator four years earlier. Summerall kicked the extra point and would add a 20-yard field goal in the second quarter to close out the scoring at 10–0.

The Browns threatened for the last time in the third period when Jim Brown, on his best run of the day, powered his way for 20 yards to the Giants' 4-yard line, dragging three tacklers the last 10 yards. But after Brown was stopped for no gain, Plum rolled out to his right and, with two receivers open in the end zone, was sacked for a 16-yard loss by left linebacker Cliff Livingston. Then on third down, the drive ended mortifyingly when Sam Huff intercepted a short Plum pass.

It was Plum's and the Browns' last stand. The second-year quarterback, outplayed and overmatched in tactical decisions by Conerly for the second week in a row, would miss the rest of the game after, first, injuring his right leg when he was tackled and crashed into the Browns' bench, and then hurting his left hand when he was sacked by Livingston. Rookie Jim Ninowski finished, but he would complete only 3 of 15 passes for 31 yards, in part because his receivers had trouble catching his bullet passes, which were thrown much harder than Plum's.

Remarkably, the Giants shut out the Browns in the second half for the third straight game they had played in 1958. And they limited Jim Brown to only 8 yards on an astonishingly low 7 carries. Since those carries included a 20-yard run, Brown actually lost 12 yards the other 6 times he had run the ball. On two of those losses, Brown was stopped at the line of scrimmage by a blitzing Emlen Tunnell, who had been in the NFL long enough to have sacked the great Sammy Baugh.

Why hadn't Brown, who averaged about 25 carries per game during the regular season, run the ball more, especially when the NFL careers of the Browns' two quarterbacks totaled only three seasons? Paul Brown had an answer, but it did not mollify Cleveland fans and the Cleveland press corps.

"We knew we had to throw because their guys in the middle are so big and strong," he said, referring to the Giants' vaunted front four and Huff. "And we could throw, but not straight enough. Of course, the Giants applied a lot of pressure, which made it tough." Which was true, mainly because of an unrelenting pass rush, especially by Robustelli and Katcavage, the two ends who, for the second week in a row, harried Plum, and later Ninowski, all afternoon. But still it begged the question as to why Paul Brown didn't have the NFL's best runner run more. After all, the previous Sunday, he had run for 152 yards against the Giants. True, 65 of those yards came on a game-opening touchdown. But even after that, he had gained 87 yards, more than all three of the Giants' running backs.

Paul Brown was effusive in his praise of the Giants' defense. "Their defense overwhelmed our offensive line," he said. "They were inspired, and the crowd was out for blood." Browns linebacker Vince Costello also lauded the Giants' defense. "They played spectacular defense. In fact, it couldn't have been more spectacular," he said.

Jim Lee Howell credited Landry with the Giants' outstanding defensive performance. "Tom Landry was the key with his great defensive job," Howell said. "He had them playing such great defense that there were no holes for Jim Brown." Howell also lauded Robustelli, who played perhaps his best game of the year. "Andy Robustelli is a great money player," said Howell, himself a former end, "and when the chips are down, he's a great leader."

Paul Brown also praised Lombardi for the double reverse and lateral to Conerly that resulted in the game's only touchdown. During practice leading up to the game, after running the second part of the double reverse, Gifford had—seemingly spontaneously and to take Conerly aback—flipped the ball to the quarterback as he trailed Gifford on the play. But if it was indeed a play, Conerly didn't know about it. "I was a little surprised when Gifford passed me the ball on that play," Conerly said. "I usually just amble along behind after

I've completed the ball handling. I never really expected anybody to throw me the thing." Gifford's take on the play was frivolous. "I tossed the ball to Charlie to protect my rushing average," he said.

Howell, though, implied that Conerly was supposed to receive a lateral on the play. "We had used the double reverse before, but this was a new wrinkle," Howell said with a smile that indicated the lateral may not have been part of the scripted play. Conerly himself gave another version later, saying, "The lateral was an option that Vinny had come up with before the game." Lombardi, never one to shrink away from taking credit, considering how much he wanted to become a head coach, finally settled the issue, saying that Chuckin' Charlie was right: It was an option. That seemed to make sense, for why else should Conerly, already pretty banged up, be trailing Gifford and thus risk being taken out by a blocker?

The statistics reflected the Giants' superiority in the game. They gained 211 yards rushing compared with only 24 yards by the Browns and outgained Cleveland 106 yards to 62 in passing. Heinrich, who again started at quarterback, completed 2 of 7 passes for 30 yards, while Conerly connected on 6 of 11 for 76 yards. The Giants had made 12 first downs against only 3 by the Browns.

"They gave us a pretty good shellacking," Brown said. "An experienced quarterback means a great deal in a game like this, and Charlie Conerly has been through the mill. And today he threw the ball very well. Meanwhile, we had two inexperienced kids at quarterback. It makes a difference." Brown seemed to have forgotten that, with the second-year Plum at quarterback during the first ten games of the season, the Browns won nine games.

Writing in the *Cleveland Press,* Howard Preston had another view as to why the Browns may have lost to the Giants on consecutive Sundays. "It appears that the first defeat by the Giants took something out of the Browns," Preston wrote in alluding to the first game the teams had played six weeks earlier.

━━

The Giants' victory put them in the NFL championship game for the second time in three years. While they had been beating the Browns, the Baltimore Colts—who would be playing in the NFL championship game for the first time—watched the game with more than just casual interest, as did coach Weeb Ewbank, who sat in the press box at Yankee Stadium. Like the Giants and the Browns, the Colts had finished the regular season at 9-3, but two of their three losses had been in their last two games after they had already clinched the Western Conference title. With 381 points, for an average of 31.8 per game, they had led the NFL, compared with the 20.5 averaged by the Giants—the third lowest in the league. Baltimore also had been second in defense, yielding 16.9 points a game, compared with the Giants' league-leading 15.3. Offensively, Unitas had come into his own, leading the NFL with 19 touchdown passes and only seven interceptions. Sixteen of those touchdown passes had gone to wide receivers Raymond Berry and Lenny Moore, both of whom had been voted to the All-Pro team along with Unitas; fullback Alan Ameche, the rookie of the year in 1955, who had scored 8 touchdowns while averaging 4.6 yards a carry to finish behind Jim Brown in rushing; offensive tackles Jim Parker and Art Spinney; defensive end Gino Marchetti; defensive tackles Art Donovan and Big Daddy Lipscomb; linebacker Bill Pellington; and defensive backs Andy Nelson and Carl Taseff—a total of a dozen players, more than any other team in the NFL.

The Giants, meanwhile, placed eight players on the All-Pro team: Rosey Brown, Wietecha, and Gifford on offense, and Robustelli, Grier, Huff, Svare, and Patton on defense.

"I'm scared to death of the Colts," said Howell, never known for his optimism. "Alan Ameche isn't Jimmy Brown, but he's right up there, and Johnny Unitas has the touch. He gets rid of the ball very quick, and he has great protection, since Baltimore has the best blocking in the league."

By Monday, the Colts had been installed as 3-point favorites in the betting, even though the Giants would be the home team for the third week in a row and had beaten the Colts at Yankee Stadium in early November. But they had done so by only 3 points, and, especially significant, Unitas had not played because of cracked ribs, which by now had completely healed. So Johnny U, as Baltimore fans had come to calling the onetime sandlot-football player, would be ready for the Giants.

18

"The Best Football Game
Ever Played"

*E*ven before the Browns-Giants play-off game was over, hundreds of fans had lined up at box offices outside Yankee Stadium to buy tickets for the NFL championship game a week later against the Baltimore Colts. An hour after the game, the line had grown to more than a thousand and continued to grow right up until midnight, when ticket sales were halted. Unlike today, when most NFL games are sold out for the season, and there are long waiting lists for season tickets, that was not the case in 1958, when the Chicago Cardinals averaged fewer than twenty thousand spectators a game, and Philadelphia, Washington, and Pittsburgh did not do much better. Only the Giants, Colts, Browns, Chicago Bears, Los Angeles Rams, and San Francisco 49ers consistently drew well—especially the Rams, who twice drew crowds of more than one hundred thousand. At any rate, the long lines continued outside Yankee Stadium on Monday and Tuesday until all seats were sold out, ensuring a crowd of about sixty-five thousand. In addition, millions more—far more, as it turned out, than had been anticipated—would watch the game across the country on NBC network television or hear it on several patchwork network radio broadcasts.

By game time on an unseasonably mild late-December day, with the temperature in the low 40s, the vast crowd, officially numbered at 64,185, included anywhere from 15,000 to 20,000 fans from Baltimore, almost all of whom had come to New York by train. (The Colts had flown to New York on Saturday.) Also from Baltimore had come the 125-member Baltimore Colts marching band, its drum majorettes, and cheerleaders, who would perform both before the game and at halftime. More than half of the spectators had traveled by subway or bus, with many coming by car or on foot from the Bronx neighborhood where the stadium was situated. Those who came by car from outside the city had to park on nearby streets, which they could do without charge, or in the few neighborhood parking garages. The Colts spent Saturday night at the Concourse Plaza Hotel, as some other NFL teams tended to do, along with many of the Giants and their families.

When the thirty-five-man Colts team took the field for pregame practice, it gave Giants fans their first look at Baltimore's twenty-five-year-old Johnny Unitas, who had become one of the best quarterbacks in the NFL. Fans could not miss the slender Unitas, with his crew cut, his old-fashioned black high-top shoes, his distinctive slope-shouldered gait, and his trademark manner of following through with his arm motion much like a baseball pitcher after having thrown a fastball, with the right palm facing down. It would also be the first time that most of the Giants would see Unitas in the flesh, although the defense had spent hours watching him on film all week. Others had seen him for the first time in 1956 when the Giants played the Colts in a preseason game in Boston. That had been Unitas's second game in a Baltimore uniform after he had been cut the year before in preseason camp by his hometown team, the Pittsburgh Steelers, and had then spent that fall playing for a local semipro team, the Bloomfield Rams, for $6 a game.

Nine days before the preseason game in Boston, Unitas had made his debut with the Colts against the Philadelphia Eagles in Hershey, Pennsylvania, where the Eagles trained. "I remember John coming into the game to replace George Shaw, who had won the starting quarterback position the year before when he was a rookie," said Ernie Accorsi, who was a fourteen-year-old high school student in Hershey at the time and would eventually become the public relations director and then the general manager of the Colts. "No one knew who he was, including the guy running the public address system, who pronounced his name 'U-*nit*-is.' You could see right away, though, that he could play, and it wasn't long after that that he threw a touchdown pass."

For Andy Robustelli, the championship game was just another game—a big one, to be sure, but, as the great Giants end put it, "Once it starts, a game is a game." But, then, Robustelli was the only player in the Colts-Giants game who had already played in three NFL championship games, two with the Los Angeles Rams and one with the Giants. For the Colts, though, the game was special indeed. After coming into the NFL in 1950 from the defunct All-America Football Conference, with Y. A. Tittle at quarterback, the Colts finished 1-11 during their first season. Then Baltimore dropped out of the league after averaging fewer than fifteen thousand spectators during its inaugural season and creating monumental debt—only to return under new ownership in 1952, when the team won three of twelve games but drew far larger crowds, averaging around twenty-five thousand. Losing records continued over the next three years, including Unitas's rookie year of 1956, until the Colts went 7-5 in 1957. That year Unitas led the NFL with 24 touchdown passes while completing 57 percent of his passes, and Raymond Berry, in his second year in the league, caught 47 passes for a league-high 800 yards. When Weeb Ewbank was hired away from Cleveland in 1954, where he had been an assistant under Paul Brown, the new coach said he would embark on a five-year plan. Appropriately enough, 1958 was the fifth year of that program.

For the city of Baltimore, the 1958 title game was huge, far bigger than it was to New York. For one thing, the Colts were the city's oldest major league franchise, at least in modern times. The Baltimore Orioles of baseball's American League had been in existence only since 1954, when the franchise, then the St. Louis Browns, was moved to Baltimore. But the Orioles had never finished higher than fifth in the eight-team league. Moreover, Baltimore did not have a team either in the National Basketball Association or the National Hockey League. Nor, of course, did it have the diverse attractions that New York did. While the Giants were more popular and drawing bigger crowds than ever, the vast majority of its residents cared little or not at all about the championship game. Thus a victory by the Colts was guaranteed to mean far more to Baltimore than it would to New York, which was accustomed to the Yankees winning so many World Series. By contrast, Baltimore, far more blue collar than New York, had never won a championship in any major league sport since the original Baltimore Orioles who won the league pennant in 1895 and 1896.

"We were like their college team," said defensive tackle Art Donovan, a native New Yorker who had played football at Mount St. Michael Academy in the Bronx. "And the support for us was unbelievable. People would run into us in stores and restaurants and tell us what we meant to Baltimore. And in the week leading up to the championship game, it seemed like everybody in Baltimore was talking about the game."

Donovan thought he remembered Robustelli from their high school days. "We went up to Stamford once and killed them," Donovan said in recalling a game from the early forties. In fact, Mount St. Michael had beaten, but not exactly killed, Stamford High, 7–0 in 1941, a year before Robustelli went out for football. The afternoon of that game, Robustelli, then a junior, was bagging and delivering groceries at Sclafani's market in his West Side neighborhood.

More so than the Giants, the Colts had a remarkably diverse group of players, starting with Unitas, who had been virtually unheard of while playing for the University of Louisville, whereas Charlie Conerly had been an All-American at Mississippi. Fullbacks Alex Webster and Alan Ameche were similar in style, but if Frank Gifford was a glamorous and handsome, if not particularly fast, halfback who had already made several movies, Lenny Moore, his Baltimore counterpart, was a fleet back who led the NFL in rushing percentage with a 7.3 average on 82 carries and seven touchdowns, the same number he scored while catching 50 passes.

If the Giants' front four was the best in the NFL, the Colts' was probably a close second, with defensive ends Gino Marchetti, who had fought at the Battle of the Bulge in Belgium during World War II and was widely regarded as the best at his position in NFL history; Don Joyce and Ordell Braase; along with All-Pro tackles Gene "Big Daddy" Lipscomb, a remarkably agile 285-pound behemoth who had never attended college; and Donovan, the puckish New Yorker whose nickname was "Fatso," and who, as a marine fresh out of high school, had fought at Okinawa in the Pacific Theater of Operations. On the offensive line were two more All-Pros in 275-pound Jim Parker, one of the best offensive tackles in the NFL, and guard Art Spinney.

As with the Giants, there was a good camaraderie among the Colts. "We all liked each other and got along very well," said Donovan, who like Marchetti, Robustelli, and Conerly did not play in the NFL until he was past his twenty-fifth birthday. "Coming into the NFL after being in the marines in the Pacific during the war was like child's play." That was a mantra of scores of players in the NFL in the 1950s, for whom football, no matter how rough, or even vicious, paled in comparison to what they had been through during World War II.

Good as they had proceeded to become as a team, many of the Colts had been unwanted elsewhere. So it was that before the Giants game, in an obvious attempt to further motivate a team that needed no motivation, knowing they had been overshadowed the last three years by the Giants and Browns, short and portly coach Weeb Ewbank played to their egos by pointing out how they had been overlooked or unwanted.

"He said the Colts wound up with Donovan because no one else wanted him, because he was too fat," recalled Marchetti. "Then he looked at Raymond Berry and told him that he also was ignored because one leg was shorter than the other"—something that Berry denied years later—"and because he had poor eyesight and supposedly wasn't fast enough to be an end. Then he turned to Big Daddy, saying how he'd been released by the Rams after sitting on the bench for three seasons before the Colts picked him up. He got on me too, saying no one had any interest in me when I played in high school— and he was right, because I was terrible—and said that I had to play two years at a community college in California before I got to play at a high level in college. Then he turned to John and said that even his hometown team, the Steelers, didn't want him before releasing him, and that he had to play with a sandlot team to prove himself.

"And even then, he wasn't done, as he kept telling other guys how they'd been unwanted until the Colts gave them a chance. Weeb even made fun of himself, saying that the Colts really wanted Blanton Collier [at the time, an assistant coach under Paul Brown at Cleveland] but when they couldn't get Collier, they picked Weeb. Did it work? I don't know, but I don't think it hurt, except for maybe a couple of egos."

It was hardly a one-for-the-ages "Win one for the Gipper" Knute Rockne oration, but for Ewbank, not renowned as an orator, it was both novel and brilliant, since it hit home with so many of his players. Of course, Ewbank was deliberately devaluing some of his players, such as Marchetti, Berry, and Donovan, who had been picked to the all-NFL team for several seasons in a row. Of course, too, there was the danger that it would boomerang by deflating the confidence of some members of the team.

In the Giants' locker room, once again the atmosphere was light-hearted. Conerly, phlegmatic as always, sat on a trainer's table having his ankles taped by John Johnson, who had started that ritual in 1948 and would be taping Giants players' ankles sixty years later, in 2008, at the age of ninety. Modzelewski, as usual, kidded Grier about his weight, while Robustelli quietly talked with Svare about strategies they planned to use. Meanwhile, Lombardi, who had driven to the stadium from Red Bank with young Vince, again not saying a word during the hour-long drive, walked around the locker room, alternating between cajoling and exhorting Giants he felt might need a dose of motivation.

Under terms of the contract negotiated between the NFL and CBS and NBC, the latter network telecast the game nationally, with Colts broadcaster Chuck Thompson and his Giants counterpart, Chris Schenkel, doing the play-by-play and the analysis. Several others broadcast the game on radio, including nationally known sportscaster Bob Wolff, who described the action—alone, no less—on a network put together by the National Brewing Company, one of a number of breweries then based in Baltimore. "They had me sitting outside below the mezzanine around the 30-yard line, where I had trouble seeing the whole field," recalled Wolff, who described thousands of college and professional football, basketball, hockey, and baseball games during his long career. "But it was worth it because it was one of the best games I'd ever covered in any sport."

Because the newspaper strike was apparently on the verge of being settled, New York sportswriters were on hand to cover the game and write their stories in the event the strike ended Sunday night—which it did, meaning that the presses rolled after midnight, and newspapers would be on the streets on Monday morning. Among those in the press box was John Steadman, the sports editor and columnist for the Sunday *Baltimore American* and the daily *Baltimore News-Post*. In a bit of literary whimsy, Steadman wrote a column for that day's editions in which he in effect predicted how the game would go. In his fictional tale, Unitas emerged as the hero who guided the Colts to a 23–17 victory, which meant that they would beat the "spread" of 3½ points that favored Baltimore.

Perched in the upper deck, even higher than the sportswriters, was Wellington Mara with his trusty Polaroid camera. As he had been doing for the last three years, Mara would take pictures of the Colts' different defenses and then, with the film encased in a stocking, would lower it by string to the Giants' bench for Vince Lombardi to see. In doing so, Mara felt that he was involved in the game and helping the team, just as he would by trying to catch punts, or at least shag them, while wearing a sweat suit in practice or do anything else on the practice field to help out.

In Red Smith's Monday column, which once again would be available to readers of the *Herald Tribune,* he would write about what he perceived to be a college atmosphere at the game, engendered largely by the Colts' band, which included fourteen cheerleaders, six drum majorettes, and a drum major, a rare scene at an NFL game. "Fillies of provocative design paraded wearing the letters COLTS across bosoms that pointedly contradicted that label," Smith wrote about the cheerleaders and drum majorettes without objecting to either the band or the "fillies" who accompanied it in their provocative fashion. At halftime, the band and the six drum majorettes, dressed in reindeer costumes that included gray skirts, red leotards, and white boots, put on a Christmas show for the big stadium crowd, which included, naturally, "Rudolph the Red-Nosed Reindeer."

―

With the Giants winning the coin toss, the Colts kicked off. But on their first possession, the Giants, with Heinrich again starting at quarterback, went nowhere and had to punt. On the Colts' first offensive play of the game, Sam Huff burst through a hole and nailed Unitas, forcing a fumble, which safety Jimmy Patton recovered at the Baltimore 37. But then Heinrich fumbled a snap from Ray Wietecha, and Marchetti pounced on the ball at the Colts' 40-yard line. On the ensuing possession, Unitas gave up the ball again when his third-down pass was intercepted by cornerback Carl Karilivacz at the New York 40. After the Giants punted again, Unitas threw a perfect 50-yard lead pass to Lenny Moore, just beyond the reach of cornerback Lindon Crow, in a play that covered 65 yards and put the ball at the Giants' 25. But then Steve Myhra, the weak link in the Colts' offense after making only 4 of 10 field-goal attempts during the season, had his 25-yard field-goal attempt blocked by Huff.

Once again, as had happened so often over the last three seasons, the Giants' defense was cheered loudly as it left the field. The ovation grew even louder when Conerly trotted out with the offense, then connected on his first pass to Triplett, after which Gifford sprinted down the left sideline for 38 yards to the Baltimore 31. Summerall then kicked a 36-yard field goal for the game's first score.

But in the second quarter, two fumbles by the usually sure-handed Gifford led to two Baltimore touchdowns. Five plays after the first fumble, at the Giants' 20, fullback Alan Ameche crashed into the end zone from a yard out to make it 7–3 after Myhra's extra point. Less than five minutes later, with the Giants at the Colts' 10-yard line after recovering another Baltimore fumble, Gifford fumbled the ball away again, with defensive end Don Joyce recovering at the 14. Unitas, behind superb protection, then completed three passes during a masterful 15-play, 86-yard drive that included a 16-yard quarterback scramble. Johnny U hit Berry in the left corner of the end zone between Patton and Emlen Tunnell with a 15-yard pass that made it 14–3 at halftime.

Apart from the sack by Huff, Unitas had barely been touched in the first half, with Robustelli rendered powerless by the huge and agile Jim Parker, and the rest of the Giants' defense also unable to do anything. If Unitas was unpredictable, he could also throw at varying speeds: short bullet passes; long, arcing throws of 50 yards or more; and soft tosses just high enough to clear the head of a charging line- man or linebacker. And, as Raymond Berry would say, Unitas was not only talented and supremely confident, but fearless, often stand- ing in the pocket until the last possible second before unloading a pass and then being plowed under by a defensive end or tackle. In all, Uni- tas completed 8 of 12 pass attempts for 115 yards during the first half as against only 39 yards by Heinrich and Conerly. On the ground, the Colts were vastly superior, gaining 83 yards compared with 47 by the home team. And the Colts had recorded nine first downs against two by the Giants.

Ferociously played as it was, the first half—and, indeed, the en- tire game, as it would turn out—was cleanly played. The only skir- mish occurred in the second quarter when, after Huff tackled Berry near the Baltimore bench, Weeb Ewbank, the fifty-one-year-old

Colts coach, threw a punch at Huff. Not only was Huff wearing a face mask, but he was about eight inches taller, around thirty-five pounds heavier, and twenty-seven years younger. "He kneed one of my men out of bounds, and he should have been thrown out," the feisty Ewbank said. Huff, who denied kneeing Berry, said, "He called me a lot of bad names, but we both got over it."

Lombardi said nothing to Gifford about the fumbles. And how could he, when Gifford had averaged 4 yards a carry on 115 rushes, caught 29 passes, and completed 3 of 10 passes for 30 yards and two touchdowns during the regular season? Rather, Lombardi calmly plotted strategy for the second half with Conerly, who he planned to have pass much more than the Giants had in the first half—if for no other reason than that the Colts had completely contained Gifford, the Giants' main running threat. Landry, meanwhile, gathered the defense around him primarily to discuss ways to penetrate the wall of blockers that the Colts had built around Unitas and to tell the defensive backs to continue to double-team Lenny Moore. Not much was said about Ameche and Berry, the Colts' other two main offensive threats.

A long drive at the start of the third quarter, highlighted by Unitas's pinpoint passing, put the Colts at the Giants' 1-yard line. A touchdown would give Baltimore a 21–3 lead and continued momentum. But once again, as it had done so often over the last three years, the Giants' Fearsome Foursome of Robustelli, Modzelewski, Grier, and Katcavage refused to bend. Two rushes up the middle by Ameche failed to gain any yardage, as did a quarterback sneak by Unitas. At that point, Ewbank signaled a time out to confer with Unitas on the sideline. "I thought of a field goal, but I decided a touchdown would kill them right then and there," Ewbank said, "so I told Johnny to go for it." Unitas then called a trick play that called for him to hand off to Ameche, who was to run right and throw to Berry or whoever else might be open in the end zone. But instead of throwing, Ameche, under pressure, was thrown for a 4-yard loss by Cliff Livingston, who came barreling in from his left linebacker position. Again, as the Giants' defensive unit walked off the field, Giants fans gave it a huge ovation.

On the ensuing possession, the Giants faced a 3rd-and-2 situation on their 12-yard line. With the Colts geared for a running play, Conerly faked a handoff and fired a 30-yard pass to Rote at the Giants' 42. One of the best open-field runners in the league, Rote then broke loose from several would-be tacklers, crossed midfield, and appeared to be on his way to a touchdown when he was hit hard by Colts safety Andy Nelson, who stripped Rote of the ball at the Baltimore 25-yard line. The ball bounced forward toward the goal line, with Nelson and Webster in pursuit. Webster grabbed it on the run and rumbled to the 1-yard line, where he was knocked out of bounds by defensive back Carl Taseff. "Thank God for Alex," Rote later said of the play, which covered 87 yards. Two plays later, Triplett banged into the end zone, and Summerall added the extra point to make it 14–10, Baltimore.

Why had Conerly called the pass on 3rd-and-2 when everyone, including the Colts, expected a run by Gifford, Webster, or Triplett—especially when Gifford and Webster had just gained 8 yards on two carries? "They were thinking run, so we passed," said Conerly, always a man of few words. That Webster had scooped up the ball and scored made it all the more meaningful to the Giants fans who loved Big Red.

Now the Giants had momentum, while the Colts' defense and the powerful offensive line, which had seemingly made Unitas untouchable, began to falter. Early in the fourth period, starting at the Giants' 19-yard line, Conerly led a masterful drive, interspersing runs with passes. After having focused on Gifford and Rote as his receivers, Conerly threw passes of 17 and 46 yards to end Bob Schnelker, while Gifford and Webster gained the additional yardage that put the Giants at the Colts' 15. There Conerly faked a short throw to Gifford, who turned as if to receive a pass, then accelerated, faking out cornerback Milt Davis and grabbing a perfectly thrown pass by Conerly along the left sideline at the 10-yard line. Gifford then ran in untouched for a go-ahead touchdown as the stadium erupted with a thunderous ovation. Summerall kicked the extra point to give the Giants a 17–14 lead.

With less than five minutes left, the Colts, though seeming to have lost their edge, drove to the Giants' 38-yard line on the strength of Unitas's passing. From there, Bert Rechichar, who was used on long field-goal attempts but had made only 1 of 4 during the season, was short on a 45-yard attempt.

A short while later, the Colts recovered a fumble by backup fullback Phil King and advanced to the Giants' 27. But Robustelli finally managed to breeze past Jim Parker for the first time to sack Unitas for a 12-yard loss. Then on the next play, Modzelewski broke through and dropped Unitas for a loss at the Giants' 47, forcing Baltimore to punt.

On the Giants' next possession, on a 3rd-and-4 situation at their own 40 with just over two minutes to play, Conerly called Gifford's number on a sweep to the right side. A first down would probably enable the Giants to run out the clock and win. But Gifford and his blockers would have to reckon with future Hall of Famers Marchetti and Donovan. As Gifford suddenly cut in, Marchetti fought off a block by Schnelker and got his hands on Gifford, as did Donovan. As Gifford began to go down, 285-pound Big Daddy Lipscomb leaped atop Marchetti, breaking his right ankle.

After the players unpiled, and Marchetti was carried off the field on a stretcher, referee Ron Gibbs placed the ball down and raised his hands, indicating that Gifford had been about five inches short of a first down. Rote, convinced that Gifford had made it, said, "The referee was so concerned with Marchetti that he forgot where he'd put the ball. I saw him pick it up at his front [left] foot, but when he put it down, it was where his right foot was."

Gifford also insisted he had made the first down. "There's no question in my mind that I made it," he said. "But before I could even complain about it, Ronnie Gibbs called out 'fourth down.' There was nothing I could do. And complaining about the call wouldn't have made any good."

Donovan recalled that Gifford did indeed complain about the call. "I said to him, 'Shut up and go back to the huddle.' "

With only two minutes to play, Jim Lee Howell felt that the Giants had to punt. During a time-out, several Giants urged Howell to let the offense go for it. "Marchetti was out, and we only needed four inches," guard Jack Stroud said. "We would have run at whoever replaced Marchetti, and we would have made it." (Marchetti's replacement was Ordell Braase, a solid defensive end who eventually would replace Don Joyce as the starting right end.) But Gifford, among some other Giants, including Robustelli, felt Howell was right. "We were very tired, and I'm not sure we would have made it. And the odds were with us. Don Chandler was a great punter—probably the best in the league—and wherever they got the ball, they'd have to go a long way, and they only had one time out."

Of course, they also had Unitas and Berry.

Chandler did his part by launching a beautiful spiral punt to the Colts' 14, where Carl Taseff called for a fair catch. That left the Colts with just over two minutes to play and 86 yards from the Giants' goal line. Against perhaps the best defense in NFL history facing them, it appeared to be a daunting task, to say the least.

Johnny Unitas would now begin the first of two drives for the football ages.

Given the short time left, the Giants expected that Unitas would pass to receivers near the sidelines so they could go out of bounds to stop the clock. So the Giants' defense was geared to stop sideline passes and long throws with a "prevent" alignment. But two of the key ingredients in Unitas's makeup were his daring and his unpredictability. Aware of what the Giants expected him to do, he did the opposite, throwing relatively short passes up the middle.

"We had to concentrate on getting the ball up the field quick, which meant we had to pass and not eat up the clock by running," Unitas said later. "The Giants knew that, so we had to pass in a way they wouldn't expect."

After failing to connect on his first two passes, Unitas needed 10 yards on third down—a crucial juncture—but got 11 when he found Lenny Moore open on the right side. Then Unitas drilled a pass to Berry, who snared it on the left side right in front of Svare at the 40 and raced to midfield. At this point, Tom Landry ordered the Giants' secondary to double-team Berry, who, slow as he was, and with poor eyesight that had to be enhanced with contact lenses, was one of the best receivers in the NFL. It did not matter. On the next play, again coming from his split-out left side, Berry got between Jimmy Patton and Sam Huff to make a leaping catch at the Giants' 35-yard line.

Some New York fans, already headed for the exits, heard the roar from the Baltimore contingent and turned back. What they saw, they would not soon forget. On the next play, which Unitas called as an audible at the line of scrimmage, Berry sprinted directly toward Karilivacz, then cut to the middle to catch his third straight pass—another spectacular reception only inches from the ground at the 20—and then ran to the 13 before he was tackled. Three straight passes to Berry, each with a defender or defenders guarding him, yet Unitas, infinitely confident, threaded the needle on every one, for a total gain of 62 yards. Myhra, who also played offensive guard, then ran onto the field along with the long snapper, Buzz Nutter, and the once-upon-a-time starting quarterback and now the holder, George Shaw. Following a perfect snap, Shaw put the ball down, laces facing the goalpost, and, with only seven seconds left and kicking from the Giants' 20, Myhra put the ball dead center over the crossbar to tie the score and send an NFL championship game into sudden-death overtime for the first time since the inaugural NFL title game in 1932.

Aptly enough, the ball landed in a section of a temporary grandstand behind the goalpost where the Baltimore Colts marching band, its drum majorettes, cheerleaders, and honor guard were seated and into the hands of George Schaefer, a member of the honor guard. Frustrated no doubt by the brilliant Colts' drive and the tying field goal, a group of Giants fans jumped on Schaefer and tried to pry away the football. Thinking as fast as Johnny Unitas under a pass rush, Schaefer deftly rolled the ball out to Danny O'Toole, a snare drummer in the band, who promptly stashed the ball in his huge drum to ensure that it got to Baltimore, while members of New York City's Finest tried to restore order.

"It was utter pandemonium," said Marge Schmidt, who along with her sister, Doris, was a drum majorette for the Colts. "Somebody even ripped the cowgirl hat off my head."

Viewing Myhra's kick from the sidelines was Gino Marchetti, who despite his pain had insisted that he be able to watch the end of the game while propped up on his stretcher. "There was no way I was going to leave at that point," Marchetti recalled. "It was my game too, and I was convinced with the way John was playing, we still had a good shot at winning." As soon as Myhra's kick sailed over the crossbar, the trainers told Marchetti they had to wheel him to safety into the locker room. "If we stay, when this game ends," one of the trainers told Marchetti, "we'll never be able to get you out of here."

From the looks of faces on the Giants' sideline, it appeared that they had lost the game. As Landry was to say later, it was evident that the Giants had gained the momentum by scoring twice in the second half, only to lose it at the end of the fourth quarter. "We had the game won, and then we let them tie it, and the momentum completely changed," Landry said. "When that happens, it's hard to get it back."

Throughout the drive, Unitas, as always, was poised, confident, and to the point in the huddle. Occasionally he might say to a receiver,

"What have you got?" But as Bob Vogel, a Colts tackle in the sixties and seventies, once said, "Once he drops his head, it's quiet. He does all the talking." Though not prone to criticizing a member of the offense, Unitas managed to get his message across if a player repeatedly missed a block. For instance, if an offensive lineman let a player break through and sack Unitas, he might turn to the player in the huddle and say, "If you can't block your man, I wonder if you can get someone who can."

John Mackey, a Baltimore tight end from 1963 through 1971, and another of the many Colts elected to the Pro Football Hall of Fame, summed up Unitas's stature when he said, "It's like being in the huddle with God."

In the press box, John Steadman was being hailed as a clairvoyant by some Baltimore writers who had seen his column predicting a 23–17 Colts victory. With the score tied at 17–17, and going into sudden-death overtime, a first in NFL history, it appeared that Steadman's fictitious account of the game, right down to the score, might come true. Steadman, of course, hoped it would happen. Although sportswriters usually adhered to the admonition of "no cheering in the press box," Steadman, as a Baltimorean who knew most of the Colts, only naturally was pulling for his hometown team.

After a three-minute rest, the captains met at midfield, where, in the coin toss, Unitas called tails. It was the only wrong call he had made up to that point. The Giants, looking spent, elected to receive. New York started at its own 20 with a run by Gifford that gained 4 yards. Conerly then overthrew Schnelker, and on 3rd-and-6, hoping to throw again, Conerly couldn't find anyone open and did something he rarely ever did: He ran to his right for 5 yards, where he was stopped by linebackers Bill Pellington and Don Shinnick 1 yard short of a first down. Again Chandler unloaded a superb punt, 51 yards to the Colts' 20. Unitas, who had been asked to get 84 yards to tie the game, now would have to take his team 80 yards to win it. Against the marvelous Giants' defense, the odds seemed to be against him.

It was only natural that Landry and his defensive unit expected Unitas, given his tremendous performance late in the fourth quarter, to throw on almost every play. But, unpredictable as always, he did not, keeping the Giants off balance. "When you thought he'd call a running play, he'd pass," Sam Huff said, "and when you were sure he was going to pass, he'd call a run."

And now, with no time constraints, Unitas had all the time in the world. On first down, he handed off to L. G. Dupre, who hadn't carried the ball at all during the Colts' final scoring drive in the fourth quarter; the 190-pound halfback from Baylor ran around right end for 11 yards and a first down. After a long incomplete pass to Lenny Moore, Dupre got 2 yards up the middle, then Unitas flipped a screen pass to Ameche, who sprinted 8 yards for a first down at the Colts' 41. Once again, Unitas handed to Dupre on a draw play that gained 3 yards. But then on second down, Modzelewski broke through and sacked Unitas for an 8-yard loss, making it 3rd-and-15 at the Colts' 36. "I had a pass play called, but Mo just wrapped me up," Unitas was to say later. An incomplete pass now—and the Giants knew that a pass was coming—and the Colts would have to punt. Again, a huge pressure play for the Colts, and Unitas knew just what he wanted to do. For the first time on the drive, Unitas called Berry's number. Berry, running straight out from his split-end position on the left side, suddenly hooked to the sideline. As he did, Karilivacz, whom Berry had burned repeatedly in the fourth quarter, slipped and fell down, leaving Berry open to grab a Unitas pass for a 21-yard gain to the Giants' 43-yard line for a first down. Giants fans let out a collective groan, and Baltimore fans roared. It was the third time that Unitas had made good on a third-and-long situation within a span of about five minutes, including the waning minutes of the fourth quarter and in overtime.

With the Giants convinced that Unitas would throw again, he instead called a draw play, faking a pass and then handing off to the six-foot, 218-pound Alan Ameche, who burst through center for 23 yards to the Giants' 20, putting the Colts within field-goal distance. "That play's not a long gainer," Unitas was to say later. "Usually we figure to get four or five yards. But Huff had been playing to the left and back, which made it an easy blocking assignment for our tackle. Huff also was playing for a pass, and the way Mo had been crashing, I figured they were right for a trap, and I hit it right."

Once more, Unitas's unpredictability had flummoxed the Giants' defense and generated one of the biggest plays of a big-play day.

Certainly now, after a run, Unitas would pass, but he didn't, instead running Dupre off tackle for no gain. On the next play, though, the Giants—now definitely expecting a pass—guessed right but could do nothing about it as Berry ran left, then cut to the center to take a slant pass. He ran it to the 8-yard line for a 12-yard gain and first down. Now, for sure, everyone felt that Ewbank, who occasionally sent in plays, not all of which Unitas heeded, would have Ameche or Dupre carry up the middle for a play, then send in Myhra for a very short field goal. But he did not. And on second down, with both Berry and Moore sprinting into the end zone on the left side, Unitas lofted a pass over the head of left linebacker Cliff Livingston and into the hands of right end Jim Mutscheller, who fell out of bounds at the 1-yard line. It seemed like a high-risk call, since, if Livingston had intercepted the ball, he had no one between him and the Colts' goal line 99 yards away. On the sideline, Ewbank, the other Colts, and most of the other players blanched when Unitas threw the pass. Daring as Unitas was, even they never expected he would throw in that situation. Some fans wondered why the Colts were taking chances by running and even passing the ball when a field goal, and a very close one at that, would win the game.

Some cynics, aware that the Colts were 3½-point favorites, depending on the bookmaker, thought that perhaps they were going for a touchdown so that bettors among their fans—and there were many, both at the stadium and back in Baltimore—along with owner Carroll Rosenbloom, who liked to gamble, would win their bets, which they wouldn't if the Colts were to win by only 3 points.

"There was no way the Colts were going to put the game in the lap of Myhra," Ernie Accorsi said. "John was going for the touchdown all the way."

Unitas had no concerns about throwing the ball so close to the goal line. "I knew they were expecting the run," he said later. "So I told Jimmy to get out there real quick. Then all I had to do was flip it up in the air and have him catch it."

Easy as that.

Now, Giants fans knew, it definitely was over. And it was, on the next down, when Unitas called a play wherein the Colts double-teamed tackle Frank Youso, a replacement for Rosey Grier, who had been injured earlier. The rest of the Colts' offensive line again did a superb blocking job on Robustelli, Katcavage, and Modzelewski while Ameche, in a low crouch and cradling the ball under his right arm, followed picture-perfect blocks by offensive tackle George Preas on Huff, Moore on Tunnell, and Mutscheller on Livingston as he bolted through a hole big enough to drive a Mack truck through for the game-winning touchdown.

"When I slapped the ball in Al's belly and saw him take off, I knew nobody was going to stop him with one yard to go," Unitas said. "They couldn't have done it if we needed ten yards."

One of the reasons for the ease with which Ameche scored was, once again, Unitas's unpredictability. "We were sure he was going to pass again, so I went to the right to help out Carl Karilivacz, and that left a big hole in the middle," said Huff, playing middle linebacker. True, but then when he tried to retreat back to the center, he encountered Preas. As for the play itself, Huff said, "That's one of the things that made Unitas great."

Within seconds, scores of Colts fans hoisted a smiling Ameche—the Colts' highest-paid player at $20,000 a season—onto their shoulders while hundreds of others tore down the wooden goalpost only a few feet from where Ameche had landed on his touchdown run. Meanwhile, the Colts marching band struck up the team's victory song, "Let's Go, You Baltimore Colts," while struggling to get back on the field, which the band finally did a half hour after the game ended.

On the Giants' side of the field, Frank Gifford, riddled with guilt over his two first-half fumbles, which led to the Colts' first two touchdowns, turned to Lombardi to apologize. "Don't worry about it, Frank," Lombardi told his crestfallen halfback. "If it wasn't for you, we wouldn't even be here."

In the press box, John Steadman was accepting congratulations from other writers. His apocryphal story in that day's *Baltimore American* calling for the Colts to win by a score of 23–17 had, for the most part, come true. For example, Steadman's flight of fancy journalism had the Colts leading at halftime, 14–7, which was pretty close to Baltimore's actual 14–3 lead at the intermission. Then he had the Giants take a 17–14 lead in the fourth quarter—which they did—and then wrote of Myhra tying the score at 17–17 with a field goal, which, of course, he had. However, Steadman wasn't clairvoyant enough to have Ameche scoring the game-winning touchdown in overtime. Instead he had Bert Rechichar, the Colts' long-distance field-goal kicker, boot two field goals in regulation to lift Baltimore to a 23–17 victory.

Most of the crowd appeared to have been left limp by the high drama in the fourth quarter and then in overtime. NFL Commissioner Bert Bell, watching from an upper-deck seat among the fans, as he was wont to do, said, "It was the greatest game I've ever seen." Certainly not many in the crowd had ever seen a more exciting game.

In the Giants' somber locker room, Jim Lee Howell had no regrets. "We have nothing to be ashamed of," the coach said. "After all, we were just a few seconds and possibly a few feet away from winning." As for Unitas's go-for-broke passes in the overtime session, Howell said, "That was smart football—not so much risky as smart football. He had our defenders bunched in for the running attack and knew just what he was doing, and he did it well."

Modzelewski, who got one of the two sacks of Unitas, agreed that the Giants had nothing to be ashamed of. "We did pretty good for a team that was so low after losing five exhibition games," Little Mo said.

While Howell offered no excuses, Gifford did. "We didn't have any life left when it went into overtime," he said. "I remember when Charlie and I were sitting on the bench during the drive that tied the score, he was exhausted. And as the drive continued, he said, 'I just can't go on anymore.' And then when they tied it, I said to him, 'Boy, you're going to have to go some more.' And he said, 'I just can't.' "

Unitas himself was asked whether he was concerned about a possible interception in what appeared to be his risky pass to Mutscheller at the 1-yard line on the play before Ameche's winning touchdown. Unitas, staring at his questioner, Dave Anderson of the New York *Journal-American*, seemed surprised at the question. "When you know what you're doing, you don't get intercepted," he said calmly but firmly.

On the basis of the statistics, the Colts deserved to win. Unitas alone, in completing 26 of 40 passes, passed for more yardage—322 yards—than the Giants gained altogether in both passing and rushing (266). In a record-breaking performance for an NFL championship game, the soft-spoken and genteel twenty-five-year-old Raymond Berry caught 12 of those passes—a record for an NFL championship game—for 178 yards. In addition, the Colts, who gained 138 yards rushing as against 88 by the Giants, recorded 27 first downs to 10 by the Giants.

Berry, who did not become a starter on his Paris, Texas, high school team (where his father was the head coach) or at Southern Methodist University until his senior year, said it was not until years later that he asked Unitas why he threw three consecutive passes to him in the fourth-quarter drive that led to the tying field goal. "I had thought about it for years, but it wasn't until John was visiting me in Colorado more than forty years later that I asked him," Berry said. "I remember how John smiled and said, 'I did it because I figured you could catch it.'"

If the Colts were trailing late in a game, Unitas often would call two plays in a huddle to be run consecutively. "Then he would call an audible on the third," Berry said. "So when he called two pass plays for me in the huddle, I wasn't surprised. But when we lined up for the third play, and he called another pass to me in his audible, I was surprised. But that was John. You couldn't predict what he might do."

Berry, who went on to become an assistant coach in Dallas, Denver, Detroit, and Cleveland, and head coach of the New England Patriots from 1984 through 1989, called the 1958 title game "a historical turning point for the NFL.

"After the game, I saw Bert Bell outside Yankee Stadium, and he had tears in his eyes," Berry recalled. "And I wondered why he was crying. Then I realized that the baby he had been nursing had been born that day."

—

When the Colts, including the injured Gino Marchetti, arrived back at Friendship International Airport on their chartered plane hours later, they were greeted by a boisterous crowd estimated at thirty thousand. At best, the fans barely got to glimpse the players, who quickly boarded a bus. Unitas, who had made about $12,000 during the season, was invited to make television appearances on Sunday and Monday that would have earned him almost $1,000, the equivalent in 2008 of about $10,000. But the quarterback declined all offers. "I want to be with the team on our big night, and I want to get home," Baltimore's most heroic sports figure was to say following his glittering performance in what would become a game for the ages.

"Never has there been a game like this," veteran football writer Tex Maule (onetime publicist for the short-lived Dallas Texans and the Los Angeles Rams) was to write in the next issue of the four-year-old magazine *Sports Illustrated,* which headlined his story, "The Best Football Game Ever Played." "It was a game which had everything, and when it was over, the best football team in the world had won the world's championship."

19

Chuckin' Charlie— Better with Age

*I*n the aftermath of the Colts' dramatic victory over the Giants, a state of euphoria gripped Baltimore, injecting a huge dose of civic pride into a city long overshadowed by New York, Philadelphia, and Washington. Not surprisingly, the Colts' triumph was emblazoned in front-page banner headlines in both the Baltimore *Sun* and the *Baltimore News-Post*.

And Johnny Unitas, the quarterback no NFL team wanted only three years before, and who the Colts, in effect, got for two eighty-five-cent phone calls, was the most popular person in town, idolized by adults and children alike, as he would be for the remainder of his football career in Baltimore and even beyond.

"Baltimore was a perfect fit for John," said Ernie Accorsi, the former Colts public relations director and general manager, who became a close friend of the fabled quarterback during the last few years of Unitas's career and after he retired. "It was a working man's town, and the people could relate to John and how he had struggled to get where he now was."

Writer Frank Deford, a native of Baltimore and a college freshman at the time, said that Unitas was in a way emblematic of Baltimore, an underdog who had been overlooked while playing in college and then while in training camp with the Steelers. "In a way, Unitas was treated like Baltimore, which, although it was the sixth-largest city in the country, had an inferiority complex, in part because it was between New York and Washington," said Deford, a longtime writer for *Sports Illustrated,* a prolific author, and a commentator for National Public Radio. "And after the Colts beat the Giants, Unitas came to represent Baltimore. And the victory itself created a tremendous amount of pride among people in the city, all the more so because it happened against the Giants and at Yankee Stadium in New York."

Even in New York, people who had been at Yankee Stadium for "the best football game ever played" or who had seen it on television raved about Unitas's performance the day after the game at office watercoolers, in factories, on subway and commuter trains, and elsewhere, and the high drama and brilliant play that the game had produced. Elsewhere in the country, sports fans who had paid little or no attention to the NFL in the past realized that in Unitas, Berry, Marchetti, Gifford, Conerly, Robustelli, Huff, and Tunnell, among others, they had seen some of the best football players ever to play football wage combat in a magnificently played game—far better than they were ever going to see in a college stadium—while under tremendous pressure. Had the league spent millions of dollars trying to promote itself, the results never would have matched what the nationally televised game had done in demonstrating the passing and play-calling genius of Unitas, the remarkable pass-catching abilities of Berry, the running of Alan Ameche, the pass blocking of Jim Parker, and the defensive play of Marchetti and Donovan, and—to a lesser degree in this particular game—of Robustelli, Modzelewski, and Katcavage. It is safe to say that the high quality of the play, coupled with the two dazzling drives engineered by Unitas at the end, convinced millions that the NFL offered football at the pinnacle of the sport, its very zenith. That the game included twelve players and two assistant coaches who would wind up in the Pro Football Hall of Fame might, of course, have had something to do with bringing the NFL out of the shadows in at least some parts of the country and in overtaking the college game in popularity.

By today's standards, the monetary reward for each of the Colts—$4,718.77, a record sum for an NFL championship game, and $3,111.33 for each of the Giants—was less than most current NFL players make in one-quarter of a game. Yet nobody was complaining; winning, and just playing in such a momentous game, was reward

enough. Robustelli went home to sell sneakers and other sports equipment, Marchetti went back to northern California to work with a construction gang, and Berry returned to Texas, where, while coaching
the Baylor University football team during spring practice in 1959,
he met and fell in love with Sally Crook, a senior at Baylor, whom
he would marry during the following summer's preseason training.*

While the greatest football game gave the NFL a huge boost,
which would dramatically increase profits, most players still had to
work in the off-season to make a living. It was also an era when teams
did not hold "minicamps" during the winter months, and players did
not visit weight rooms to lift weights and run on treadmills. Most of
the slightly more than four hundred players in the NFL might be
asked to stay in shape by their coaches, but it was voluntary and usually meant playing basketball at the local YMCA, which Robustelli,
for example, often did in Stamford, or going out for an occasional
run or a round of golf. And though the Giants lost to the Colts, the
gripping game certainly helped make many of the New York players
marketable in off-season business ventures. By 1959 Robustelli had
six children, had opened a second sporting goods store in Stamford,
and was operating a summer camp in his hometown known as the
All-American Day Camp. Its staff consisted largely of former high
school and college teammates and Nick Pietrosante from Ansonia,
Connecticut, a recent Notre Dame star who was now playing for the
Detroit Lions.

Maybe a lot of people thought the Colts-Giants game was the
greatest football game ever played, but Robustelli certainly was not
one of them. "I had a bad game, mainly because of Jim Parker, who I
always had trouble with, and we wound up losing a game we should
have won," Robustelli said. "Our defense didn't hold them during

---

*In addition to finding a wife, Raymond Berry found someone to throw to him during
the off-season. "Sally had never touched a football in her life until we met, and I taught
her how to throw," the extraordinarily dedicated Colts left end said in referring to his
five-foot-seven, 130-pound wife. "I'd run a series of drills and have Sally throw the
ball low at my feet, high over my head, and also throw it to the sidelines, where I could
practice catching the ball out of bounds while keeping my feet inside. Sally became very
good at it, even when I asked her to throw it to me when I had my back to her and would
have to catch the ball without completely turning around. These drills, which we usually did in a park near our home in Texas and also at times in Cambridge in Maryland
helped me a lot." And how far could Sally Berry throw? "Sally could throw it up to
twenty-five yards," said Berry, "and she was pretty accurate."

the series when they tied the score or in the overtime. I know the game was great for the NFL, but when it was over, I never felt worse, because we let it get away after it looked like we had it won."

—

The off-season following the classic Colts-Giants game would prove to be extremely notable for the Giants, mostly in a negative way. First, in January, Vince Lombardi, who had harbored hopes of becoming a head coach for more than a decade, accepted an offer to become the head coach and general manager of the woefully inept Green Bay Packers, who hadn't had a winning season since 1947; over the last three seasons, the team had won only eight games while losing twenty-seven and tying one. Lombardi, of course, had hoped that he would eventually succeed Jim Lee Howell as the Giants head coach, but who knew when big Jim Lee was going to quit? And Green Bay, both because of its location in the tundra of northern Wisconsin and its perennially poor teams, was not exactly what Lombardi, or his wife, had had in mind. But, then, teams had not exactly been knocking down Lombardi's door with coaching offers, had they? So after talking it over with the Maras and his wife and two teenage children, Lombardi decided to take the job. Just maybe, he thought, with outstanding young players like Paul Hornung, Bart Starr, Jerry Kramer, Forrest Gregg, and Max McGee, he could turn this team around. He'd seen these young guys in preseason games—none of them had been in the league more than two years—and had been impressed; all of them, he could see, were talented football players. Maybe they just had to be worked a bit harder and jell together better as a team. Assisting him would be Emlen Tunnell, now thirty-seven and a Giants defensive back since 1948; Lombardi, in one of his first moves as coach of the Packers, convinced Wellington Mara to trade Tunnell to Green Bay, where he would be a playing coach.

At any rate, if things didn't work out well at Green Bay for Lombardi, and Jim Lee Howell finally did quit, Wellington Mara had already indicated the Giants probably would want him back in New York; maybe the Packers would let him out of his five-year contract so he could go home.

Then on February 16 came the news that Tim Mara, the founder and owner of the Giants and the patriarch of the Mara family, had died of a heart attack at his Park Avenue apartment at the age of seventy-one. Though for years he'd had little to do with the Giants, leaving the running of the team to his sons Jack and Wellington, it was Mara who had taken advantage of an opportunity to buy a New York franchise in the NFL and then watched it grow into a multimillion-dollar family operation. As Arthur Daley, the sports columnist for the *New York Times* and a close friend, wrote, in Mara's later years, "pro football was booming far beyond his most visionary dreams," reaching a peak during the Colts-Giants classic two months before he died.

In perhaps the biggest surprise of the off-season, Frank Gifford, the Giants' best runner and best receiver, wrote a letter to Jim Lee Howell informing him that he wanted to try out for quarterback. Though no doubt stunned, Howell told him that he'd be given every chance to succeed. What made Gifford's plan all the more surprising was that the incumbent quarterback, thirty-eight-year-old Charlie Conerly, showed no signs of slowing up, and, moreover, was Gifford's best friend on the team. More than a few of the Giants veterans, who looked up to the laconic Conerly as the leader of the offense, did not take kindly to Gifford's hope of supplanting the old Marlboro Man. It also did not seem to make sense, since not only was backup quarterback Don Heinrich returning, but the Giants had obtained the Colts' backup to Johnny Unitas, George Shaw, in a trade for four high draft choices; *and* they had picked All-American quarterback Lee Grosscup in the first round of the draft, apparently as the heir apparent to Conerly whenever he decided to retire. Concerned about his friend's reaction to his decision, Gifford flew to Mississippi to inform Conerly of his plans, which he did while they were fishing. Conerly—not surprisingly, given his nature—told Gifford that his decision was fine with him. Whether Conerly was actually troubled by his friend's hope of getting his job would never be disclosed. However, Conerly's wife, Perian, said her husband was not upset by Gifford's decision. "It didn't bother Charlie," Mrs. Conerly said. "He even offered to help Frank, and he did."

Gifford's rationale, as he was to explain, was that he'd always wanted to be a quarterback—and, in fact, had been one in high school and at USC, only to wind up at halfback each time—and because he thought it could diversify the Giants' attack. That seemed to defy logic, since Gifford's role at halfback already had diversified the team's attack, for the Giants had set plays in which Gifford would run the "option," wherein he could either continue to run or pass. As he himself pointed out to Howell, he already had thrown 43 passes and completed 19, 12 of them for touchdowns, since 1952.

Howell, of course, did not think much of the idea. For one thing, who was going to replace his All-Pro halfback at the position? And for another, what was going to happen to Conerly? Was he supposed to retire? Or, if Gifford succeeded in outplaying Conerly in preseason, was Conerly supposed to accept becoming the backup to a reformed halfback? Perhaps to assuage Gifford, and in light of all that he had done for the team, the least he could do was to give Gifford a chance to show what he could do. Gifford, meanwhile, assured Howell that if his grand plan failed, he would gladly go back and play halfback again.

To replace Lombardi as the Giants' offensive coordinator, Wellington Mara had decided on the 135-pound onetime Brooklyn College quarterback Allie Sherman, the master of the T formation, who had rejoined the team in 1957 as a scout after three years as head coach of the Winnipeg Blue Bombers of the Canadian Football League. Greasy Neale, the Pro Football Hall of Fame coach of the Philadelphia Eagles, had called Sherman "the smartest football player I ever coached." That was saying something, considering how Sherman, as a backup quarterback for the Eagles for five years, played sparingly after being signed primarily to teach the team's starting quarterback the fundamentals of the T formation.

All of a sudden, Sherman found himself a very desirable commodity. Art Rooney, the owner of the Pittsburgh Steelers, had made a trip to New York to offer the thirty-six-year-old Sherman his team's head-coaching job, and Lombardi had urged Sherman to come to Green Bay as his offensive coordinator. "Marie Lombardi even called me to try to convince Al to go to Green Bay," Joan Sherman, Allie's wife, recalled later. Joan, a New Yorker like her husband, was not crazy about the thought of moving to Green Bay, especially after three seasons in Winnipeg, which she conceded could have influenced Sherman's decision to become the Giants' offensive coordinator. Another major consideration, Sherman said, was his sense that Howell might soon retire and that he might very well be next in line to become the team's head coach, since Tom Landry, the most logical choice as Howell's successor, was on the verge of giving up his coaching job with the Giants to go into the business world in Houston. "Jim Lee had been telling me for several years that he might be retiring soon, and I realized that I might have a shot at the head-coaching job," Sherman said. "And when I was offered the job as offensive coordinator, there were indications that I would probably replace Jim Lee."

Besides quarterbacks Shaw and Grosscup, the Giants also had added rookies Joe Morrison, a versatile third-round draft pick out of the University of Cincinnati, who, like Gifford, could run, catch passes, and play defensive back if necessary; defensive back Dick Lynch, a native of Queens in New York City who had been a star running back at Notre Dame and had spent one unhappy season with the Washington Redskins before being traded to the Giants for a draft pick, to replace Carl Karilivacz at right cornerback; Tom Scott, a linebacker and defensive end who had been obtained in a trade with the Eagles and would join Jim Katcavage as a long-distance commuter from Philadelphia and thereby take over the Pennsylvania Railroad seat usually occupied by Emlen Tunnell; guard Darrell Dess, obtained from Pittsburgh in a trade; cornerback Dick Nolan, who, after a year with the Chicago Cardinals, had been reacquired; and the team's second-round draft pick, Buddy Dial, an All-American offensive end out of Rice University. Given those talented additions, it appeared that the Giants would be even stronger in 1959 than the team that came close to winning the NFL title the year before.

After having spent the summer of 1958 at Willamette University in Salem, Oregon, the Giants returned to Saint Michael's College in Winooski Park, Vermont, for preseason training. Vermont, though more than three hundred miles from New York, was, in a way, a good venue for the Giants in late summer. By now, not only were the Giants hugely popular in the New York area, but, because their games were televised throughout New England, the team had added thousands of fans in the five New England states beyond Connecticut.

Of particular interest at Saint Michael's College was Gifford's effort to supplant Conerly at quarterback. To that end, Allie Sherman spent considerable time teaching him the intricacies of the position—which, under Sherman, would be more pass oriented—to the twenty-eight-year-old Gifford, just as, ironically enough, he had taught Conerly to be a T-formation quarterback eleven years earlier.

Grosscup, who for a while held the National Collegiate Athletic Association record for pass-completion percentage, reported three weeks after training camp began after preparing for and playing in the College All-Star game in Chicago. Not surprisingly, he received a frosty reception. During his senior year at the University of Utah, Grosscup had written a series of letters to Murray Olderman, a syndicated sportswriter and cartoonist, and gave *Sports Illustrated* permission to print some of the letters, including one in which he described the Giants as "good drinkers"—an assessment based on having met some of the players before the Colts-Giants championship game. That Grosscup also described the Giants as a "great bunch, fine gentlemen, very spirited, close-knit" did not matter. What the Giants remembered was Grosscup's assessment of the team's drinking, hardly an unusual aspect of a team's social life. Nor, in a milieu of crew cuts did some of the players appreciate Grosscup's long hair or, apparently, his taste for classical music. Shunned throughout training camp, Grosscup made things worse when he told a sportswriter that Gifford had been his boyhood idol and that his mother was younger than Conerly.

But then in his first appearance, late in an exhibition game in which the Giants held a 24–0 lead over the Detroit Lions, Grosscup, on his first play, threw a 50-yard touchdown pass to Joe Morrison.

"Son, you're batting a thousand," Jim Lee Howell said when Grosscup came back to the sidelines. "The only way you can go now is downhill."

"I'll try to stay at the same level, sir," Grosscup replied.

Moments later, Sam Huff, never a shrinking violet, walked over to Grosscup and, smiling, said, "Nice going, kid. Now you ought to be ready to write another letter." Aware that Huff had made his comment in jest, Grosscup smiled, pleased that at least one Giant was talking to him.

Through the remainder of the preseason training and the five-game exhibition schedule, some other veteran players also reached out to the young quarterback. But along the way, Sherman, who had opened up the offense with a "man in motion"—wherein a back begins to run laterally before the ball is snapped—along with more play-action (faking by the quarterback), and more passing, felt that with Shaw and Heinrich backing up Charlie Conerly, Grosscup wasn't going to make it. "He had a good arm, but he didn't have the feel for the game or the footwork that our other quarterbacks had," Sherman was to say years later. "We also just had too much experience at the position."

Cut before the season started, Grosscup, despite his All-American status, was unclaimed by the remaining eleven teams in the NFL and was placed on the Giants' nonplaying taxi squad, which included players who were paid and could practice with the team but could not dress for games. Things improved, but not much, during the next three seasons as Grosscup, the Giants' third-string quarterback, got into sixteen games and threw 173 passes, 126 of them during his final season, after which he was released. After failing a tryout with the Minnesota Vikings, Grosscup spent part of the 1962 season with the brand-new New York Titans of the American Football League and a year in the Canadian Football League before flunking tryouts with the San Francisco 49ers and the Oakland Raiders. He wound up as a publicist with the Raiders while battling drinking and drug problems before straightening himself out and starting his own health food company.

Still, Grosscup, intelligent, articulate, and sensitive, came away with at least one pleasant memory of his time with the Giants. Entering a game against Washington at Yankee Stadium, with the Giants well ahead, he threw two interceptions, but then fired a long touchdown pass. "I got a standing ovation from a crowd of sixty-five thousand," he said years later. "Then I went over to the bench and just sat there and started to shake, and then I started crying. At least I had that. I know what it is to have a standing ovation at Yankee Stadium."

Not only had the Giants cut their top draft pick, they also cut their second-round pick, Buddy Dial, demonstrating how strong the team's roster was. Dial, however, fared better than Grosscup in the long run, eventually spending five seasons with the Pittsburgh Steelers and three with the Dallas Cowboys. Ironically, two far lower draft picks, halfback and defensive back George Scott, out of the University of Miami of Ohio, and Joe Biscaha of nearby Passaic, New Jersey, an offensive end from the University of Richmond—drafted nineteenth and twenty-seventh, respectively—made the team, although both would last only one season. Two other newcomers, both defensive backs, were Bill Stits, who had played for three NFL teams in five years, and Don Sutherin, a ninth-round draft choice from Ohio State the year before, who would be traded to Pittsburgh in midseason.

Gifford's attempt to replace his friend at quarterback lasted about as long as Grosscup's. Though he performed fairly well during an intrasquad scrimmage, Gifford saw limited action in the Giants' first two preseason games against the Eagles and the Colts, where he spent more time at halfback. "By then I had told Frank that it was going to be tough for him to make it with us at quarterback, and that he did a much better job at halfback," Sherman said in an understatement almost a half century later. "And he said he understood."

Meaningless as the game was, the Giants still felt embarrassed when the Colts trounced them, 28–3, after the Eagles had beaten them, 21–17. But the defense stiffened in the next two games, shutting out both Detroit, 38–0, and then Green Bay, 14–0, in the Giants' first meeting with the Packers under Lombardi, in Bangor, Maine. "That Giants defense might be the best one in the history of the NFL," Lombardi said after his offense—featuring running backs Paul Hornung and Jim Taylor, quarterback Bart Starr, and receivers Max McGee and Boyd Dowler—had been unable to score. The Giants then closed out their preseason schedule with an 18–6 loss to the Chicago Cardinals and, in a homecoming of sorts for Grosscup, a 17–13 victory over San Francisco in Salt Lake City.

Despite the wealth of talent at quarterback, the big question for the Giants was how well Charlie Conerly would hold up. Approaching forty, Conerly was the oldest quarterback in the NFL and was the same age as Sammy Baugh, the legendary Redskins quarterback, was when he retired after the 1952 season. Conerly had started slowly in 1958, but then finished strong, getting better as the season progressed. The always laconic Conerly, asked how he felt going into the 1959 season, said, "I feel fine, and I think I'll be okay."

As it would develop, Conerly would be more than okay.

Once again, the Giants opened their regular season on the West Coast, but this time against the Los Angeles Rams, no longer the scourge of the league's Western Conference. Norm Van Brocklin had been traded to Philadelphia, and Bob Waterfield, Crazylegs Hirsch, Tom Fears, Tank Younger, and Glenn Davis had all retired. Indeed, neither Robustelli nor Svare recognized anyone from his days with the Rams. Recognizable, though, were cornerback Carl Karilivacz, whom the Giants traded to the Rams during the off-season, and running backs Ollie Matson, the former Chicago Cardinals halfback, and Jon Arnett, who had established himself as one of the best runners in the NFL. Meanwhile, in Billy Wade, the Rams had a good quarterback—but one whose best years lay ahead with the Chicago Bears in the 1960s.

In the first NFL game of the season, played on a warm Saturday night at the Los Angeles Coliseum before a crowd of 71,297, Conerly was as good as ever, completing 21 of 31 passes for 321 yards. Without Alex Webster, who had suffered badly bruised ribs in the final preseason game, the Giants took a 17–0 lead in the first half. But the Rams responded with three touchdowns to go ahead, 21–17, going into the last quarter. Largely behind Conerly's passing, the Giants drove deep into Rams territory twice in the last quarter to set up field goals by Pat Summerall, the last one, his third of the night, from the 18-yard line with less than two minutes left in the game to give the Giants a 23–21 victory. It was a dramatic start for the Giants and a bad omen for the Rams, who would end up at 2-10 for the season.

Returning to New York on a high, the Giants, for a rare change, had Yankee Stadium all to themselves, since the Yankees had failed to make it to the World Series for the first time in five years. And as their early-autumn claim on the stadium would not last, neither would the high they felt from their first victory. But as usual, the Giants' first three games were on the road, since schedule makers understandably had assumed the Yankees would be in the World Series, as they would be again for the next five years. After practicing all week at Yankee Stadium, with almost half the team and their wives again ensconced at the Concourse Plaza Hotel, the Giants were crushed in Philadelphia by the Eagles, 49–21, New York's worst loss since 1953, when they yielded 62 points to the Browns in Steve Owen's last season as head coach. Tommy McDonald, the five-foot-nine All-Pro flanker and kick-return specialist for the Eagles, had a spectacular afternoon, catching three Norm Van Brocklin passes for touchdowns and scoring a fourth on a punt return.

It would be one of only two losses the Giants would endure during the 1959 season. Bouncing back the next week in Cleveland, the Giants beat the Browns for the fourth straight time, 10–6, in a defensive struggle marked by only one touchdown and three field goals, two by Groza and one by Summerall. But that day would be marred by sadness in the NFL, as Bert Bell, the commissioner since 1945, died of a heart attack at the age of sixty-five while watching a game at Franklin Field in Philadelphia between two teams he once co-owned, the Eagles and the Pittsburgh Steelers. Adding to the coincidence, Bell, a native Philadelphian, had been a quarterback for the University of Pennsylvania, which played its home games at Franklin Field. Bell would be succeeded temporarily by NFL treasurer Austin Gunsel and then, the following winter, by thirty-three-year-old Pete Rozelle, the general manager of the Los Angeles Rams.

By 1959 the Giants were drawing near-capacity crowds on a regular basis, clearly demonstrating how a Giants home football game had become the hottest ticket in town. Readily recognizable, Giants players became marquee stars in Manhattan—among them the handsome and fun-loving twenty-three-year-old cornerback Dick Lynch, who roomed in a midtown apartment with another bachelor, the equally fun-loving linebacker Cliff Livingston. As bachelors, Lynch and Livingston were a rarity with the Giants, and they lived bachelor life to the hilt, showing up often at popular Manhattan nightspots like Downey's and Eddie Condon's, where they met and mingled with up-and-coming actors like Ben Gazzara and John Cassavetes and more than a few actresses, some of whom they dated.

"I think a lot of them came to those places to meet the players rather than the other way around," Lynch said, although that was not necessarily true in the case of Lynch and Livingston, who obviously enjoyed the attention and, more than that, meeting Broadway and Hollywood actresses.

One of the young women Lynch met and dated became one of the world's best-known movie actresses, Kim Novak. The appearance of the handsome dark-haired football star and the beautiful blond actress together made it into several of the newspaper "gossip" columns popular at the time, which wound up on a bulletin board in the Giants locker room. Beneath the columns was a crayoned note, no doubt written by one of Lynch's teammates, that read: "In one date with Dick, Kim learned more defensive maneuvers than Lynch has been able to absorb in two whole years as a pro."

When the matter was brought to Lynch's attention a half century later, he laughed and said, "Oh, I don't think I want to talk about that; I'm a married man."

Had it not been for the army, Lynch might never have played professional football. "I was drafted by the Redskins, but when I graduated from Notre Dame, I had no intention of playing pro football and had a job lined up with the *Encyclopaedia Britannica* in Chicago," recalled Lynch, who in 1957 scored the only touchdown in Notre Dame's 7–0 upset over the University of Oklahoma to end the Sooners' forty-seven-game winning streak. "But I knew I might be called up for service, since I had been in the ROTC [Reserve Officers'

Training Corps] while at Notre Dame, which meant you could have to serve for six months. But then I got drafted and was ordered to report for two years of service in the army in January of 1959. So, since I had some time to spare, I decided to sign with the Redskins and made the team. But while I was practicing for the College All-Star team that summer, I said in a television interview that I couldn't take the job with the *Encyclopaedia Britannica* because I was going to be stuck in the army for two years. Well, an army colonel heard what I said and called Notre Dame and raised hell, saying, 'What kind of men is the ROTC at Notre Dame turning out?' and 'We don't want people like him.' So I ended up serving just six months as a second lieutenant at Fort Monmouth in New Jersey after spending the '58 season playing with Washington. But then I didn't enjoy playing with the Redskins and didn't plan to go back, and they knew it, and so they traded me to the Giants. How lucky could I get? My family was living in Bound Brook, New Jersey, and my dad worked in New York, and here I am going to play for the Giants."

As it turned out, the Giants were lucky to get Lynch. During his eight years with the team, Lynch would become one of the NFL's best cornerbacks, known for his pass-intercepting and running skills, developed while he was a two-way player at Notre Dame. Lynch would go on to lead the NFL in pass interceptions, with nine, in 1961 and 1963, a Giants record. In the latter year, Lynch ran back three of his nine interceptions for touchdowns, another team record that would outlast the century. That same year, 1963, Lynch gained 251 yards in running back interceptions to tie Emlen Tunnell for yet another team record.

"When you have Andy Robustelli, Rosey Grier, Dick Modzelewski, and Jim Katcavage coming at a quarterback, you're going to get to make a lot of interceptions," Lynch said graciously. "I always kidded Sam Huff about being in on so many tackles after our front four had slowed down a runner. I would say to him, after the guys in the front four had made a tackle, 'Hey, Sam, is it okay for everybody to get up, or do we still have to wait until you jump on the pile and they take the pictures?' I was kidding, of course, because Sam was a great linebacker. We just didn't want to let him get carried away with all the publicity he got."

Like most of the defensive players, Lynch looked up to Robustelli. "Andy was the leader of our defense, no doubt about it," Lynch said. "But in social situations, he sometimes could be strict. For example, if a player put an arm around a girl, he'd come over and say, 'Get your hand off her.' But don't get me wrong. Andy was a great teammate, but I'd like to have fun with him at times, like getting on one knee and asking if I could kiss his ring."

———

Unlike the Baltimore Colts and the Washington Redskins, the Giants still did not have a band when they played their home opener on October 18 before a standing-room-only crowd of 68,783, but they unveiled ten new cheerleaders to rouse Giants fans. But then who needed rousing, what with the team's superb defense, and, with the addition of Joe Morrison in the backfield, an improved offense? Indeed, with the defense—by now introduced before every home game, and usually drawing more applause and cheers than the offense—yielding only 68 yards, the Giants responded to an early Philadelphia touchdown by scoring 24 unanswered points—the first on a 70-yard run by linebacker Harland Svare after he intercepted a pass from the Eagles' Norm Van Brocklin. For Svare, the touchdown was his first in seven years in the NFL.

During that scoring spree, the crowd got to see Allie Sherman's new man-in-motion offense, which involved Frank Gifford and Alex Webster and led to the first two Giants touchdowns. They also got to watch one of Charlie Conerly's two backup quarterbacks, George Shaw, make his debut in a New York uniform and throw his first touchdown pass as a Giant.

A week later in Pittsburgh, Conerly threw two first-quarter touchdown passes to Gifford in less than a minute's time to give the Giants a 14–0 lead before the Steelers responded with a touchdown and a field goal by placekicking quarterback Bobby Layne. But then Pittsburgh went ahead, 16–14, in the last quarter on another field goal by Layne. By then Conerly had left the game with a rib injury, leaving the quarterbacking to Shaw and Don Heinrich. Once again, though, the defense came through in the clutch, as Huff scooped up a fumble by Steelers fullback Larry Krutko at the Pittsburgh 6-yard line and ran in for the go-ahead touchdown that made it 21–16.

With time running out, the Giants' defense, which held the Steelers to a paltry 33 yards rushing, was called on for another goal-line stand. With first-and-goal at the Giants' 6-yard line, Tom Tracy, one of the league's best fullbacks, hit the line repeatedly, only to be repulsed as the Giants' vaunted front four once again preserved a victory. It left the Giants atop the Eastern Conference with a 4-1 record. Now the team would return to Yankee Stadium for Vince Lombardi's home-coming with the Green Bay Packers, who after five games already had two more victories under the former Giants offensive coordinator than the one game they had won during the 1958 season. Lombardi had promised Green Bay fans that he would turn around a perennial loser, but no one had expected even the ingenious Lombardi to do it so fast.

For the third game in a row, the Giants' unforgiving defense held an opponent to fewer than 100 yards rushing, as the Giants beat the Packers, 20–3, before another standing-room crowd of 67,837. That was a remarkable achievement, since, in Paul Hornung and Jim Tay-lor, the Packers had two outstanding young running backs, and in Forrest Gregg, Jim Ringo, Fuzzy Thurston, and Jerry Kramer, an offensive line that soon would establish itself as one of the best in the league's history. All the while, Lombardi stood on the sidelines in a raincoat, sports jacket, tie, and gray fedora, waving a clipboard, ex-horting his players on, and, at times, berating the officials.

As Max McGee was to say, "Vince is great in preparing us for a game, but during the game, he's absolutely useless, just hollering at us and yelling at the officials." Fortunately, as McGee pointed out, Lombardi had top-flight assistants in Phil Bengtson, John Cochran, Norb Hecker, and former Giants Bill Austin and Emlen Tunnell.

Alex Webster scored both Giants touchdowns on power sweeps—a play that Lombardi had implemented into the New York playbook—after Conerly had taken the home team downfield with pinpoint passing, while Summerall kicked two 49-yard field goals. The Packers, who gained only 112 yards passing with only 7 comple-tions in 27 attempts, managed only a 29-yard field goal by Hornung in the second quarter. The victory, the Giants' fifth in six games, left them with a one-game lead over Cleveland in the Eastern Con-ference. When the game was over, Lombardi heaped praise on his former team. "They're the greatest defensive team in football," he said. "These guys just don't make mistakes."

Conerly's leadership and passing ability were made evident by his absence in most of the next two games, against the Chicago Cardinals and then the Pittsburgh Steelers, both at Yankee Stadium, because of an ankle injury. But even though he was merely employed as a holder for Summerall in the first game, his deft hands proved invaluable, as

Summerall accounted for all of the Giants' points. Summerall's three field goals enabled the Giants to beat the Cardinals, 9–3. Conerly's main backup, George Shaw, fared well, completing 9 of 13 passes, but he was unable to get the Giants in the end zone before he suffered a sprained right thumb in the third period and had to be replaced by Don Heinrich. But on the other side of the ball, the Giants' defense largely accounted for the victory, holding the Cardinals to 108 yards rushing and only 68 yards in the air on 8 of 20 pass completions. By now it was evident that, even with the loss of Emlen Tunnell, the Giants' secondary of Dick Lynch, Dick Nolan, Jimmy Patton, and Lindon Crow was perhaps the best in the NFL.

A week later, the Giants again were held without a touchdown, as Summerall again accounted for all of the team's points with three field goals. Conerly started, but reinjured his right ankle in the first quarter when, after holding for Summerall on a blocked field-goal attempt, he made a rare tackle, evoking a roar from the crowd of 66,786. Heinrich, the only available backup quarterback, managed to connect on only 7 of 24 passes, while Steelers quarterback Bobby Layne completed 13 of 30 throws, two of them for touchdowns in Pittsburgh's 14–9 victory.

By now Allie Sherman was furious over the ineptness of the Giants' offense. Neither Howell nor Landry was happy about it either. Nor was the defense, which was spending far more time than usual on the field. Fortunately, the touchdown drought was about to end against the Chicago Cardinals. Before it did, though, the defense—tired of having to spend so much time on the field for the third game in a row—could not resist a dig at the offense for its lack of scoring. At one point during the first half as the defensive unit was going off the field and the offensive unit coming on, Andy Robustelli called out to Kyle Rote, "Let's see if you can hold them for a little while," an odd request from a defensive player, since such a request normally comes from offensive players. Sam Huff, the most vocal of the Giants, frequently needed the offense when it was giving up the ball quickly, but not Robustelli, who apparently said what he did to Rote at least partially in jest. Given the source of the comment, Rote could not help but smile.

Summerall, the league's leading scorer, kicked three more field goals against the Cardinals, giving him sixteen, but this time—finally—he had some offensive help. Though still hobbled by a sore ankle, Conerly threw two touchdown passes and Gifford one, on an option maneuver to Alex Webster. That play accounted for the Giants' first touchdown over a span that encompassed 173 minutes and 23 seconds, almost the equivalent of three full games. But, again, the offense was overshadowed by the defense, which outdid itself. In a remarkable display, the Giants' defense held the Cardinals to zero yards on the ground, while quarterbacks King Hill and M. C. Reynolds completed 6 of 12 passes. Yardage gained on those completions, though, was negated by losses sustained in sacks by Robustelli, Katcavage, and Modzelewski.

The 33–20 victory, in a game played as a home game for the Cardinals in Minneapolis, which was bidding for an NFL franchise, put the Giants back on top of the Eastern Conference, since Cleveland lost to Pittsburgh, 21–20, and fell into a tie for second place with Philadelphia.

Conerly, reviled by Giants fans during his early years at the Polo Grounds, had, at the age of thirty-eight, become something of a folk hero and the most popular Giant, no doubt because he was having the best year of his long career. Justifiably, he was honored before a game against the Redskins at Yankee Stadium on November 29. Cheered wildly by a crowd of more than sixty thousand when he walked onto the field with the team chaplain, Father Benedict Dudley, Conerly was joined by Perian, whereupon they were showered with gifts, ranging from a new Cadillac (for Charlie) and a new Corvette (for Perian), a new wardrobe for Charlie, a fishing boat, wristwatches, luggage, cameras, a variety of jewelry, a ton of fertilizer, enough cotton seed to cover the fields at Conerly's farm in Mississippi, and a trip to Europe.

"I've had my ups and downs here with the Giants," Conerly said when he took the microphone, "and I want to thank you all for sticking by me." "All" might have been a bit overly gracious considering how, even during his best years, Conerly would hear scattered boos, probably out of habit from fans with long memories.

If the ceremony and $25,000 in gifts made Conerly nervous, it didn't show once the game began. The quarterback was brilliant, as he had been all season, throwing three touchdown passes in the first half and then sitting out the second half as the Giants drubbed the Redskins, 45–14, to go to 8-2 in the standings. The win assured them of at least a tie for first place, since Cleveland and Philadelphia both lost.

That same week, Sam Huff, who was having another outstanding season as the pivotal figure in the 4-3 defense created by Tom Landry, found himself on the cover of *Time* magazine and the principal figure in a story entitled "Pro Football: Brawn, Brains & Profits."

Huff at first had been inclined not to cooperate on the story when he found out there would be no reimbursement, but he decided to do it when he was promised the original portrait on the cover. Suddenly, tens of thousands of people with no interest whatsoever in football knew who number 70 of the New York Giants was: middle linebacker Sam Huff, who, as the story said, was "a confident, smiling fighter fired with a devout desire to sink a thick shoulder into every ball carrier in the National Football League." To say the least, the story was flattering, both to Huff and to the NFL. More national acclaim would come to Huff the next year.

—

The Sunday following "Charlie Conerly Day," the Giants wrapped up their second Eastern Conference title in a row, and their third in the last four years, when they demolished Cleveland, 48–7, at Yankee Stadium. Again Conerly was superb, completing 14 of 21 passes for 271 yards and three touchdowns. Overall, the Giants, in their most awesome offensive display of the season, amassed 526 yards against only 146 by the Browns. Stymied by the Giants' Fearsome Foursome up front and their tenacious secondary, quarterback Milt Plum was able to complete only 6 of 20 passes. Jim Brown, hit so hard by Sam Huff that he had to sit out most of the second period, was able to gain only 50 yards in 15 carries.

The glittering victory over the archrival Browns was tarnished, though, when, with just under two minutes left to play, about three thousand fans bolted onto the field and began tearing down the goalposts—a longtime collegiate celebratory tactic that some NFL spectators had begun to adopt at the end of big games—and then surrounding the Browns near their bench and throwing punches at some of the players. As police and security officers tried to restore order, Paul Brown and his team dashed off the field while public address announcer Bob Sheppard warned that unless the field was cleared, the Giants would lose by forfeit, which, under NFL rules, was possible. Sheppard, also the voice of the New York Yankees baseball team, hadn't been instructed to say that but felt it would be effective in ending the small-scale riot, which it was. Eventually the teams returned to finish the game.

In all, the Giants had drawn almost 390,000 fans to Yankee Stadium for an average of 65,000, in 1959, a team record.

Seven days later, in a meaningless final regular-season game, the Giants, down 10–7 at halftime, came back to beat the Redskins, 24–10, in Washington. On target consistently once more, Conerly threw two touchdown passes, while Summerall converted after all three touchdowns and kicked a field goal to finish with 90 points, a remarkable number for a placekicker. However, Summerall, who began the day as the NFL's leading scorer, was overtaken by Packers halfback/kicker Paul Hornung. The former Notre Dame star scored three touchdowns and kicked four extra points to finish with 94 points. It would be the first of three straight years in which Hornung led the NFL in scoring. Summerall, displaying his versatility, also got into several games briefly at tight end and caught two passes for 32 yards. He also returned one kickoff, albeit for only 3 yards, but, then, at six-foot-four and 225 pounds, no one really expected Summerall to break loose.

In his finest season to date, Summerall made all 30 of his extra-point tries and led the league by converting on 20 of 29 field-goal attempts. Conerly, too, enjoyed his best season, completing 113 of 194 passes for a percentage of 58.2, his highest in eleven seasons, while throwing for 14 touchdowns and only four interceptions, also an NFL best. For that outstanding season, Conerly was named the NFL's most valuable player, making him the oldest player ever to receive that honor.

With their 10-2 record, the Giants had posted the best record in the league since 1953, when Cleveland went 11-1. By scoring 284 points and averaging 23.7 points per game, the Giants led the Eastern Conference and finished second to Baltimore, which amassed a staggering 374 points for an average of 31 points, the highest total since the Los Angeles Rams accumulated 392 points in 1951, Robustelli's rookie year with the Rams. Not surprisingly, the Giants, who yielded an average of only 14.2 points per game, led the NFL in that category. Baltimore, by contrast, gave up an average of 21 points over the twelve-game season.

Unlike the Giants, Baltimore had to go right down to the wire to qualify for the championship game for the second year in a row. Led by Johnny Unitas, the Colts beat the Rams in Los Angeles, 45–26, in their final game before a crowd of sixty-five thousand. And so a rematch of the 1958 NFL title game was set for Baltimore's Memorial Stadium, home of the baseball Orioles, on Sunday, December 27, between the highest-scoring team in the NFL and the team with the league's best defense. The question people were asking was: Could the game possibly come even close to matching that epic encounter of the year before?

20

Colts-Giants Redux

*W*ith the 1959 championship game scheduled for Sunday, December 27, once again not many of the Giants got to spend Christmas at home. But those who spent the holiday in New York did their best to make it a joyous occasion. At the Concourse Plaza Hotel in the Bronx, lighted Christmas trees adorned the apartments of the roughly fifteen players and their wives and about twenty-five children who spent the season at what had become their home away from home.

"Most of us would have liked to have been home, but we also realized that spending Christmas in New York meant we were in the championship game and still got to spend the holiday with good friends," Perian Conerly, the designated team den mother, recalled.

While gifts were exchanged, Santa Claus usually left a note for the players' children saying that big presents, such as bicycles and toy fire engines, were being left at Grandma's house back home, where they'd be able to pick them up in a few days. "Some of us would get together for dinner at the hotel or go out to a restaurant," Perian said, "and so we still managed to get into the Christmas spirit, even though our husbands usually had to practice that morning after we had opened our presents." In the case of the Conerlys, that usually meant joining with Kyle Rote and his wife, Betty, who had three children living with them at the Concourse Plaza. The oldest was Kyle Jr., an entrepreneur by the time he was four, who would charge five cents to deliver mail and perform other delivery services for the players and their wives—and also, unbeknownst to his parents, sold autographed photos of his famous father to children in the park across from the hotel for ten cents.

Refreshed after not having played in almost two weeks, thus allowing some players to recover from injuries, the Giants left by train for Baltimore the day after Christmas and worked out in late afternoon at Memorial Stadium. Because of their strong finish, the Giants were far more confident than they had been before the title game a year ago when they had to beat Cleveland two Sundays in a row and then face the Colts the following week. And why not? The team had averaged 39 points in its last four games, and the defense had given up an average of only 10 points over the final seven.* Also, Charlie Conerly, who one might think would slow down at the end of a season, especially after having been hurt, was on a roll, getting better with each game, and Frank Gifford was coming off another strong season during which he had once again led the Giants in rushing and receiving. Moreover, in Pat Summerall, the Giants now had the most accurate placekicker in the league, and in Don Chandler, who averaged 46.6 yards a punt, second only to Yale Lary's 47 yards, one of the NFL's best punters.

Nevertheless, once again the Colts were favored to win, and again by the same 3½ points that most oddsmakers had set the year before, mainly because of the team's offensive juggernaut. Tom Landry's strategy was to concede a touchdown, or maybe even two, to Lenny Moore, the Colts' most dangerous deep threat, and thus cover him with only one man. That would enable the Giants' secondary to double-team wide receivers Raymond Berry and Jim Mutscheller. That way, Landry thought, the Giants could hold the Colts to two touchdowns and most likely win by a field goal or a touchdown. Berry had enjoyed another outstanding season, leading the league in receptions with 66 and in touchdown catches with 14, while Johnny Unitas had thrown an NFL record 32 touchdown passes—twice as many as Norm Van Brocklin, who was second with 16. Conerly also would be confronted with one of the best secondaries in the league. Two of the

---

* Asked in 2008 to compare the strong Giants defense that helped upset the New England Patriots in the Super Bowl that February with the defense he played on in 1959 and during the early 1960s, Dick Lynch, by then a longtime radio broadcaster of Giants games, said, "This team's defense is very good, but we had an all-star at every position"—a slight exaggeration, but not too far off the mark.

Colts' defensive backs, Milt Davis and Don Shinnick, had tied with Dean Derby of Pittsburgh for the league lead with seven interceptions. As for the Giants' secondary, with Carl Karilivacz gone, Dick Lynch, at right cornerback, would be primarily responsible for covering Berry, who had scorched Karilivacz and several other Giants defensive backs in the 1958 title game.

Again the two rosters would be studded with Pro-Bowlers. Eleven players from each team were picked to play in the game, usually held at the Los Angeles Coliseum two weeks after the championship contest. On the Giants' side, Conerly, Gifford, Brown, Stroud, Wietecha, Schnelker, Robustelli, Katcavage, Grier, Huff, and Patton had been named All-Pros, while for the Colts, Unitas, Berry, Parker, Spinney, Ameche, Moore, Marchetti, Lipscomb, Davis, Shinnick, and Nelson had been selected. Nine of those players would achieve an even greater honor: eventually being voted into the Pro Football Hall of Fame.

In the week leading up to the title game, Perian Conerly, in a syndicated weekly column she had been writing for the *New York Times,* among other papers, wrote that she had detected "a bit more enthusiasm, confidence, and—if I may be old-fashioned—desire in the attitude of the team as a whole than was apparent in last year's championship game. Last season we were fighting with our backs to the wall from the seventh game on."

Mrs. Conerly, who also wrote a separate weekly column for the Conerlys' hometown paper, the *Clarksdale Press Register,* in Mississippi, did not pretend to be impartial and rarely if ever broke a major news story. Rather, her column read more like a diary of daily events in the lives of football players and their wives and children in New York City, but also contained nuggets of information about players that she described as "locker-room gossip." Her laconic husband was not always a good source, prompting her to interview other players and their wives, mainly those who also lived at the Concourse Plaza Hotel.

—

Where between 20,000 and 30,000 Colts fans had attended the previous year's title game, only a few thousand Giants fans appeared to be among the capacity crowd of 57,545, which included Vice President Richard Nixon, a big football fan, in Memorial Stadium. For the second straight year, it was unseasonably mild, with the temperature in the low 50s at game time. And once again, the Baltimore Colts marching band, its drum majorettes, and its cheerleaders were on hand to both dazzle and entertain the Colts fans, arguably the most fervent in the NFL. This time around, though, John Steadman, the sports editor of the *Baltimore American* on Sunday and the *Baltimore News-Post* the other six days of the week, did not try to predict how the game would go, as he had done so remarkably well the year before, apparently choosing to rest on his laurels.

Before the game started, Huff, who called the defense signals, gathered the rest of the defense around him in the locker room and, using a large equipment trunk as a blackboard, scribbled out *X*s and *O*s with white chalk to denote a series of defensive maneuvers. Across the room, offensive coordinator Allie Sherman, puffing away on a cigarette and surrounded by the team's offensive unit, discussed the first series of plays the Giants would use on offense. Overall, the atmosphere in the minutes before the Giants headed for their bench along the sideline was quiet and businesslike, devoid of the levity that usually prevailed in the Giants' clubhouse before a game. No doubt it was because the Giants remembered all too well how they let victory, and an NFL title, slip away from them in the last two minutes of the championship game against these same Baltimore Colts a year ago. And these Colts, more experienced now and with a few strong additions, were even better than the 1958 team.

Those hoping for a game comparable to the classic of a year before were disappointed. Once again Baltimore took the lead less than five minutes into the opening quarter when Unitas faked a handoff to Alan Ameche, then feigned throwing twice to Berry on the left side before drilling a 21-yard pass to a wide-open Moore along the right sideline, and the swift flanker sprinted 38 yards into the end zone. But that would be the Colts' only score until the fourth quarter. As was the case in the game of a year ago, the Giants led going into the fourth period after three field goals by Summerall from 23, 37, and 22 yards out put them ahead, 9–7. The lead could have been larger. In the first quarter, the Giants reached the Colts' 6-yard line, but the strong Baltimore defense, led by Gino Marchetti and Art Donovan, pushed them back to the 19, and New York had to settle for Summerall's first field goal. Then in the second period, the Giants reached the Baltimore 29-yard line, where Jim Lee Howell decided to go for it on fourth down and inches, but Alex Webster, usually a sure thing in such situations, was stopped for no gain.

"That was the turning point," Howell said later. "From then on, we were on the defensive."

Indeed, the Giants were. After Webster was stopped, the Colts drove 71 yards for a go-ahead touchdown, highlighted by a 36-yard pass from Unitas to Moore, after which the quarterback sprinted 4 yards around right end for the touchdown. "It was an option play, and when I saw Jim [Mutscheller] wasn't open, I ran it in," said Unitas, understating his effort as usual.

Only minutes later, the Colts added another touchdown when cornerback Andy Nelson intercepted a Conerly pass at the Giants' 31 and ran to the 14-yard line. After double pumping and faking a pass to Berry, Unitas then connected with rookie Jerry Richardson in the end zone to make it 21–9 and trigger a scoring blitz that the Giants could not counter.

Under tremendous pressure from the Colts' front four, Conerly was intercepted twice more, both times by cornerback Johnny Sample, who ran back the first interception 41 yards for a touchdown and then set up a 25-yard field goal by Steve Myhra with his second interception, which made it 31–9. By then the Colts had scored three touchdowns and a field goal within a span of ten minutes.

The cocky and outspoken Sample, in only his second year in the NFL, taunted Gifford from the outset. "You'll never catch any balls today," he said to the Giants' flanker and kept up his verbal needling throughout. Miffed over Sample's taunts, Gifford said later, "He hasn't been in the league long enough to have any class." As it developed, Sample would not change his abrasive image, neither with the Colts nor, later, with the New York Jets.

Conerly, who completed 17 of 38 passes for 205 yards, got the Giants their only touchdown in the last half minute of play with a 32-yard pass to Bob Schnelker. Unitas, though under more pressure than a year ago, connected on 18 of 29 passes for 264 yards with no interceptions, although the Giants managed to sack him a half dozen times, with Robustelli making four of the sacks. Robustelli obviously had learned a lot in the previous championship game, when he was kept at bay by the 275-pound Jim Parker, and, later, by watching film of the game. For the second year in a row, Unitas was voted the game's most valuable player, an honor that got him a new car. Both defensive lines turned in solid performances—the Giants' front four holding Colts runners to 73 yards rushing, while Baltimore yielded only 118 yards to the Giants.

Baltimore coach Weeb Ewbank agreed with Howell that stopping Webster on fourth down in the third quarter was crucial. "Holding them to less than a yard on that play was the key," Ewbank said. "That was a great team that we beat."

Years after he retired, Robustelli implied that Allie Sherman had a "penchant for changing the offense" and had done so in advance of the Colts game. Robustelli said that Sherman apparently did so in the belief that he would surprise the opposition instead of going with what was already working well. Sid Gillman, Robustelli said, had done the same thing with the Los Angeles Rams in the 1955 NFL championship game loss to Cleveland. "It doesn't make any sense to change a system that's been successful," Robustelli said.

Of course, the Giants hadn't done much on offense during the regular season, going almost three entire games at one stretch without scoring a touchdown, in large measure because of injuries to Conerly. Still, the 284 points the Giants scored in 1959 were more than they had scored in the four previous years when Vince Lombardi was the offensive coordinator.

Besides losing, the Giants also took a physical beating. Defensive back Jimmy Patton suffered a pulled muscle in his foot in the second quarter and did not play the rest of the game. Rote had to be helped off the field after he suffered an apparent concussion when he was hit while trying to catch a pass in the end zone in the first quarter, but he returned in the second half. And Lindon Crow was knocked unconscious when he caught a knee while trying to tackle Lenny Moore in the last quarter, but, although dazed, he remained in the game.

Arthur Daley, in his column in the *New York Times* the next day, wrote that the game "wasn't even a pale carbon copy of 'the greatest game ever played.' "

For Conerly it was a depressing ending to a brilliant season. As Daley said, Conerly "threw hurriedly and badly, and almost seemed at times on the verge of panic." That seemed an unfair assessment, since, in fact, the Giants' graying thirty-eight-year-old quarterback was under unrelenting pressure from a very good front four and the frequently blitzing linebackers Don Shinnick, Bill Pellington, and Dick Szymanski. Indeed, after the game, Jim Lee Howell said, "They just overpowered us along the line."

Still, it did not diminish the wondrous year Conerly had after fighting off challenges for his position from four younger rivals, including his best friend on the team. And yet again, the almost perennial postseason question would arise once more: Would Charlie Conerly return for another year? One thing was certain, though: If he did come back for a thirteenth season, Gifford would not challenge him for the quarterback's job.

21

Frank Gifford, Meet
"Concrete Charlie"

*N*ot only did Charlie Conerly decide to return in 1960, when he would be thirty-nine, but so too did Andy Robustelli, who would turn thirty-five during the season. Robustelli said that he had been offered jobs as a defensive coach at two colleges but had turned them down. And Harry Wismer, the sportscaster and president of the new New York Titans of the new American Football League, had indicated in late 1959 that Robustelli might be the team's defensive coach when the league started play in the fall of 1960. However, Robustelli, still one of the best defensive ends in the NFL, and giving no signs of slowing down, said at the end of the 1959 season that he would return for the second year of his contract. "You have to honor a contract," he said.

The Titans were to be one of the eight teams in the AFL, which would play 14-game seasons followed by a championship game. The others would be located in Boston, Buffalo, and Houston in the Eastern Conference, and Los Angeles, Dallas, Oakland, and Denver in the Western Conference.

Whereas Conerly and Robustelli would return for the 1960 season, Tom Landry would not. For a number of years, Landry had been planning to retire from football and go into the industrial engineering field in the Houston area, where he lived during the off-season. But Dallas had been promised the first new franchise in the NFL since Baltimore, Cleveland, and San Francisco were absorbed into the league following the collapse of the All-America Football Conference in 1949. As a native of Texas and a onetime star halfback at the University of Texas, Landry was immensely popular in the state, so Clint Murchison Jr. and Bedford Wynne, the co-owners of the new Dallas franchise, to be known as the Dallas Rangers, offered him the job as head coach before the title game between the Giants and Colts. Landry flew to Dallas the next morning, signed a five-year contract, and, later that day, was introduced as the head coach. Ironically, that same day, newspapers were carrying a story put out by United Press International that Landry was on the verge of accepting the head-coaching job with the new Houston Oilers of the AFL. A month later, when the NFL officially approved Dallas as the league's thirteenth team, Murchison announced that the team had changed its name to the Dallas Cowboys.

"I liked the way Tom talked," said general manager Tex Schramm, the former GM of the Los Angeles Rams. "He was determined, he wasn't cracking any jokes, and he was all business. It was what I was looking for. I had kept hearing what players thought of him. They talked about him like he was a god or something."

Coming a year after the departure of Vince Lombardi to the Green Bay Packers, the loss of Landry, though not totally unexpected, was a severe blow to the Giants. But then, no other assistant coach in the NFL had been as coveted as Landry, who had never intended to become a head coach. To the Maras, Landry's departure also meant that neither he nor Lombardi would be available to replace Jim Lee Howell, who had already indicated to the Maras in late 1959 that he would like to retire. At management's request, he agreed to return to finish out the last year of his contract and then accept a newly created job as the team's director of personnel. Given that Wellington Mara knew, even before the 1959 season ended, that Howell wanted to step down, that begs the question as to why the Giants didn't ask Landry to become the head coach starting in 1961, or perhaps even let Howell retire after the 1959 season and offer the coaching post to Landry. In truth, there would have been no guarantee that Landry would have accepted it, since he was anxious to return to Texas for good.

The Maras also knew that the American Football League would be looking for coaches and that Landry almost assuredly would be coveted as a head coach. But, for whatever reason, so far as is known, they did not offer the head coaching job to Landry. Of course, it's possible that the Giants had broached the subject with Landry, and that he had let them know that if he was to become a head coach, it would have to be in Texas.

Now that Landry was gone, rather than replace him with another full-time defensive coordinator, Wellington Mara took a novel—and money-saving—approach, naming three veteran players as playing coaches. Under the new arrangement, Harland Svare would become the defensive coordinator, Andy Robustelli was to be the defensive line coach, while also calling defensive signals on the field, and Jimmy Patton would coach the defensive backs. Even with the added responsibilities, none of the three would make more than $20,000, an above-average NFL salary at the time, including Robustelli, a perennial All-Pro defensive end. But, then, Jim Lee Howell, in his seventh year as the head coach and after having won three Eastern Conference titles in four years, was making about the same as his three playing coaches, as were offensive coordinator Allie Sherman, end coach Ken Kavanaugh, and line coach Ed Kolman.

Apart from Dallas's having been granted an NFL franchise, the other major development was the move of the Chicago Cardinals, who had been playing before more empty seats than spectators at Comiskey Park, to St. Louis. This would give the Missouri city two teams named Cardinals, although the football Cardinals would hardly turn out to be a rousing success in a red-hot baseball town. Indeed, neither quarterback King Hill nor wide receiver Bobby Joe Conrad would come close to rivaling Stan Musial as drawing cards at Busch Stadium.

The day after the Giants-Colts championship game in 1959, Howard Cosell, the sportscaster and a close friend of Robustelli's, accompanied Robustelli to Stamford Hospital to see his eighth child, Mike, who was born while Robustelli was in Baltimore. The next day, Robustelli went back to work at his Stamford sporting goods store, waiting on customers and stocking shelves. By then Robustelli also was a sales representative for a Chicago steel company whose clients included the Pennsylvania Railroad. Robustelli knew nothing about selling steel when he accepted the job a few years before, but he was a quick study and did well while working out of a New York office. "Andy still spent an awful lot of time in our Stamford store," his partner, Ed Clark, recalled. "And with all of his kids, I don't know how he found time to sleep." By 1960, too, Robustelli had moved his family of ten into a newly built home in Stamford, which would be the family homestead well into the twenty-first century.

For the fourth and final year, the Giants would train again at Saint Michael's College in Winooski Park. Maybe the Giants were now a hot sports entity in New York, but during preseason training, they were still out of sight and thus out of mind with football fans. Even now few sportswriters ventured to Vermont to watch them practice, although well-known New York sports columnists such as Red Smith, W. C. "Bill" Heinz, and Frank Graham would occasionally come up for a day, or, more likely, make a side trip to Winooski Park after an assignment in Boston.

But with the AFL about to start its first season, the NFL, and the Giants, were confronted with competition. The Maras would realize, early on during the 1960 preseason, that the new and unproven New York Titans were getting more press coverage than the Giants because they were training in the Metropolitan area. Thereafter, in order to maintain a competitive press balance with the Titans—so named because in Greek mythology, titans were the largest form of giants—the Giants would make it a point to stay within a fifty-mile radius of New York for the next thirty-five years.

Wellington Mara was fiercely opposed to the new league, particularly because it would bring a second professional football team to New York. Not that it hadn't happened before. Before the All-America Football Conference folded at the end of the 1949 season, New York had as many as three pro football teams: the Giants who played at the Polo Grounds; the New York Yankees, who played in Yankee Stadium; and the Brooklyn Dodgers, who played at Ebbets Field. But Mara perceived the AFL as a more serious threat, since the owners, except for those of the New York Titans, had deep pockets and could endure a few seasons in the red. Furthermore, the new league had negotiated a multimillion-dollar contract with NBC to televise its games. Mara finally gave up his effort to keep the Titans out of the AFL when the Giants received an indemnity fee of $10 million, which managed to assuage his bitter opposition.

—

Among those missing from the Giants' 1960 roster was Don Heinrich. After six years as the backup quarterback to Charlie Conerly, Heinrich had been claimed by the new Dallas Cowboys franchise.

But Heinrich, now thirty, would still remain a backup, since the Cowboys had also picked up little Eddie LeBaron as the team's starting quarterback and had drafted quarterback Don Meredith from Southern Methodist, who would eventually become one of the team's most popular and best players. Also gone was Al Barry, who had started at offensive guard for the Giants the last two years but had jumped to the Los Angeles Chargers of the AFL. With Heinrich's departure, that left George Shaw and Lee Grosscup (added to the roster after a year on the taxi squad) as Conerly's backups. As it turned out, Chuckin' Charlie would need a lot of backup in 1960.

The most highly touted newcomer was the Giants' top draft choice, Lou Cordileone, a 250-pound defensive lineman from nearby Jersey City, New Jersey, by way of Clemson University. Cordileone would play in all twelve games in 1960, his only season with the Giants before he figured in one of the team's most famous trades and one of football's most memorable quotations. Otherwise, all of the starters from 1959 would be back. Still, everyone conceded that the team would not be the same without Landry. Given how fortunate the Giants had been to have had Landry and Lombardi as assistant coaches, losing both of them in consecutive years was a double-edged blow almost beyond comprehension. And the Maras, if not the players, knew that at the end of the 1960 season, Jim Lee Howell also would be gone.

To say the least, the Giants did not look good in their first four preseason games, in what seemed like a barnstorming tour of non-NFL cities. The team scored only two touchdowns over the first three games. After losing to the Chicago Bears in Toronto, and the Green Bay Packers in Jersey City, the Giants hit a low point when they were beaten in Louisville, 14–3, by the fledgling Dallas Cowboys, whose lineup was stocked primarily with players that other NFL teams had been willing to part with and others who no one else wanted, along with a few promising rookies like Don Meredith. Then, in the first professional football game ever played at the hallowed Yale Bowl in New Haven, the Giants tied the Detroit Lions, 16–16, before closing out their exhibition season with their only victory, a 17–13 win over the L.A. Rams in Los Angeles.

Though it was only an exhibition, the game against the Bears on August 15 was a milestone of sorts for the NFL. It would be the setting for the action part of a documentary to be televised by CBS in late October entitled *The Violent World of Sam Huff*, which would be watched by millions and give viewers a close-up look at the NFL, both on and off the field, with Huff, the focal figure of the show. "They approached me during the off-season about the idea and had offered me five hundred dollars, which was big money for an NFL player in those days," Huff said. "The idea was to give TV viewers a feel for what pro football was like, and I was to be wired during the exhibition game against the Bears."

To give the documentary a cachet that would hopefully attract non–football fans too, the narrator was CBS's most highly esteemed news personality, Walter Cronkite, on whose weekly program *The Twentieth Century* the show was to be aired. The hour-long program included three segments: Huff at home in West Virginia, walking on his high school field and standing in front of the mine where his father had worked and where seventy-nine miners would die a few years later; the Giants on the practice field and in the locker room at Saint Michael's, with scenes of Rosey Grier playing his guitar, Dick Modzelewski singing Polish folk songs, and Harland Svare diagramming defensive plays; and Huff in action against the Bears.

At the beginning of the documentary, which was broadcast on October 30, 1960, Cronkite set the stage when he said, "Today you will play pro football, riding on Sam Huff's broad back. We've wired him for sound with a tiny transistorized radio transmitter. It's not allowed in regular league play, and it's the first time it's been done on television." Cronkite went on to say, "You're going to be closer to pro football than you've ever been before. This is our story, *The Violent World of Sam Huff*."

Aware that CBS cameras were filming the game, some of the Bears seem to have gone out of their way to get into the act. At one point, Bears wide receiver Harlon Hill appeared to have hit Huff after a play was dead, whereupon Huff turned to him and said, "Harlon, for Godsake, you never hit anyone in your life, so what the hell did you do that for?"

"Aw, Sam," Hill replied, "I was just trying to get on TV."

At several other points, Huff, always an emotional player, was seen screaming at Bears players who he thought had been unnecessarily rough. Those exchanges, along with the sound of colliding bodies, grunts, and occasional taunts, enhanced the documentary and made Huff an overnight celebrity across the country. For the NFL, the show was a bonanza. Writers who had never written about football wrote about the stark realism that the documentary displayed, along with, of course, the violence, which could not only be seen but heard. Huff said he received hundreds of letters related to the program, which was the talk of much of the country the next day.

"It all came out perfect," Huff reflected. "It was well photographed, well written, and Cronkite was Cronkite. And it came at a time when the NFL was just beginning to attract a lot of attention."

Huff conceded there had been resentment toward him, and that some players thought that Bill George of the Bears or Ray Nitschke of the Packers, also outstanding linebackers, should have been chosen to star in the documentary instead of Huff. "There was quite a bit of jealousy toward me around the league," Huff said, "but I realized that I probably was picked because I played for the New York Giants in the media capital of the world. Then, too, there were guys like Art Donovan of the Colts, who told me that every defensive player in the league owed me a debt of gratitude for showing the world what it was like to play on defense. After all, for a long time, all the glory went to offensive players."

Along with some resentment, there was another downside to Huff's newfound celebrity. "Because I had become recognizable from the *Time* cover and the CBS documentary, some guys who'd had too much to drink or were trying to impress a girl would try to provoke me into a fight at a bar, but I wouldn't bite; it would have been stupid," Huff said.

Some people also thought that Huff's name helped him get the role. *The Violent World of Bill George*, it was generally conceded, didn't have as good a ring as *The Violent World of Sam Huff*. Huff, as in tough.

Even Huff's number, seventy, became famous. The following summer, Don Smith, the public relations director for the Giants, was in Los Angeles for a meeting with the Rams' general manager, Elroy "Crazylegs" Hirsch, in advance of an exhibition game with the Rams. The talk got around to Huff's national celebrity, and it gave Smith an idea. "I told Hirsch that I was sure I could just write 'number 70' on the address of a postcard, and nothing else on the card, and that it would get to Huff in New York," Smith said. "Hirsch thought I was crazy. Anyway I did, just wrote '70' on the address side of a postcard, and several days later, the card arrived at the Giants' offices in Manhattan. That's how well known Sam had become."

Thanks to the CBS documentary and his portrait on the cover of *Time* the year before, everyone, it seemed, knew exactly who number 70 was and where he played. No name or address was necessary.

———

In what would turn out to be an omen for the Giants in 1960, Alex Webster tore ligaments in his left knee against the Cowboys and would miss the first four games of the season, depriving the team of its most consistent runner on short-yardage situations, one of its best blockers, and an outstanding pass receiver. Surprisingly, in light of their poor preseason play and Webster's injury, the Giants won their first three regular-season games—all on the road, as usual. First they beat the 49ers, and then the Cardinals in their opening game at their new home in St. Louis, as Shaw threw four touchdown passes before only 26,000 spectators—about what the Cardinals would have drawn against the Giants at Comiskey Park in Chicago. Two of Shaw's touchdown passes were caught by Joe Morrison, who had replaced Webster at fullback and proved to be about as versatile. In the third game, the Giants defeated the Steelers, 19–17, when, with less than a minute left and New York trailing by 5 points, Gifford tore the ball away from Steelers cornerback Fred Williamson, who appeared to have made an interception of a Conerly pass on the Pittsburgh 5-yard line, and ran in for the game-winning touchdown. Even with a swollen right arm, the old pro came through in the clutch again.

"When I have a bad game, I'm old and over the hill," Conerly said. "But when I do okay, I'm an old pro."

During that road trip, two more injuries befell the Giants. Conerly hurt his elbow and Don Chandler, one of the league's best punters, was hurt while making a tackle and would miss five games. In his place, Conerly, though unable to pass, became the punter. Old number 42, who had punted often for the Giants during his first four years, did reasonably well, averaging 37 yards on 18 punts. But that was far below Chandler's 44-yard average.

Then in their home opener, before a crowd of 60,625, the Giants played to a 24–24 tie against the woeful Redskins, who would win only one game in 1960. That was disappointing, but then when they lost to the Cardinals at home, 20–13, Jim Lee Howell was furious. "Professional football players are men and should be treated like men," an angry Howell told reporters in alluding to the team's poor play. "But there are times when they must be disciplined."

Practices during the following week were far more strenuous than usual, as Howell instructed Svare, Robustelli, and Patton to push the players harder than in the past, especially with the Browns, the Giants' next opponent, in Cleveland. Somehow, once again, the Browns brought out the best in the Giants, who upset favored Cleveland, 17–13. Before a crowd of 82,872, the largest ever to watch the Browns play at Municipal Stadium, the Giants again held Jimmy Brown in check, allowing him only 28 yards in 11 runs. This, during a season in which he would average 5.8 yards a carry and run for more than 100 yards seven times. The Browns netted a total of 6 yards rushing, due partly to sacks of quarterback Milt Plum—who would lead the NFL with a 60.4 pass-completion percentage—by Robustelli, Katcavage, and Modzelewski. Suddenly the Giants were 4-1-1 and, despite all the injuries, only a half game back of Philadelphia in the Eastern Conference.

A week later, three touchdowns by Frank Gifford, followed by a 30-yard field goal by Summerall with less than a minute to play at Yankee Stadium, lifted the Giants to a 27–24 victory over Pittsburgh to keep them a half game behind the Eagles, their next opponent in two memorable back-to-back games.

With Conerly relegated again to punting and holding for Summerall, George Shaw guided the Giants to a 10–0 halftime lead over Philadelphia at Yankee Stadium before another capacity crowd on November 20. But then late in the fourth quarter, thirty-four-year-old Norm Van Brocklin, in his thirteenth and last NFL season, threw for a touchdown, Bobby Walston kicked a field goal, and defensive back Jimmy Carr scooped up a fumble by Mel Triplett and ran 38 yards for a touchdown to give the Eagles a 17–10 lead. Then came a play that no one in attendance was likely to forget.

Far and away the most dangerous area for a pass receiver is in the zone patrolled by a team's linebackers, since when a pass is caught in that zone, the receiver usually knows he's apt to be clobbered by a linebacker as soon as the pass reaches him. And by 1960, practically all thirteen teams in the NFL had adopted Tom Landry's three-linebacker set. In thirty-five-year-old Chuck Bednarik, the Eagles had one of the best and most ferocious linebackers in the NFL, which was saying a lot, given the likes of such contemporary linebackers as Sam Huff, Bill George, and Ray Nitschke, who, like Bednarik, would wind up in the Pro Football Hall of Fame.

As the last of the two-way players in the NFL, Bednarik also played center and on special teams, which meant that he usually was on the field for more than fifty-five minutes of a sixty-minute game. Renowned as he was for his defensive play, Bednarik was as good on offense, where he was a relentless blocker both on running and passing plays. What made him all the more popular was that the native Pennsylvanian had been an All-American at the University of Pennsylvania in Philadelphia and a waist gunner on a B-24 bomber in the Army Air Corps during World War II. Bednarik flew thirty missions over Germany, and his planes were hit often and had to make three crash landings.

Playing almost the entire game as usual, Bednarik was at his best against the Giants. Late in the fourth quarter, he would make what may well have been the most memorable tackle in NFL history. With the Giants trailing by 7 points but deep in Eagles territory, Gifford, coming out of his right halfback slot, caught a pass from Shaw and cut inside to the Philadelphia 10-yard line. As he did, the 235-pound Bednarik hit him with a devastating blind-side tackle that knocked the ball out of Gifford's hands and was recovered by another Eagles linebacker, Chuck Weber. Even veteran players on the field were stunned by the sound of the tackle and then the sight of Gifford lying motionless on the grass. Elated that his tackle had resulted in a fumble recovery by the Eagles, ensuring a Philadelphia victory, Bednarik literally jumped for joy over the fallen Gifford, unaware of how badly he had been hurt.

"The fucking game is over!" Bednarik screamed. "The fucking game is over!"

But then the huge crowd grew silent as an unconscious Gifford was placed on a stretcher, put in an ambulance, and rushed to St. Vincent's Hospital in Manhattan. At first it was feared that he had suffered a fractured skull, and Gifford was actually given last rites. Further observation showed, however, that it had been an extremely severe concussion; Gifford would not play for the rest of the season, if ever again.

"I saw Frank coming, and as soon as he caught the pass, I hit him up high, and his head snapped, and the ball went flying," Bednarik recalled almost a half century later from his home in Coopersburg, Pennsylvania, not far from his hometown of Bethlehem. "I hit him good, but I hit him clean. And when they carried him off the field, I was concerned. I had no idea he had been that badly hurt."

Distraught over Gifford's injury, Bednarik sent a telegram and a basket of fruit to the Giants star at the hospital. A few days later, Gifford, still hospitalized, exonerated "Concrete Charlie," so called because of his off-field job as a salesman for a concrete company in Philadelphia, and not, as many people thought, because of his jarring tackles. "He didn't mean it; it was a clean play," Gifford said. Gifford's linebacker teammate Huff agreed, saying it was a tackle linebackers dream of making.

"Over the years, whenever we ran into each other, Frank would say to me, 'I made you famous,'" Bednarik said. "I liked Frank; he was a good guy, and he never held the tackle against me."

Bednarik, for his part, tended to downplay the tackle. "People remember that tackle because it happened in New York and because it involved a big star like Frank Gifford," Bednarik said. "If it had happened anywhere else against a lesser player, it never would have been remembered."

In a rematch in Philadelphia the next Sunday, the Giants again blew a lead—this time a 17–0 first-quarter advantage—in a must-win game and were beaten 31–23 by the Eagles, who intercepted four passes by George Shaw.

Losing to the Eagles was one thing, but the following week, the Giants squandered yet another lead, a 21–7 edge over the first-year Dallas Cowboys, and had to settle for a 31–31 tie. This one was humiliating, since the Cowboys had lost all ten of their previous games and would lose another to finish at 0-11-1 in their inaugural season under Tom Landry, who was welcomed back to Yankee Stadium with an ovation before the game. It also eliminated the injury-plagued Giants from play-off contention.

The Giants would finish the season by beating the Redskins, 17–3, in a snowstorm in Washington and then losing to the Browns, 48–34, at Yankee Stadium to land in third place behind the conference champion Eagles and Cleveland at 6-4-2. The Eagles would go on to beat Green Bay, 17–13, to win the NFL title, with Bednarik again making a crucial tackle: stopping Packers fullback Jim Taylor at the Eagles' 9-yard line as time ran out.

Jim Lee Howell, as anticipated, formally announced his retirement as head coach after the Redskins game to take the newly created job of personnel director. For the Giants, it had been a hugely disappointing season, mainly because of injuries. Elsewhere in the league, not much had changed. Jim Brown again was the leading rusher, Raymond Berry the leading pass catcher, and Paul Hornung the leading scorer. But now it all looked different to the Giants. Not only were they getting older and, apparently, more injury prone, but they needed a new head coach. Then, too, would Gifford and Conerly return?

22

High School Handball Star
to Coach the NY Giants

*W*ellington and Jack Mara knew that the most important task during the off-season was to hire a new head coach in 1961. The first choice was obviously Vince Lombardi, who had worked wonders during his first two years in Green Bay. After leading the perennially losing Packers to a 7-5 record during his first year, the Packers won the Western Conference with an 8-4 record in 1960 before losing to Philadelphia, 17–13, in the championship game. But with three years left on his contract, and with a very good young team, the former Giants offensive coordinator would certainly be difficult to lure back to his hometown, much as he loved New York.

For five years as the Giants' offensive coordinator, Lombardi had hoped to succeed Jim Lee Howell once Howell retired. But now it was too late. Lombardi's initial reaction when he heard that Howell was quitting was not surprising: He was furious. *Why the hell didn't he tell me he was going to quit while I was still there?* Lombardi thought to himself. *Then I would have stayed.* Lombardi still explored the possibility, talking it over with Wellington Mara—and his wife, who probably wanted to leave Green Bay more than Vince did, since she never really adjusted to the area. But then he decided to stay in Wisconsin, both because the Packers' board of directors was reluctant to let him out of his five-year contract, because of potential problems with the league if he tried to break the contract, and because he knew that he already had a team that could dominate the NFL for many years.

"He definitely wanted to go back and coach the Giants," Vince Jr. said. "New York was his town, and his dream was to coach the Giants. But then he realized there was no way he could do it. But I think he got over it all."

The Maras, again reluctant to go outside the organization for a coach, which they hadn't done since 1929, four years after the franchise was founded, decided on Allie Sherman. The new coach had been with the organization on and off since 1948, when he was brought in to teach Charlie Conerly the T formation. After three years as a head coach in the Canadian Football League, he replaced Lombardi as offensive coordinator in 1959. Now, ironically, Sherman was getting the job that Vince had coveted for years.

It was not a particularly popular choice. Sportswriters and other members of the media criticized the Maras for not succeeding in bringing back Lombardi or Landry, or, failing that, getting an established, well-known coach from the outside. Though the thirty-eight-year-old Sherman was personable and cooperative with the media and acknowledged as a very creative offensive strategist, he didn't seem to fit the mold of an NFL coach. Like Lombardi, he had grown up in Brooklyn. But Sherman had not even played high school football—although he had been captain of his school's handball team. Then he had been a 135-pound quarterback at Brooklyn College, which was hardly a big-time football school. Seemingly lost on many sportswriters was the fact that Sherman became good enough to be a backup quarterback with the Philadelphia Eagles for five years. But even then, some writers felt that he had managed to make the Eagles' roster solely because Earle "Greasy" Neale, the head coach, had hired him to teach his starting quarterbacks the intricacies of the relatively new T formation, which was in large measure true. Then, too, at about five-foot-nine, Sherman, with his inexplicable Southern accent, was a drastic counterpoint to the six-foot-six Howell and his commanding presence and booming voice. As it would develop, for all of his football knowledge, quite a few of the Giants would never quite get used to Alexander Sherman.

"I knew the Giants wanted Vinny Lombardi and that I was the second choice, but it didn't bother me," Sherman said. "It was just a thrill for me, a kid from Brooklyn, becoming head coach of the New York Giants. And I knew I could prove that I belonged."

Given his early football background, Sherman may well have been one of the most unlikely players ever to make it in the NFL.

"I went out for football at Boys High School in Brooklyn as a sophomore, but the coach, Wally Mueller, took one look at me—I was only thirteen years old and weighed about one hundred twenty-five pounds—and said I was too small for the football team and that maybe I should go out for the handball team," Sherman recalled. "I did, and became captain. But I kept playing football weekends against much bigger guys at the Parade Grounds in Brooklyn, sometimes getting on a subway train after a morning game and then riding to another part of Brooklyn to play in another game in the afternoon, always against much bigger kids."

When he got to Brooklyn College, Sherman made the football team, but played sparingly. But the coach, Lou Oshins, decided to institute the T formation during the 1940 season and felt that little Allie Sherman, his smartest if not necessarily best quarterback at the time, was the one most likely able to make it work. With that in mind, Oshins gave Sherman a copy of a book on the T formation that had been written by Clark Shaughnessy, George Halas, and Ralph Jones, coaches who had been instrumental in developing the modern version of the T and asked him to study it while he was spending the summer working as a waiter in the Catskills. "Not only did I study it every day, I also took a football with me and practiced by throwing it at trees to improve my accuracy," Sherman said. "I became the starting quarterback during the 1940 season, when we were one of the few colleges in the country using the T. And it worked wonders for us, since everybody had a hard time following our fakes and movements, and we had a lot of success."

At one point, during Sherman's senior year, Brooklyn College played a practice game—a "scrimmage," as such games are called—against the Brooklyn Dodgers, then in the NFL. The matchup appeared to have the makings of a disastrously one-sided affair. "We played at our field, and, as I recall, I had a good game and completed seven straight passes," Sherman recollected.

Not long after, Sherman got a questionnaire from the Eagles. Greasy Neale, an eventual Hall of Famer, had planned to become only the second coach in the NFL to institute the T formation the following season. Halas, with Sid Luckman and the Bears, was the first. "I was overjoyed to get the questionnaire," Sherman said. "Maybe it was because of how I did in the scrimmage against the Dodgers or because we were one of the few schools using the T. I certainly never expected to play pro ball, even though I did pretty well in college. It was against teams like Ithaca, Panzer, and Cortlandt State; not exactly big-time football schools. But just the thought of a little Jewish kid— and I was only nineteen—from Brooklyn College, who couldn't even make his high school team, getting a chance to play with the Eagles just didn't figure."

Of course, the fact that so many NFL players had gone off to war by 1943 helped Sherman make it in the league. Their absence created a shortage of players and prompted Commissioner Elmer Layden, the former Notre Dame player and coach, to combine the Eagles and Steelers into a team with the awkward and unappealing name the Steagles.*

Greasy Neale may have been interested in the little quarterback from Brooklyn College, who had now grown to about 150 pounds, but Sherman was not among the twenty-eight players drafted by the Eagles in 1943, few of whom made the team. Though he thought he was doing well, Sherman found himself being berated frequently by Neale and some other coaches. Eventually, Sherman, feeling he was out of his element and with twelve quarterbacks in camp at Saint Joseph's College in Philadelphia, felt that he'd had enough and had no chance of making the team. "I told Coach Neale that I apparently had no future with the Eagles, since he was always getting on me, and that maybe I should go home. I told him it seemed that everything I was doing was wrong," Sherman said.

Neale, who had played for Jim Thorpe's Canton (Ohio) Bulldogs before the NFL was founded and spent eight years with the Cincinnati Reds as an outfielder, looked Sherman right in the eye and, in a stern tone, said, "Let me tell you something. If I didn't care about you, I wouldn't be talking to you at all. The fact that I do—even when I complain about something you do—means I do care, and I want you to stay."

---

*That name change, not surprisingly, did not sit well with either Eagles or Steelers fans. Most Philadelphians called the Steagles the Eagles, while Pittsburgh fans called them the Steelers. The Steagles, playing four games in Philadelphia and two in Pittsburgh, averaged about twenty thousand spectators per game—far more than each team had the year before. The Steagles did fairly well too, finishing at 5-4-1 and only one game out of first place in the Eastern Conference. By the following year, the Eagles were again a separate entity, while the Steelers merged for one season with the Chicago Cardinals. This time they were called Card-Pitt, which also did not catch on. If their name was bad, the team was worse, losing all ten of its games and leading Dan Rooney, the owner of the Pittsburgh franchise, to call it the worst team in the history of the NFL.

What Neale and his assistants saw in Sherman was, of course, his familiarity and skill with the T formation, his passing ability, his quickness, his creativity, and his intelligence. "The truth of the matter is I knew how to handle the ball in the T better than any of the rest of the quarterbacks," Sherman said. Signed for the paltry sum of $150 a game, Sherman was expected to teach the intricacies of the T formation to the new quarterback, Roy Zimmerman, who had been acquired from the Redskins, where he had played the last three seasons. Though an apt pupil, Zimmerman showed he was no Sid Luckman, completing only 34.7 percent of his passes and being intercepted 17 times. Still, somehow—perhaps because it was a war year—he was named to the All-Pro team at quarterback along with Luckman and Sammy Baugh. Sherman, meanwhile, who hardly expected to play at all, got into nine of the Eagles' twelve games in 1943, mostly at cornerback and safety—it was still the era of the two-way player—and connected on 16 of his 37 passes, two of them for touchdowns, for a 43.2 percentage. By then Sherman had become friendly with Luckman, who was also from Brooklyn and, with Sherman, was one of only three Jewish players in the NFL; Marshall Goldberg, a fullback for the Chicago Cardinals, was the third. "We would spend some time together in the off-season and became friends," Sherman said. "And Sid taught me a lot about the T." It was in 1940, with Luckman directing the Bears' new T-formation offense, that the Monsters of the Midway demolished the Washington Redskins, 73–0, at Griffith Stadium in Washington in the worst beating ever inflicted in an NFL title game.

Sherman remained with the Eagles as a backup quarterback and defensive back through the 1947 season, when the Eagles lost to the Chicago Cardinals, 28–21, in the NFL championship game. Through those five seasons, the diminutive quarterback completed 66 of 135 passes for a respectable 48.9 percentage and nine touchdowns, while running for four more. He also played safety on defense in at least a part of every game, including the NFL championship game in 1947. Retiring from the Eagles at the end of that season, Sherman spent the 1948 season as a player-coach with the Paterson Panthers, a strong minor league team in New Jersey, across the Hudson River from Manhattan.

Years later, Greasy Neale, who had taken a chance on an undersized quarterback from Brooklyn College, called Allie Sherman "the smartest football player I ever coached." Similar tributes would come from two other legendary NFL coaches. "The man is amazing," said Tom Landry after coaching against Sherman when they both became head coaches after having worked together as assistant coaches with the Giants. "In the first half, he'll stop everything we wanted to do. Then we'll make adjustments at halftime, but he'll have anticipated every single one of them, and he'll stop us again."

George Halas, the patriarch of NFL coaches, also had high praise for Sherman. "If I'm watching a game between two evenly matched teams, and Allie Sherman is coaching one of them, that's the team I'll pick, because he'll find a way to win."

—

Now in 1961, Sherman was put in a position of proving himself again, this time as the head coach of his hometown team—and without the team's best offensive player, Frank Gifford, who had retired after recovering from the severe concussion suffered late in the 1960 season. Almost everyone else was back, except for right-side linebacker Harland Svare, who had retired at the age of thirty after eight years in the NFL to become the Giants' defensive coordinator, and Mel Triplett, the fumble-prone fullback, who had been sent to the new Minnesota Vikings franchise, which was to start play during the 1961 season. The NFL was now a fourteen-team league and would play fourteen games instead of twelve. In the draft, the Giants got running back Bobby Gaiters—who also would turn out to be fumble prone—and guard Greg Larson. In trades, they obtained end Joe Walton from Washington, and a hard-hitting defensive back, Erich Barnes, from the Chicago Bears. Perhaps the most interesting acquisition was Allan Webb, a speedy twenty-eight-year-old defensive back and kick returner who had been a teammate of Robustelli's at little Arnold College and had been playing with a semipro team in Robustelli's hometown of Stamford, after a tryout with the Los Angeles Rams, two years in the navy, and one season in the Canadian Football League. Robustelli had recommended him to Wellington Mara. Not only would the relatively unknown Webb make the team, but he would be a starting defensive back for five years. Eventually Webb would become an assistant coach with the Giants and the Cleveland Browns, and then director of player personnel for the Browns and, later, the San Francisco 49ers. "I couldn't have made the team at a better time," Webb said years later, "and I've got to thank Andy for recommending me."

The coaching staff remained the same, except for the additions of Svare and Don Heinrich, the bright and highly analytical former backup quarterback, who now became a backfield coach after one season with the Dallas Cowboys. Once again, the one element missing in an otherwise solid team, and Sherman knew it, was a pass receiver who would pose a fast, deep threat to opposing teams. Also, with George Shaw gone, the Giants were left with Lee Grosscup as the only backup quarterback. Sherman was hardly enamored of the second-year quarterback, especially after having spent so much time with Charlie Conerly, the very antithesis of the Shakespeare-reading and Mozart-loving Grosscup.

For their preseason training, the Giants, wanting to be closer to home to compete for media coverage with the New York Titans, selected Fairfield University, a picturesque campus in Fairfield, Connecticut, about fifty-five miles from Manhattan—and, of course, a Jesuit school with a Catholic chapel where Wellington Mara could attend Mass every morning. For many of the Giants, the setting was ideal, since about a dozen of them lived in nearby Stamford, although during the week the players, including the thirty-five-year-old Robustelli and the forty-year-old Charlie Conerly, had to stay in a campus dormitory and eat in a dining hall in the dormitory's lower level. Evenings, the players were free to frequent bars and restaurants such as the Black Angus, the Surfside, the Nautilus, and the Beachside along with a few others in the Fairfield beach area on the fringe of Long Island Sound.

Once the preseason schedule began, however, the team switched campuses, moving to Willamette University in Oregon, where the Giants had trained twice in the past, mainly because their first two games were in Portland, Los Angeles, and Albuquerque, New Mexico. By then Sherman, convinced Lee Grosscup wasn't the answer, realized that the Giants needed an experienced quarterback to back up Conerly, who over the last few seasons had become increasingly vulnerable to injury.

Surprisingly enough, the most available one happened to be one of the NFL's best and most durable quarterbacks, Yelberton Abraham Tittle, who at thirty-four was a touch younger than Conerly, although he appeared as old, if not older, since he was prematurely bald. Tittle had become available because Red Hickey, the head coach of the San Francisco 49ers, had decided to go with a shotgun formation, wherein the quarterback lines up about 5 yards back of the center, similar to the by now outmoded single-wing formation, rather than directly behind the center in the classic T-formation pattern. The system lends itself to a mobile quarterback who can run, and Hickey had more than one in the much younger John Brodie, Bob Waters, and rookie Billy Kilmer. Thus, Tittle, after ten productive but nonchampionship years as the 49ers' starting quarterback, had become expendable; he was a classic "pocket" passer who, in Hickey's opinion, did not fit in a shotgun-oriented offensive system.

As it turned out, the Giants were on the verge of trading for Tittle when they met the 49ers in the exhibition in Portland on August 12, 1961. Thus the word had spread among the Giants to go easy on Y. A., as he was called. Fortunately, the Giants did not have to worry about not hurting Tittle until the last quarter, when he finally got into the game. Even Tittle, who had no idea he was about to be traded to the Giants, conceded later that he was surprised how the rough and tough Giants defense had treated him so deferentially, at Sherman's orders, in a game that the Giants won, 21–20, when Dick Lynch blocked an extra-point attempt. Several days later, though, he realized why when he was traded to the Giants for Lou Cordileone. When Cordileone was informed that he had been traded for the perennial All-Pro Tittle, the young lineman, obviously stunned by what many others considered an inequitable exchange, asked, "Just me? For Y. A. Tittle? You've got to be kidding!" If nothing else, the trade did wonders for Cordileone's ego.

Along with the trade for Robustelli in 1956, the trade for Tittle would stand among the best ones the Giants ever made.

However, Tittle, who, like Conerly, had been in the NFL since 1948, was reluctant to leave the San Francisco Bay Area because of his wife and three children and his insurance business in Palo Alto. Tittle also was unsure of what his role would be with the Giants. He got the answer when Sherman called him at his home. "You'll get all the football you want with the Giants, Y. A.," Sherman said. "Conerly is my quarterback right now, but I have an open mind. The best man will play. Besides, we have some concern that Charlie can go all the way at his age." A short while later, Tittle got another call, this one from the now-retired Frank Gifford, a longtime friend. "Charlie

Conerly is my best friend, Y. A., but I don't believe he can do it by himself this year," Gifford said. "The Giants need you."

Convinced that the Giants really wanted him, Tittle joined the team at Willamette University, where they were preparing to play the Rams the next Sunday. Despite Gifford's call, Tittle's reception was hardly cordial, apparently because many of the Giants felt that he was going to take over for Conerly. "Hardly anyone talked to me, and no one asked me to join them for a beer or for dinner after practice," Tittle recalled. "I felt like a complete stranger and began to wonder if I'd made a mistake."

It got worse in Tittle's first game as a Giant. Though he had practiced with the team for only a few days and hardly knew any plays, Sherman, after telling him what plays to call, put him into the game against the Rams in the last quarter. "On the very first play, I fumbled the exchange from Ray Wietecha, then scooped up the ball and started to run, something I didn't do very well," Tittle said. "Before I got very far, two big Rams hit me, and as I was going down one hit me in the back with his knee, and I felt a severe pain up and down my back. When we got back in the huddle, I tried to call out the next play but couldn't talk because of my injury. And someone said, 'C'mon, what's the play?' I imagined they were thinking 'What's the matter with this old guy? And why in the world did we get him?' At that point, I signaled to the sidelines that I had to come out. Boy, was it embarrassing."

X-rays the next day showed that Tittle had fractured two transverse processes in his back and would be out for about five weeks. In breaking the bad news to Tittle, team doctor Francis Sweeny didn't exactly cheer him up. "And don't forget," Dr. Sweeny, who was then sixty-eight, told Tittle, "it takes even longer with us old fellows."

"I felt bad enough as it was, and that's all I had to hear," Tittle said. "I really didn't appreciate being reminded of my age."

After another exhibition game against Dallas in Albuquerque, the Giants returned to Fairfield University, where, for the most part, Tittle, unable to practice, still didn't much feel part of the team.

"My first day on the beautiful campus at Fairfield University, which looked more like a country club than a college, I was miserable," Tittle recalled. "It was a Sunday, and I had just arrived there on a bus from the airport in New York with some other players. Most of the guys had stayed in New York, and the rest left the campus as soon as we arrived, since we had the day off. So I found myself alone in Loyola Hall, where the Giants stayed, and kept trying doors on the second floor until I found one that was unlocked, and, with no means of transportation, stayed there the rest of the day. I could not have been more homesick. Then the next morning, I went down to the dining hall and found myself sitting alone. It was all pretty miserable." All the more miserable because Tittle was an outgoing and likable individual who thrived on companionship.

Though Tittle was unable to practice because of his injury, he helped the Giants immeasurably in another way when Allie Sherman called him to his room and asked what he thought of Del Shofner, who had been an All-Pro receiver with the Rams but had spent most of the previous season on the bench and had caught only 12 passes. Shofner, Sherman told Tittle, was now available, and the Giants were considering trading for him.

"I told Allie that I thought the Rams lost confidence in Del after he had dropped a couple of passes and had a couple of muscle pulls the last year, but that I was sure he could help the Giants, and that there was no receiver in the league I'd rather throw to," said Tittle, who had thrown to Shofner in a Pro Bowl game. "I also reminded Allie that Del was one of the fastest receivers in the league, something the Giants had lacked." Based to a considerable extent on what Tittle had told Sherman, several days later the Giants obtained the slim twenty-six-year-old for two future draft choices. When he walked into the team's locker room, most of the players couldn't believe their eyes. Listed at six foot three and 185 pounds, Shofner looked like Ichabod Crane, the tall and gaunt-looking schoolteacher in Washington Irving's *The Legend of Sleepy Hollow*. A chain-smoker who coughed frequently and had stomach ulcers, Shofner also had hollow cheeks on a very thin face. One thing he did not look like was a football player. Yet he had been an All-Pro with the Rams twice. He also was a superb athlete, having played varsity football and basketball and freshman baseball and run track at Baylor, where he was a member of the Western Athletic Conference 440-yard championship relay team. But after he showed up at the Giants' training camp at Fairfield University, one player said, "He looks more like a clarinet player after a hard one-night stand than a football player."

Maybe, but Shofner, despite his fragile appearance, was almost certainly the best all-around athlete on the team. Besides excelling at football, basketball, baseball, and track, he was a scratch golfer, a good tennis player, and a whiz with a cue stick. Don Smith recalled how Dave Klein, a sportswriter for the Newark *Star-Ledger* and a good pool player, came into the players' dormitory at Fairfield University one night looking for a game. "Dave was so good that he carried his own cue stick in a case," Smith said, "and on this night, he said he'd be willing to play anyone on the team—for money, for his watch, jewelry, anything. I had heard that Shofner was a good player, so I went upstairs and asked Del if he could do me a favor and play Klein. But he said he'd rather not, because, for one thing, he hadn't played in a long time, and, secondly, because he didn't want anyone to know that he played because of his Baptist background and the reputation pool had at the time. Anyway, he finally agreed to play after I told him no one would see him because we would play in nearby Bridgeport. So the three of us sneak out of camp—Klein with his pool cue in its case—and to this sleazy poolroom that one of the workers at Fairfield U. had told me about.

"Once we get a table, Klein breaks, meaning, of course, that he goes first," Smith went on. "Then Del picks up a cue and proceeds to run the table three straight times, sinking almost fifty balls in a row before he finally misses. Klein, meanwhile, can't believe his eyes, nor can a number of guys who had gathered around the table after noticing how good Shofner is, even though they have no idea who he is. As it was, Klein never had a chance against Del. Then on the way back to Fairfield U., Shofner is apologizing to Klein, saying he can't believe how well he did, since he hadn't played in such a long time. But that was Del Shofner; he was great at any sport or game he ever tried."

—

Tittle also missed the last two preseason games, at Green Bay and at the nearby Yale Bowl, where the Baltimore Colts demonstrated once again that with Johnny Unitas at quarterback, they could beat the Giants anywhere. Having already defeated the Giants in the last two championship games in New York and Baltimore, they did the same in New Haven, routing the Giants, 49–20, before a crowd of more than fifty thousand as Unitas threw five touchdown passes in the first half, including four in the first quarter, and then sat out the second half in the 90-degree heat. The only encouragement the Giants were able to take from the drubbing was the performance of

Shofner, who, in his first game as a Giant scored two touchdowns on pass plays that covered 62 and 73 yards. It would prove to be a good omen on an otherwise bad day for the Giants, during which Conerly suffered a broken nose in the first quarter and had to give way to Lee Grosscup, the lone available backup quarterback.

Before the Colts game, the Giants shifted their practice site to Fordham University in the Bronx. Tittle joined the large Giants' family contingent at the Concourse Plaza Hotel, where he would room with Del Shofner once Tittle's wife returned to California to be with their three children. Following the first practice on the Tuesday after the game, Sherman asked Conerly and Tittle to come into his small office in a building near the football field. Sherman shared the space with his assistant coaches, except for Robustelli and Patton, who dressed with the rest of the team. It was to be a momentous meeting.

"Charlie and Y. A., I called you here because I need your help," a tense Sherman said in his Southern drawl. "You are both outstanding veteran quarterbacks, and I'm fortunate to have you both on the team. But it creates a problem for me. This has been Charlie's club for thirteen years, but I'll eventually have to make a judgment as to whether you, Charlie, or you, Y. A., will be the starter. Charlie will be at the start of the season, but that could change. I want you both prepared to play in every game, regardless of who starts. I know that's asking a lot because you've both been starters for a long time. But I want to win a championship, and if we all work together, I think we can do it because we have a good ball club. I'm also going to ask you to put your faith in me, since I'll need your help along the way. Is that okay with the both of you?"

Conerly spoke first. "Hell, Allie, you know me. I've been here a long time, and I don't care who starts; all I want to do is win."

"Same thing here, Al," Tittle said. "I just want what's best for the team."

"Thanks, guys," said Sherman, looking very relieved. Then, shaking hands with both Conerly and Tittle, he said, "You're real men, and with men like you, we can win it. See you at practice tomorrow."

When the Giants opened at home against the St. Louis Cardinals, it was the first time in the team's thirty-six-year history that it had played its first game at home. True, they had opened in places like Newark and Orange in New Jersey, which were considered "home" games, but never in New York. Strangely enough, they did so even though the New York Yankees were still playing during the regular season. But on September 17, 1961, the Bronx Bombers were on the road with Roger Maris in pursuit of Babe Ruth's record 60 home runs in 1927.

Shofner again excelled, catching six passes on a day when Conerly, playing with a broken nose, was sacked repeatedly. As Joseph Sheehan of the *New York Times* put it in his account of the game, Conerly "spent a large part of the sunny afternoon on his back or fleeing desperately from hordes of Cardinal linemen who stormed into the New York backfield virtually unimpeded." Indeed, it got so bad that by late in the game, with the Giants trailing, 21–10, Giants fans, having already forgotten Conerly's MVP year in 1960, began to chant, "We want Grosscup!" Allie Sherman obliged them shortly thereafter, but Grosscup was hardly an improvement, completing only 3 of 11 passes and unable to guide the Giants to another score. It was hardly an auspicious start for Sherman. Looking on from the Giants' bench, Tittle, who had been cleared to practice during the week although his back was still sore, hoped to get in, especially with both Conerly and Grosscup being hammered. Afterward, in the locker room, Sherman came over to Tittle and, knowing he was upset about not having played, said, "I could have used you today, Y. A., but the way things went, it probably wouldn't have done any good. And it might have done a lot of harm to you."

Those were consoling words for Tittle, who had begun to think that Sherman had forgotten about him. But he realized that the coach's rationale made sense, and that he was looking ahead when he said, "We have a long way to go, Y. A., and I know you'll be ready when I need you."

A week later, Sherman found that he needed Tittle. With the Giants trailing Pittsburgh 14–10 in the third quarter, Conerly was shaken up after being sacked twice in a row, whereupon Sherman called on Tittle. Determined to show his teammates, and Sherman, what he could do under pressure, Tittle completed three passes in a row to Shofner on a square-out, a slant, and a pass down the middle that put the ball on the 5-yard line, after which Tittle, using Shofner as a decoy to the left, fired a pass to Joe Morrison in the end zone for the game-winning touchdown.

Before he was done, Tittle had completed 10 of 12 passes, including his first 8, for 143 yards and a 17–14 Giants victory, with a field goal by Summerall making the difference. "I had already thrown a lot of touchdown passes in my long career, but none had given me such a thrill as the one to Morrison," Tittle said. "My back still hurt a bit, and I had taken some good shots in the game, but I passed the test physically and couldn't have felt happier sitting in the locker room after the game."

Suddenly, forty-year-old Charlie Conerly and the rest of the Giants realized how important Y. A. Tittle was going to be during the 1961 season. But who the starter would be during most of the rest of the season remained to be seen. And the amity that seemed to prevail between Sherman and his two veteran quarterbacks almost came asunder the following Sunday.

Playing the Redskins in Washington, the Giants got off to an early start when the Redskins fumbled away the opening kickoff and, minutes later, Conerly threw a 17-yard touchdown pass to Kyle Rote. But the Redskins quickly responded with a touchdown to tie the score. Then on the ensuing Giants possession, Conerly underthrew Shofner; the pass was intercepted and run back 48 yards for a touchdown. By then Sherman already had Tittle warming up on the sideline. Following the next kickoff, the coach sent him into the game. Conerly, in a rare display of emotion, stormed past Sherman, slammed his helmet to the ground, and sat down at the end of the bench, assuming he had been taken out because of the interception. As Sherman explained to Conerly later, he had planned to put Tittle in for a series or two to give Conerly a chance to study the Redskins' defensive alignment and then send him back in, but Conerly wasn't buying it. "I throw one interception early in the game, and you embarrass me in front of everyone by taking me out," Conerly, still seething, said to Sherman later.

"You know better than that," Sherman replied. "Y. A. was warming up, and I decided to take you out for a while. The interception had nothing to do with me taking you out." That Sherman had planned to take Conerly out in the first quarter of a game that was tied 7–7 did not seem to make sense. If he was having trouble, it would be understandable, but he wasn't and had accounted for the Giants' score with a touchdown pass.

As it was, Conerly never did return to the game. Tittle finished it, connecting on 24 of 41 passes for 315 yards as the Giants edged Washington, 24–21, with a Summerall field goal again the margin of victory. Conerly realized he was wrong when he got back to the

Concourse Plaza that night, and his wife, Perian, who had watched the game on television with Betty Rote, told her husband that what Sherman had told him was right; he'd had Tittle warming up before Conerly threw the interception. At the next Giants practice on Tuesday, Conerly apologized to Sherman. "Sorry, Al, for the outburst," he said. "I misunderstood, but shouldn't have lost my head."

Whether it was because of Conerly's tantrum or Tittle's strong performance, Tittle was now the first-string quarterback, and Conerly, for the first time in his thirteen-year career, was the backup. Sherman's decision could hardly be questioned, as Tittle performed well, and the Giants won their third and fourth straight road games by beating St. Louis, 24–9, and Dallas, 31–10. But, back at Yankee Stadium the following Sunday, Tittle seemed to lose his touch, completing only 6 of 18 passes as the Giants fell behind the Los Angeles Rams, 14–10, in the third quarter. As Charlie Conerly began warming up on the sideline, Perian Conerly, who had become increasingly nervous at games because of her husband's uncertain status, said later, "I almost got sick to my stomach." Sherman then inserted Conerly, who, to the delight of a crowd of 64,000, threw touchdown passes to Kyle Rote and Shofner to lift the Giants to a 24–14 lead and their fifth straight victory. After the first touchdown pass, Perian Conerly and Rote's wife turned to each other and said, in unison, "Do you have an extra Kleenex?"

Even Allie Sherman was emotionally moved. "I got chills during Charlie's performance," Sherman was to say. "I was even on the verge of tears when he did what he did."

Suddenly, Conerly had won back the starting position at quarterback, at least for the following Sunday's game against Dallas. "In other years, being benched after one bad game would have bothered me, but not now when we were winning," Tittle said. Trying to soften the blow, Sherman told Tittle the day before the game, "I'm starting Charlie because he played well last week, not because you played poorly." Still, Tittle was upset.

But Conerly and the Giants' offense in general could do little against Dallas and lost, 17–16. Tittle, back at quarterback, threw three touchdown passes the next two Sundays in a row, as the Giants crushed Washington, 53–0, and Philadelphia, 38–21, to take over first place in the Eastern Conference. With the offense on a roll, the Giants continued to win, trouncing Pittsburgh and Cleveland to go to 9-2 in the standings, while averaging an awesome 42 points per contest over a four-game span. In the process, Tittle, now the leader of an explosive Giants offense, had become a folk hero in New York. His bald pate made him look at least ten years older than his thirty-five years, so that Tittle, without his helmet on in pregame practice, looked more like an average middle-aged fan than a football player. Indeed, at times he had to convince people he *was* a football player. On at least one occasion during a team charter flight, Tittle, without a hat and wearing glasses, asked a flight attendant for a soda, where-upon she said, "I have to take care of the football players first."

"But I *am* a football player," he replied to the dubious flight at-tendant, who finally asked a few of the Giants nearby whether this bald-headed man with the reading glasses *really* was a football player. After first feigning ignorance of who Tittle was, the players laughed, and one of them said, "Yeah, believe it or not, that old guy's a player." Tittle, blessed with a good sense of humor, also laughed. By then, of course, all of the Giants not only were talking to the man they called "Yat," but were thankful they had him as a teammate.

By then, too, Giants fans realized how lucky the team was to have Tittle. Bill Wallace, who covered the Giants for years, first for the New York *Herald Tribune*, and then for the *New York Times*, recalled the day he drove Tittle to the village of Southport, a part of Fairfield in Connecticut, while the Giants were training at Fairfield Univer-sity, so that Tittle could mail some letters. "The three clerks in the post office were astounded to have Tittle in their presence," Wallace said, "and Y. A. signed some autographs, and we left. Afterward we drove over to my house, which was nearby, and sat on the porch hav-ing a Coke. While we were there, my daughter, Polly, who was three, saw Y. A. and went back inside and said to my wife, 'What's that funny-looking old man doing out on our front porch?' "

But then, of course, Tittle's roommate, Del Shofner, also didn't look like a football player. He wasn't much of a roommate, either, since, as Tittle said, he spent more time with his fiancée than with Y. A. Even when he was around, Shofner, reserved and quiet, didn't say much. "Del never did say anything unless he had to," Tittle said. "Sometimes we'd be in a room at Fairfield during training camp or at the Concourse Plaza, and we wouldn't talk for hours, and I'm a talkative person. Del also wasn't much for going out with the guys for a beer during training camp. Instead he'd stay in the room reading a

Western novel and, sometimes, talking to me. When we first got to New York, he and I—a couple of guys from small towns in Texas—were fascinated by the subway and, for lack of anything else to do, would ride it from Yankee Stadium downtown and back. But don't get me wrong; Del was a good companion, my kind of guy on and off the field."

—

Tittle and Conerly, by contrast, could not have been more different in personality; the yin and yang of quarterbacks. Conerly was laid-back and quiet and rarely showed any emotion. Whether he had thrown a touchdown pass or an interception, his expression, as he trotted to the sideline, was about the same. In the huddle, he also was a man of few words, calling out a play and saying nothing else, not even if he had been sacked because an offensive lineman had missed a block. Tittle, by contrast, was fiery and emotional. Unlike Conerly, he was talkative and inspirational in the huddle, trying to exhort his teammates on. "Let's go, guys!" he often called out as the Giants broke their huddle. Also, when Tittle threw a touchdown pass, he might literally jump for joy, whereas if he fumbled or was intercepted, he verbally berated himself. In one of several memorable pictures of Tittle, he stood over a fallen Bobby Gaiters, his helmet off and his bald pate in full view, chastising the young Giants halfback for 1 of his 11 fumbles in 1961. Only minutes later, though, after Gaiters ran for a substantial gain, Tittle patted him on the back and called out, "Attaboy, Bobby!" as Gaiters returned to the huddle.

Although New York had won four games in a row for the second time during the 1961 season, the Giants' defense had given up an average of 21 points over the last three games. And on December 3 in Milwaukee, where Green Bay played some of its home games, the suddenly porous defense allowed 270 yards to a powerful Green Bay running attack, led by Paul Hornung—who was on a weekend pass from army service at Fort Riley in Kansas—and punishing fullback Jim Taylor, enabling the Packers to win, 20–17, and clinch the Western Conference championship for the second year in a row under Vince Lombardi. That loss dropped the Giants into a first-place tie with Philadelphia, their next opponent, with two games to play.

Playing at Franklin Field in Philadelphia, Tittle hooked up with

Shofner for a touchdown on the fourth play of the game, but then faltered, and the Eagles went ahead, 10–7. Late in the second quarter, Sherman sent in Conerly, who, on his first play from scrimmage, threw a 45-yard touchdown pass to Joe Walton, then threw two more touchdown passes in the second half to give the Giants a 28–24 victory and assure them of the Eastern Conference title if they beat or tied Cleveland at Yankee Stadium the following Sunday.

"You might think I'd be upset about being taken out like I was," Tittle said. "But on the contrary, I admired how Charlie could lose his starting job at quarterback and be able to come off the bench, calm and poised, and do what he did without ever complaining."

With Tittle starting again, the Giants had to settle for a 7–7 tie against Cleveland in the last game of the regular season—a contest made notable by Alex Webster, who, playing with a pulled leg muscle, accounted for 91 yards in 21 carries, which enabled him to finish in third among the NFL's rushing leaders. It was a remarkable achievement when you consider that Sherman and the Maras had expected Webster would likely be a nonfactor in the team's offense, due to a series of injuries.

The championship game in frigid Green Bay, where it was near zero at game time on December 31, pitted the Giants' last two offensive coordinators, Vince Lombardi and Sherman, against each other. It turned out to be no contest. The Packers, seemingly unbothered by the frozen field and bitter cold, held the Giants to 31 yards rushing, while Paul Hornung alone gained 89 yards and scored a title-game-record 19 points as Green Bay demolished the Giants, 37–0. Tittle, under swift and unrelenting pressure, had his worst game of the year, completing only 6 of 20 passes and being intercepted four times, before being relieved by Conerly, who did not fare any better.

Sherman refused to offer any alibis. Some of the Giants thought the weather could have been a factor, but the Giants' rookie head coach said, "The weather wasn't a factor, nor was the condition of the field. It's true that we did more slipping and sliding, but that's because the team that's behind is pressing harder and loses footing more often. The big thing was that we made a number of mistakes early in the game, and they always capitalized."

Tittle was not quite as composed after losing. "I was furious," he said later. "Here I finally made it to the championship game after thirteen years, and I blew it. I was awful, overthrowing, underthrowing—

terrible." Tittle's favorite target, Del Shofner, who said he found it hard to cut on some pass patterns, did not catch a pass until late in the third quarter, and that was from Conerly who some thought might be playing his last NFL game.

The Giants knew, though, that they would not have reached the championship game without Tittle—and Conerly too. Not to mention Shofner, who Tittle had urged Sherman and Wellington Mara to sign and who, with a team-record 68 catches, finished third among NFL receivers. For Tittle, considered over the hill by the 49ers at the age of thirty-five, it had been an outstanding season. He completed 57.2 percent of his passes and threw for 17 touchdowns, good enough to be voted the NFL's most valuable player for the second time. Remarkably, thirteen Giants were named to the All-Pro team, including the entire defensive front four, and Huff, Livingston, Patton, Barnes, and Lynch, the latter of whom led the league with nine interceptions. On offense, Tittle, Shofner, Stroud, and Wietecha were also voted to the All-Pro team. And in scoring a team-record 368 points, the Giants led the Eastern Conference, while finishing second in the NFL to Green Bay's high-powered offense, which scored 391 points. The Giants' defense was just as, if not more, impressive, leading the league by limiting opponents to a total of 220 yards during the regular season for an average of 15.7 points per game.

For managing to survive the loss of Frank Gifford and Harland Svare, and convincing two veteran quarterbacks that they could coexist, along with opening up the Giants' offense with his acknowledged football creativity and a spread offense that often had six eligible receivers, Allie Sherman was named NFL coach of the year.

"I couldn't be with a smarter bunch of football players," Sherman said.

23

"I'm in Love with Yelberton Abraham Tittle"

*A*fter years of threatening to retire, Charlie Conerly finally did following the 1961 season, when, for the first time, he had found himself as a backup quarterback, and yet still one of the best quarterbacks in the NFL. On the flight back to Mississippi three days after the Giants lost to the Packers, Conerly told his wife that this time he definitely was all through. Charlie had said in the past that when a player was still hurting on game day from the previous Sunday, it was time to get out. And that, Chuckin' Charlie said, was how he often felt during the last few seasons. No more would the Conerlys return to spend about four months in the Concourse Plaza Hotel in the Bronx. He'd been the oldest Giant, both in terms of age, at forty, and service, at thirteen seasons. It was indeed the end of an era, one that spanned a time when the Giants played in front of as few as ten thousand spectators at the Polo Grounds to a time when they hosted standing-room-only crowds of almost seventy thousand at Yankee Stadium; when NFL quarterbacks switched from the traditional single-wing to the T formation; when players started wearing face masks; and when the goalposts were moved ten yards back from the goal line. Conerly had also gone from being reviled by Giants fans to becoming a beloved figure, admired for his capacity to play while hurt, his leadership qualities, his soft-spoken demeanor, and his penchant for coming through in the clutch, as he had done several times during his last season.

Appropriately enough, Conerly's retirement was formally announced in February 1962 at a testimonial luncheon in his honor at
his and Perian's favorite restaurant, Toots Shor's. The very restaurant where so many of the Giants and their wives had gone after home
games so many times. The very restaurant where a future Hall of
Fame quarterback made a scene in the bar area when told that he
and his party had to wait awhile for a table, whereupon Toots Shor
himself said angrily, "Who do you think you are, Charlie Conerly?"

At the luncheon, Allie Sherman, the man who had taught Conerly
the T formation fourteen years earlier, said, "Charlie was a great per-
former, whether he was with a fair team or a great team. And I love
the man." Jack Mara, the president of the Giants, then presented
Conerly with an engraved watch and said to him, "If you change your
mind and decide to return, you can still keep the watch. Meanwhile,
it won't seem like the Giants without you." Mara knew, though, that
old number 42 would not return.

When the Giants began preseason training again at Fairfield
University in July of 1962, others missing included Pat Summerall,
who had retired at thirty-two after having made all 108 extra-point
attempts during his last three seasons. Some of his teammates josh-
ingly told Summerall they were convinced he was retiring because
he had lost his holder—meaning Conerly. In fact, he said, he had
quit because of wear and tear on his knees and to pursue a full-time
career as a television sportscaster. That left the placekicking up to
Don Chandler, the Giants' punter, who in six years with the team
had made all three extra points he attempted and would do well as
Summerall's replacement. Also retiring to become the team's backfield coach was thirty-four-year-old Kyle Rote, for years the most
popular player among his teammates. During his eleven years with
the Giants, Rote, after injuring both knees in his first three seasons,
was switched from running back to become one of the league's best
receivers. When he retired, Rote had caught 48 touchdown passes, a
Giants record that stood until broken by Amani Toomer in 2007. A
heralded All-American halfback at Southern Methodist, Rote's career fell into the realm of "what might have been," since his knee
injuries robbed him of the spectacular open-field running talent that
in the late 1940s and early 1950s made him one of the most coveted
college players ever. Another player for whom the Giants had reasonably high hopes, quarterback Lee Grosscup, the team's top draft

choice in 1960, was released after getting into only four games in each of the previous two seasons.

Gone in trades were Dick Lynch's onetime roommate and fellow man-about-town companion, linebacker Cliff Livingston (to Minnesota for defensive back Dick Pesonen), and, once again, Dick Nolan, to Dallas for a draft pick. Also leaving in 1962 was Harland Svare, who after one season as defensive coach, moved to Los Angeles. There, at the age of thirty-one, he would become the youngest coach in the NFL. His former team, the now-hapless Rams, would finish 1-12-1 that year and would also endure losing seasons the following three years. In the annual draft, the Giants picked up guard Bookie Bolin; end Jim Collier; linebacker Bill Winter; and halfback and kick-return specialist Johnny Counts, from nearby New Rochelle, New York. Counts, after playing with the same Stamford semipro team as Allan Webb, had, like Webb, been recommended by Robustelli. It was hardly a fruitful draft, since, of that foursome, only Bolin and Winter would spend at least three years with the Giants.

To back up Tittle, the Giants acquired Ralph Guglielmi, a five-year NFL veteran from St. Louis who previously had spent four seasons with Washington, all but the last one as a backup quarterback. Far and away the most surprising addition to the thirty-six-player roster was thirty-two-year-old Frank Gifford, who had retired at the end of the 1960 season after having suffered that famous, or infamous, hit by the Eagles' Chuck "Concrete Charlie" Bednarik, but was making a comeback as a flanker. Asked why he was returning after having been so grievously injured, Gifford, alluding to the Giants' ever-growing popularity, said with tongue in cheek, "I was having trouble getting tickets."

Having Gifford as a pass catcher was not new, since, as a halfback, he had caught 257 passes, 26 of them for touchdowns, for the Giants over a nine-year period and had led the team in receptions five years in a row. But as a flanker, Gifford would be running different routes. Instead of running to his left out of his left halfback position, he would be lined up far to the right and would run to the right side. He also would not be inclined to run short routes between the line of scrimmage and linebackers—the no-man's-land for receivers, where he had been crushed by Bednarik. Gifford also would have to get used to a new passer in Tittle, whose sidearm throws came with far greater velocity and a different trajectory than Conerly's, but who

also could throw farther. Given Gifford's athleticism and football instincts, Allie Sherman had no qualms about using him exclusively as
a receiver, although, as Sherman expected, it took time for Gifford
to adjust to Tittle. In training camp and in the first few exhibition
games, Gifford dropped as many passes as he caught and began to
wonder if he and Tittle would ever click. "He could zip that sucker
like a bullet," Gifford was to recall, in contrasting Tittle's rifle shots
with Conerly's sharp, but not as penetrating, passes. Gifford's comeback also was slowed by a series of minor injuries, which at times gave
him pause as to whether the comeback was such a good idea after all.
During his brief retirement, Gifford had done a nightly sports show
for CBS Radio and worked for the Giants, scouting future opponents,
writing out scouting reports, and exercising fairly vigorously. During
the 1961 season, he also worked out with the team several days a week
at Yankee Stadium, mostly running pass routes and catching passes
thrown by Tittle, albeit not as hard as he would throw them in a game.

For Gifford, perhaps more than any other Giant, preseason camp
at Fairfield University would be stranger than ever; Charlie Conerly,
his best friend on the team, was missing from a Giants training camp
for the first time since 1948, and he and Gifford had played together
from 1952 through 1960. "Giff," as Conerly called his friend, would
especially miss Conerly in the evening, when many of the Giants
would go out for a beer or two. Only then, under prodding, would
Conerly talk about his wartime experiences in the Pacific, only to cut
it short by saying, "Oh, who gives a shit, Giff. Let's have another
beer."

Gifford also would be playing under Allie Sherman as a head
coach for the first time. Like many of the Giants, Gifford found
Sherman to be an offensive coaching wizard, innovative and creative,
and a good teacher—but someone who sometimes had a difficult time
dealing with players on a one-on-one basis. "He used to deal with
each one of us psychologically," Gifford was to say in his book *The
Whole Ten Yards*. "Then he'd play these little mind games with us
that not only were debilitating for him but weren't very effective."
Other players thought that Sherman wanted to be liked, but tried too
hard at it, yet was smart enough to realize that tack wouldn't work,
especially with a veteran team.

Gifford, one of the few players who didn't like Jim Lee Howell,
also was one of the few offensive players critical of Sherman, who

during his first season seemed to have done a masterful job of coaching a team without its biggest star—Gifford himself—to the Eastern Conference championship and his Coach of the Year award.

Still, Gifford, as always, was supremely optimistic whenever doubts were raised about the Giants' chances. After absorbing a 42–10 thrashing by Tittle's old team, the San Francisco 49ers, in the Giants' second exhibition game—on the road, of course—Tittle told Gifford that he doubted if the Giants could repeat as Eastern Conference champions. "Look what those guys did to us out there today," an embarrassed Tittle said. "They murdered us."

"We're going to win, Y. A.," Gifford replied. "Don't worry about that."

Still dubious, Tittle then pointed out that the Giants had lost Conerly, Rote, Summerall, Livingston, and Nolan, and that Gifford himself had been nursing a variety of injuries.

"Listen, Y. A.," Gifford said. "We will win because we always win." That had become a Gifford mantra, which Gifford, the team's biggest optimist, had expressed often to teammates whenever they began to despair of the Giants' chances.

Clearly repudiating what Gifford had said about the Giants always winning, New York lost its opening game in Cleveland to the Browns, 17–7, as Tittle threw three interceptions. Tittle responded a week later by throwing two long touchdown passes to Del Shofner, while the defense blocked three field-goal attempts, as the Giants beat Philadelphia. Then, in Pittsburgh, Tittle threw four touchdown passes in a 31–27 win over the Steelers. Week four brought an easy 31–14 victory in St. Louis. At last, on October 14, the Giants opened at home with a 3-1 record. But, in a rematch, the Steelers, led by thirty-six-year-old Bobby Layne, ran for 231 yards and upset the Giants, 20–17. Tittle was sacked four times by Big Daddy Lipscomb, who had been traded to Pittsburgh by the Colts the year before, and eventual Pro Football Hall of Fame tackle Ernie Stautner.

But then Gifford and the other four new starters began to jell, and the Giants ran off one of the longest winning streaks in the team's history, capturing their last nine games to win the NFL Eastern Conference championship for the second year in a row with a 12-2 record. Making the season all the more enjoyable for Tittle, he had moved his wife and three children into a rented house in Tuckahoe in Westchester County, not far from where Gifford and Sherman and their families were living in Scarsdale. Interestingly enough, the Tittles had named their two boys Pat and Mike. "Those are not short for Patrick and Michael; they're actually Pat and Mike," Tittle said. "People used to assume, and may still do, that they're Irish, but they're not, since we're Scottish and English."

Why Pat and Mike?

"After being kidded all the time when I was in school about my name, Yelberton Abraham, I vowed that if I ever had boys, they wouldn't have any fancy names," Tittle said. "So the boys became Pat and Mike. Nothing fancy, but real simple names." Same thing with Tittle's daughter, who was named Dianne and became a poet, artist, and writer, and who wrote a touching biography about her father.

———

With the Giants scoring more than 40 points three times, Tittle set an NFL record by throwing 33 touchdown passes, including 7 in one game against Washington on October 28 at Yankee Stadium. The 33 touchdown passes broke an NFL record shared by Johnny Unitas and Sonny Jurgensen. Tittle's seven touchdown passes against the Redskins matched an NFL record achieved by two other quarterbacks, Sid Luckman (in 1943) and Adrian Burk (in 1954).

"We had the ball first and ten on the Redskins' two-yard-line late in the game with a big lead, and the guys were telling me to go for a new record, but I told them I just couldn't do it because it would be rubbing it in. So I called a running play, and we scored," Tittle said forty-five years later. "Looking back now, I wish I had gone for the record because a couple of us are still tied at seven touchdown passes in a game." As impish as ever many years later, Tittle smiled when he said that, leaving a listener convinced that if had been able to relive that moment, he most likely would have still called a running play and resisted entreaties from his teammates that he go for a new record.

Against a Washington team that was unbeaten in six games—and had in its lineup its first black player, halfback Bobby Mitchell, whom the Redskins had obtained from Cleveland*—Tittle, behind superb blocking, completed 27 of 39 passes for 505 yards, a team record, to lead the Giants to a 49–34 victory. At one point, Tittle connected on twelve passes in a row to come within one of the then-NFL record.

"They did everything right on offense," Redskins tackle and defensive captain Bob Toneff said. "Their protection was perfect, their timing was excellent, and Tittle was just unbelievable."

Among those who did "everything right" was Del Shofner, who caught 11 passes for 269 yards and one touchdown. Shofner's yardage gained on those passes was still a team record forty-five years later.

"Del was the best receiver I ever worked with," Tittle was to say of the fleet Shofner, who was probably the best long-pass threat in the NFL. "Not only was he lightning fast, but he had great hands and great moves, which is a pretty good combination for a receiver." Robustelli recalled that although he was so slim that his teammates called him "Blade," Shofner reminded him of Crazy-legs Hirsch, with whom Robustelli played with the Rams, since, like Hirsch, he had powerful leg drive and thus was able to break tackles and run away from defenders.

A week later Robustelli would catch his only pass as a Giant on a fake field-goal play when Ralph Guglielmi, Tittle's backup, connected with him for a 28-yard gain that set up a touchdown in the Giants' 31–28 victory over the St. Louis Cardinals. Robustelli's only other catch in the NFL came when he was with the Rams and was for 49 yards and one of the five touchdowns he scored during his NFL career.

Not counting Robustelli, Tittle's receiving corps was as good, if not better, than any in the league. Complementing Shofner were Gifford, who while not as fast as Shofner, was even more deceptive; Joe Walton, a sure-handed receiver, particularly on short-yardage third-down situations; and fullback Alex Webster, who at the age of thirty-one not only carried the ball more than he ever had in the NFL—207 times for 743 yards—but also caught 47 passes, most of them screen passes, a Tittle specialty, for 477 yards and nine touchdowns.

In a season of many remarkable accomplishments, Don Chandler's may have been the most remarkable. With Summerall gone, Chandler, helped along by a Giants legend and Hall of Famer, former halfback, defensive back, and kicker Ken Strong, succeeded beyond Allie Sherman's wildest dreams. The twenty-six-year-old Chandler

---

*George Marshall, the owner of the Redskins, was virtually forced to add a black player to the Washington roster, since federal funds were being used to build a new stadium for the team, and the government, under pressure from several black organizations, said Marshall would have to sign a black player if the funds were to be allocated.

made good on 19 of 28 field-goal attempts for a league-leading 67.9 percentage, and also was successful on 47 of 48 extra-point attempts to give him a total of 104 points, a new Giants record. In addition, he punted fifty-five times for an average of 40.6 yards, slightly below his average, but still very respectable.

In only his second year as a Giant, Tittle became as big a sports hero in New York as Yankees slugger Mickey Mantle. So much so that the "Bald Eagle" as Tittle was called by some sportswriters, became one of the few New York sports figures to have a song written about him and played on radio stations throughout the New York area.* Written and recorded by Martha Wright Manuche, a Broadway musical star and the wife of the owner of Mike Manuche's, a Manhattan steak house popular with the Giants, the humorously affectionate song was entitled "I'm in Love with Y. A. Tittle." Reminded of the song while sitting in the lobby of the Algonquin Hotel in Manhattan in the late fall of 2007, Tittle, always playful, broke into a smile and started to hum and sing it with obvious glee.

Tittle, like so many players who had been traded to the Giants, was struck by the team's collective intelligence and dedication to work. "Coming to New York late in my career was the greatest thing that ever happened to me," he said, forgetting at least momentarily the cold shoulder he got when he first joined the team. "It was a joy to play with the Giants because they were such a smart team and such great guys," Tittle said, "and they were very close together and always incredibly prepared.

"I also had the desire, but I think I became a better player when I came to the Giants because of their tremendous preparation. For example, the defensive players always seemed to be studying their playbooks or talking about defensive strategy. The young players coming in see this, and they realize they have to do it too. It's contagious. Preparation on the offensive side was just as intense, with everyone constantly watching films and memorizing most of what the guys saw, and it was because of Allie Sherman, who was an absolute perfectionist."

---

* Joe DiMaggio was the subject of the most popular song ever produced about an athlete when it was recorded in 1941 and entitled " 'Joltin' Joe' DiMaggio." Many years later, the duo of Simon and Garfunkel recorded a song entitled "Mrs. Robinson," which lamented DiMaggio's passing from the sports scene with the lyrics "Where have you gone Joe DiMaggio" and "Joltin' Joe has left and gone away."

Tight end Joe Walton, who also joined the Giants in 1961, after four seasons with the Redskins, echoed Tittle's sentiments. "They were a very intelligent group of guys and very close together," said Walton, who preceded Joe Namath as a star at Beaver Falls High School in Pennsylvania and then played at the University of Pittsburgh. "My years with the Giants were magical ones, both because we got along so well together and were treated like celebrities everywhere we went in New York. If there was a New York Yankee mystique, I think there was a New York football Giant mystique, too."

Throwing 375 passes in 1962, more than he had tossed during any of his twelve previous seasons in the NFL, Tittle completed 200 of them for 3,224 yards—also a career high—and a 53.3 percentage, marking the thirteenth consecutive season in which he completed more than half his passes. Six of Tittle's thirty-three touchdown passes were thrown in the last game of the season. Del Shofner, whom Tittle called his "home run threat," caught 53 for 1,133 yards and 12 touchdowns, while Frank Gifford hauled in 19, including 12 for touchdowns. By scoring 398 points for an average of 28.4 a game, the Giants broke the team record set the previous year. Only Green Bay scored more, 415 points for an average of 29.6 points a game, while yielding an average of 10.8 points a game compared with the 20.2 that the Giants allowed. Thus, not surprisingly, the Packers, who lost only one of fourteen games, were a one-touchdown favorite to beat the Giants for the second straight year in the NFL championship game on Sunday, December 30, at Yankee Stadium. "Thank God," Alex Webster said, "that we're not going to have to play in Green Bay again."

Tittle would be one of ten Giants named to the All-Pro team. Also named on the offensive side were Shofner, Brown, Stroud, and Wietecha. The defensive players named were Robustelli, Katcavage, Grier, Barnes, and Patton, the quiet 180-pound safety who could hit as hard as a 250-pound linebacker and who would spend hours watching film at Robustelli's home in Stamford, where Patton and his wife lived during the season.

Because home games of all NFL teams were still blacked out within a radius of seventy-five miles, more Giants fans than ever—estimated to be in the thousands—traveled as far as one hundred miles to watch the team's games on out-of-town television stations, most notably WTIC-TV in Hartford, Connecticut, at motels, bars, and restaurants in Connecticut and even as close as northern Westchester County. Some enterprising establishments erected tall antennae to pick up the telecasts, and, in many cases, had to turn fans without reservations away. For those who neither saw the Giants play at Yankee Stadium nor headed east or north to watch them on television, their only source of information about the games was on radio and television because of another newspaper strike. This one, the second in five years, shut down all of the city's daily papers, four of which would never publish again.

Meanwhile, Wellington Mara's fears about the New York Titans drawing attention away from the Giants proved to be unfounded. After attracting about 105,000 spectators to the Polo Grounds for six games in the AFL's inaugural season, attendance plummeted to less than 30,000 in 1962, when the Titans rarely drew as many as 5,000 spectators, finished last in the Eastern Conference, and had to be taken over by the league after players' checks began to bounce like fumbled footballs, bringing the franchise to the verge of bankruptcy.

———

In the week before the title game, *Time* magazine ran a story about the Packers, with a portrait of Vince Lombardi on the cover and a cover line that read, "The Sport of the '60s." The newsweekly may have been a bit late, since, by the late 1950s, pro football had already become the hottest sport around. Never before had New York—by now a wildly rabid pro-football town—been as caught up in a football game as in the days leading up to this championship game. No doubt it was because of Tittle's spectacular year, Gifford's comeback, and the signature Giants defense, as well as the homecoming of the charismatic Vince Lombardi, the pride of Sheepshead Bay in Brooklyn. And, of course, in Allie Sherman, Lombardi would be going up against another Brooklynite, who had succeeded him as the Giants offensive coordinator and had declined his invitation to follow him to Green Bay. Lombardi, who had to wait so long to show what he could do as a head coach, had showed plenty, taking a perennial loser to the NFL championship game for the third year in a row in his fourth straight winning season since going to Green Bay. In doing so, he became the most popular sports figure in all of Wisconsin with the possible exception of Milwaukee Braves sluggers Hank Aaron and Eddie Mathews and pitcher Warren Spahn.

Beginning in 1961, Sherman had the team spend the night before a home game at the Roosevelt Hotel in midtown Manhattan. Like so many things in professional football, that practice had been started years before by Paul Brown, who put the Cleveland Browns up in a hotel before home games.

The prevailing feeling among coaches, football writers, and others who knew football was that the only way the Giants could beat the Packers was through Tittle's passing game and his outstanding array of receivers. Running wasn't going to do it, even though Joe Morrison and Phil King had both averaged better than 4 yards a carry, and Alex Webster had put up another good year. But in the Packers, they'd be running against a defense that allowed barely more than 10 points a game. Also, Green Bay, by contrast, had in Taylor and Hornung the best one-two running punch in the NFL, with Taylor having ended Jim Brown's streak of leading the NFL in rushing for five straight years. Taylor gained 1,474 yards and averaged 5.4 yards a carry while scoring a league-high 19 touchdowns. Moreover, Taylor and Hornung functioned behind a fiercely aggressive offensive line. And if they had to pass, they had, in Bart Starr, a veteran quarterback who led the league in passing with a 62.5 percentage on what was essentially a run-oriented team.

In Lombardi, the Packers had a coaching legend in the making, who in only four years had become an icon in Green Bay and, indeed, in most of Wisconsin. Though hardly beloved by all of his players, Lombardi was highly respected as a coach. And why not? In his four years as the head coach, the Packers had won thirty-nine games and lost only thirteen, after having won only eight games in the three seasons before he took over. Asked once whether the volatile Lombardi treated some players, such as Hornung, Taylor, and Starr, for example, different than others, Henry Jordan replied, "No. He treats us all the same—like dogs."

As to whether Lombardi actually said, "Winning isn't everything; it's the only thing," a latter-day player, center Bill Curry, who played with the Packers in 1965 (when Green Bay won another title) and 1966 before being traded to the Baltimore Colts, maintained that the oft-attributed quote was close but not entirely accurate. "What I recall him saying many times," Curry said, "was that 'Winning isn't the most important thing; it's the only thing.' "

"After having played for Bobby Dodd at Georgia Tech, I hated

Lombardi's guts," said Curry, who spent two years at Green Bay and then six with Baltimore and one year each with the Houston Oilers and the Los Angeles Rams before becoming the head coach at Georgia Tech, Alabama, and Kentucky. "I couldn't abide the man until I got to understand him years after I left the Packers when the hatred turned to respect."

Besides Taylor, Hornung, and Starr, the Packers had other perennial All-Pro players such as offensive linemen Forrest Gregg, Jim Ringo, Jerry Kramer, and Fuzzy Thurston, defensive tackle Henry Jordan, linebackers Ray Nitschke, Dan Currie, and Bill Forester, and cornerback Jesse Whittenton. But Hornung's injured right knee had forced Lombardi to use Kramer for extra points and field goals (the only offensive guard in the league to do so at a time when it was still not unusual for position players to do the placekicking—still being done in straight-ahead style) because of the thirty-six-man rosters. Veteran receiver and free spirit Max McGee was pressed into duty as a punter, which he had done on a fairly regular basis in the past, because regular kicker Boyd Dowler had turned up lame on the day of the game.

"Thanks for telling me, Coach," McGee said to Lombardi with a touch of sarcasm before Green Bay left the locker room for pregame practice, aware that punting, like passing, was going to be extremely difficult on this blustery December Sunday. As it happened, it felt even colder than it had been at the title game a year ago in Green Bay. That was because the game-time temperature of 18 degrees— and falling—was combined with winds of around forty miles an hour that made it feel well below 0. Even Lombardi had to adjust to the elements, forgoing his traditional camel-hair coat for a heavy parka, ski cap, heavy gloves, flat-soled shoes, and thick white socks. Before and during the game, a blizzard of paper and other debris flew wildly throughout the stands and across the playing field, making matters even worse for fans and players alike.

The Yankee Stadium turf was even harder and more rutted than it had been when the Giants wore sneakers to get better traction on the frozen field during the 1956 championship game against the Chicago Bears. Twenty-year-old Vince Lombardi Jr., a running back at the College of St. Thomas in Minnesota, had made the trip to New York on Friday aboard the Packers' chartered plane with his parents and his sister, Susan. He jogged on the rock-hard field before the game and said it was like running on an asphalt parking lot.

Wellington Mara and some longtime followers of the Giants said they could not recall the Giants ever playing in worse conditions. Even the blizzard in December of 1958, when Pat Summerall had kicked a long and memorable field goal to beat the Browns and force a play-off the following Sunday, was, they agreed, mild by comparison. Nevertheless, Giants fans able to secure tickets were not going to miss the game for the world, and by kickoff at two o'clock, every seat in the frigid and windswept House That Ruth Built was filled with another thousand or so standing—more than sixty-five thousand in all.

In pregame practice, both Max McGee and Don Chandler watched as punts that normally would have traveled 50 yards were pulled back by what sportswriter Red Smith described as "polar gales" after going 30 yards or less, and realized they would have to try to keep their kicks on a lower trajectory. Similarly, both Tittle and Starr found their passes fluttering in the gusty crosswinds, and reasoned that short passes would have to be the order of the day. Knowing that the Packers would expect Tittle, the Giants' best offensive weapon, to pass often, Sherman had decided that he would try to surprise Lombardi and the Packers by almost exclusively running the ball at the start of the game—meaning going right at their strength, a defensive line that, while overshadowed by the Giants' heralded Fearsome Foursome, had given up an average of only one touchdown a game during the regular season.

For unknown reasons, Sherman had not asked Robustelli to outfit the team with rubber-soled basketball shoes from his sporting goods stores, as Robustelli had during the 1956 championship game against Chicago, a stratagem that had helped the Giants in trouncing the Bears, 47–7. So, apart from Gifford, who wore sneakers, the rest of the Giants, and the Packers too, were shod with cleatless rubber-bottomed football shoes.

In a bruising game reminiscent of the NFL in its earliest days, most of the action occurred in the trenches, at the line of scrimmage. The Giants' vaunted front four was as good as ever, forcing five fumbles, only to have all five recovered by the Packers. Conversely, the Giants fumbled only twice, but both were recovered by Green Bay's All-Pro linebacker Ray Nitschke. Far and away the best player on the field on this frigid day, Nitschke deflected a pass by Tittle intended for a wide-open Joe Walton in the end zone in the first half that was intercepted by linebacker Dan Currie.

After testing out the winds before the game, Tittle said to Sherman, "This is not our kind of day. The wind is going to raise hell with our passing."

Noting that there was nothing the Giants could do about the wind, Sherman replied, "Don't throw long if you can help it." Eventually, though, Tittle would have no other choice.

In the only sustained drive of the game, in the opening quarter, the Packers drove to the Giants' 26-yard line, from where Jerry Kramer kicked a field goal for the game's first score. The second score came in the second period when Giants halfback Phil King fumbled at the Giants' 28-yard line, and Nitschke recovered for Green Bay. Two plays later, Jim Taylor bulldozed through a big hole opened up by the Packers' offensive line and scored untouched to make it 10–0.

Mainly because of the wind, Lombardi's strategy was to give the ball often to the six-foot, 214-pound Taylor, a highly aggressive and punishing runner who, like Jimmy Brown, could inflict as much damage on a tackler as the tackler might on him. Time and again, Taylor would crash through the Giants' line, knees churning and fists flying as the Giants' front four and Huff tried to stop him, often with as many as three players. Belted by Huff, who was then aided by Grier and Katcavage, Taylor at one point was slammed violently to the ground. "Is that your best shot, Sam?" Taylor said, glaring at Huff as he arose from the frozen turf. "That didn't hurt at all." Another time, Taylor, at the bottom of a pileup, tried to bite Huff but bit Dick Modzelewski instead. "Sorry, Mo," a surprisingly contrite Taylor said, "I thought you were Sam." The taunting kept up, but Taylor, racked with assorted bruises and pain, resolutely kept plowing into and through the Giants' defensive line and inevitably landing on the rutted and rock-hard turf. After the game, Bart Starr would say of Taylor's effort, "I've never seen a back take such a beating."

Before the day was done, Taylor carried the ball 31 times and gained 85 yards, almost as much as Giants running backs King, Webster, and Morrison gained combined. The Giants, who had now gone six quarters through two title games against the Packers without scoring, finally scored in the third quarter when cornerback Erich Barnes broke through and blocked a punt by McGee, who was kicking from his end zone. Rookie defensive end Jim Collier pounced on the ball for what would be his one and only NFL touchdown. That score electrified the chilled crowd and made it 10–7.

Green Bay's third score—a second field goal by Jerry Kramer—was set up after a punt by McGee was fumbled by Sam Horner, a Giants kick returner in his first and last year with the Giants. The ubiquitous Ray Nitschke, who, justifiably, would be named the game's most valuable player, recovered the ball. That increased the Packers' lead to a touchdown at 13–7.

With the Giants unable to move on the ground, Sherman gave Tittle the go-ahead to throw more. After throwing only 13 passes in the first half, the Bald Eagle unloaded 28 tosses in the second half, some of which fluttered short of their targets or, when the wind was behind Tittle, sailed over the heads of Giants receivers. Starr, by comparison, threw only 21 times, content to give the ball to Taylor and Hornung once the Packers had taken the lead. "They had us backed against the wall all afternoon, and in the last quarter, we had no choice but to throw," Tittle said. That was especially true when, with just under two minutes left, Kramer connected with his third field goal from 30 yards out to seal the Packers victory at 16–7.

"The wind became a mental and physical problem," a dejected Tittle said later. "It shook my confidence. I was concerned about the ball fluttering and staying up long enough to be intercepted, and then when I had the wind behind me, I had to worry about overthrowing my receivers. And Henry Jordan and other guys on the defensive line were coming at me all afternoon. I now had had two straight chances to win an NFL title and had blown it both times." Tittle, now thirty-six, had to wonder if he would get a third chance.

Most Giants fans were understandably disappointed to lose an NFL title game for the fourth time in five years. But this one was easier to take. Hey, it was to a team coached by one of New York's own, Vinny Lombardi from Brooklyn, who had coached and helped develop many of the players on this Giants team when he was the offensive coordinator. If only he had stayed and become the head coach of the Giants, maybe things would have been different. But then the guy the Giants had coaching them, also from Brooklyn, had won two straight NFL Eastern Conference championships with teams that weren't supposed to win. Sherman was named NFL coach of the year for the second straight time, so how could Giants fans complain?

24

The Last Hurrah?

*U*nlike major league baseball, the National Football League was not touched by a major scandal during its first forty years. The closest it had come was on the day before the 1946 championship game between the Giants and the Chicago Bears at the Polo Grounds when Tim Mara was told by New York City mayor William O'Dwyer that two of his Giants, quarterback Frank Filchock and fullback Merle Hapes, were under investigation for reportedly not having disclosed receiving bribe offers from a gambler and convicted felon named Alvin Paris to fix the game.

At a meeting at the mayor's office at city hall, Hapes, who was twenty-seven, said that he and the thirty-year-old Filchock, who had been voted the Giants' most valuable player for the 1946 season, had been offered $2,500 each plus a $100 bet if they would make sure that the Giants lost by more than the 10 points by which the Bears were favored. Hapes was immediately suspended from the championship game by Commissioner Bert Bell, but Filchock, who denied having received an offer, although he conceded knowing Paris, was allowed to play. After being greeted with a chorus of boos on game day, December 15, Filchock broke his nose in the first quarter but played very well, throwing passes for both Giants touchdowns as they were beaten by the Bears, 24–14. That meant that Giants bettors, with their 10-point spread, would wind up with the same amount of points as the Bears, 24, resulting in a tie—at least in the eyes of oddsmakers and gamblers. In the end, no one betting on the game won or lost. In gambling parlance, it was a wash.

Subpoenaed to testify at Paris's trial, Filchock finally admitted to having received a bribe offer to try to fix the title game, and he too was suspended indefinitely. Filchock returned to play in one game for the Baltimore Colts in 1950, in which he threw three passes, but Hapes never played in another NFL game.

During the winter and spring of 1963, investigators hired by NFL Commissioner Pete Rozelle began looking into reports that more than a few NFL players were betting on league games—a violation of league rules. The investigation eventually led to Paul Hornung of the Packers and another All-Pro player, tackle Alex Karras of the Detroit Lions. Hornung, after initially denying that he had placed bets on NFL games, became increasingly aware that the NFL had strong evidence that he had and admitted having bet on the Packers, while Karras conceded that he had made wagers on the Lions and some other teams. Rozelle, after meeting with Hornung and Karras separately, suspended both of them indefinitely, and fined five other members of the Lions $2,000 each for betting on the 1962 championship game between the Packers and the Giants.

The story was front page news across the country. For all of his high style of living, Hornung was Vince Lombardi's favorite player—almost like a second son—and the coach was devastated by what the "Golden Boy" from Notre Dame had done, although he agreed that Rozelle had no choice but to suspend both players. Lombardi, who discussed the matter with Hornung on the phone, told Packers broadcaster Ray Scott, "I think he thought he was pulling something on the Old Man." He also told friend and writer Tim Cohane that he thought Hornung had bet "for the thrill of it" and that "the thrill lay in the fact that it was forbidden."

Without Hornung, the Packers would still do well in 1963, but they definitely missed their versatile halfback, on the practice field, in the locker room, and, especially, during a game. Meanwhile, Rozelle gave no hint as to when Hornung and Karras would be allowed to return. The suspensions were a wake-up call for all fourteen teams. No Gambling signs were posted in locker rooms, and the league sent representatives to training camps during the summer of 1963 to warn players about violating the NFL rules against gambling on games.

Finally catching up with baseball, the NFL opened a Pro Football Hall of Fame on September 7 of that year in Canton, Ohio, where the Canton Bulldogs, an original franchise, once held forth. Among the initial seventeen inductees were Tim Mara, and Giants linemen Cal Hubbard and Mel Hein, along with such legendary stars as Bronko Nagurski, Red Grange, Jim Thorpe, Ernie Nevers, and Sammy Baugh. More Giants would follow, including a remarkable seven from the 1963 team, which was more than from any other Giants team ever.

By far the biggest news in the NFL during the winter of 1963 was the firing of Paul Brown, the only coach the Cleveland Browns had known since they were formed in 1946 in the old All-America Football Conference. Brown's teams never had a losing record, winning all four AAFC titles before the league disbanded following the 1949 season, and then three NFL championships in the 1950s. In addition, the Browns appeared in the title game three other times during their first six years in the league. That meant the Browns had been in a title game ten years in a row under Brown. But they had not appeared in a championship game since the 1957 season, and that bothered Art Modell, who bought the Browns in 1961 for a then-record price of $4 million. That Paul Brown's teams had posted winning records of 8-5-1 and 7-6-1 over the last two seasons mattered not at all to Modell, a brash and very wealthy advertising man from New York who had been a season-ticket holder to New York Giants games. What did matter was that the Browns hadn't won the NFL title since 1955 and Paul Brown's dismissive attitude toward Modell, who insisted on sitting in on team meetings and film sessions. On one occasion, the owner stayed in the locker room while Brown gave his ritualistic pregame pep talk, which prompted Brown to tell Modell never to do that again, further exacerbating his situation and worsening his relationship with Modell. Brown had lost his chief assistants Weeb Ewbank to the Colts and Blanton Collier to the University of Kentucky—although Collier did return in 1962—and his relationship with Jim Brown had deteriorated.

Finally, in January of 1963, Modell summoned Brown to his office and, in a move that stunned the NFL establishment, told him he was being dismissed. Brown would resurface as head coach of the new Cincinnati Bengals franchise in the American Football League in 1968, where he would remain through the 1975 season. Modell would shock the football world again in 1995, when he announced that he was moving the Browns to Baltimore the following year, leaving Cleveland without its beloved Browns for the first time in fifty years. Commissioner Paul Tagliabue pledged that Cleveland would get a new NFL franchise within three years—which it did—with the Browns name.

—

In what some saw as the beginning of a dismantling movement, the Giants—meaning Allie Sherman and Wellington Mara—traded popular thirty-one-year-old Rosey Grier to the Los Angeles Rams for twenty-seven-year-old tackle John LoVetere. The trade of Grier, a Pro Bowl choice three times since joining the Giants in 1955, ended a seven-year run with the same front four of Robustelli, Katcavage, Modzelewski, and Grier, and marked the end of Grier's guitar playing and needlepointing in the locker room. Also gone was the Giants' no-look All-Pro center Ray Wietecha, who retired at the age of thirty-four after ten years with the Giants. He had joined New York in 1953 as a twelfth-round draft choice after forgoing a highly promising baseball career.

Once again, the draft would be of little value to the Giants. The team's picks included linebacker Jerry Hillebrand, a first-round draft choice; fourth-round pick Glynn Griffing, who had broken most of Charlie Conerly's passing records at Mississippi but would last only one season as a third-string quarterback with the Giants; and tackles Lane Howell, who would last two seasons, and Lou Kirouac, who would last one. Not a good omen for the future, to be sure.

The most surprising newcomer on the 1963 team was future Hall of Famer Hugh "The King" McElhenny, now thirty-four years old and definitely past his prime, but still one of the greatest runners and kick returners in NFL history and also an outstanding receiver. A first-round draft choice of the San Francisco 49ers in 1952, McElhenny had been a perennial All-Pro while scoring 35 touchdowns, many of them on runs of more than 50 yards, before he was traded to the new Minnesota Vikings franchise in 1961. With the Giants, McElhenny would be reunited with Y. A. Tittle, with whom he had played during all nine of his years with the 49ers.

"Hugh was one of the greatest backs I ever saw," Alex Webster said. "He was amazingly quick off the ball. He would run sideways, even backward, and then race forward, and they still had a hard time getting him down."

Even George Halas, who seemingly had seen everything in more than fifty years in football as a player and coach, was left incredulous by McElhenny. Against the Bears in 1952, the rookie sprinted upfield from his 6–yard line after fielding a punt, then swerved to his right and stopped as two defenders collided. Back into overdrive, McElhenny then raced to his right past another would-be tackler before changing pace to avoid another Bear and sprinting to his left at full speed and finally into the open for a touchdown. On the sideline, Halas looked on in awe after watching McElhenny run at least 125 yards on an officially charted 94–yard touchdown punt return. "That was the damnedest run I've ever seen in football," said Papa Bear, who thought he'd seen it all. In the following years, there was much more of the same from the dazzling "King."

By 1963, though, McElhenny was a shell of what he had been. Employed by the Giants as a backup running back and receiver, and occasionally to run back punts and kickoffs, where he had always been at his best, McElhenny would rush 55 times for a 3.2 average, far below his 4.7 career average. But McElhenny still came in handy, catching 11 passes for 91 yards and two touchdowns, and running back six punts for 136 yards.

Across the Harlem River from Yankee Stadium at the Polo Grounds, New York's struggling entry in the then four-year-old American Football League had a new owner, David "Sonny" Werblin, an entertainment mogul who had once headed the Music Corporation of America, better known as MCA, who had immediately changed the name of the team from the Titans to the Jets. Werblin also was the key figure in negotiating a television contract with NBC that guaranteed each of the eight teams in the AFL $900,000 a year, only $100,000 less than what CBS was paying NFL teams for television rights. The contract meant that teams like the Jets, who had drawn poorly, could at least stave off potential bankruptcy. In buying the team, Werblin also intended to move the Jets to a new stadium being built in Queens for the New York Mets baseball team, which had been playing at the Polo Grounds since starting operations in 1962.

Following a third preseason training at Fairfield University in Connecticut, the Giants won three of five preseason games, with one of the losses coming against the Packers in Green Bay. Though it was only an exhibition game, a record crowd of almost forty-three thousand spectators turned out to watch Green Bay beat the Giants yet again, 24–17. During the preseason games, the Giants got an opportunity to adjust to the new placement of the goalpost, ten yards back of the goal line in the end zone, meaning that running backs would no longer have to worry about colliding with the two posts when running across the goal line.

In the Giants' opening game in Baltimore, Tittle picked up where he left off at the end of the 1962 regular season, throwing three touchdown passes before he had to leave with injured ribs suffered when he scored the winning touchdown on a 9-yard bootleg run as the Giants won, 37–28. In beating the Colts for the first time since Johnny Unitas joined the team in 1956, the Giants had to overcome an 18-point halftime deficit. Tittle missed the second game, a 31–0 trouncing in Pittsburgh—during which Ralph Guglielmi and Glynn Griffing passed for fewer than 100 yards—but returned to fire a total of five touchdown passes in victories over the Eagles and the Redskins. In the game against Philadelphia, Dick Lynch, by now one of the premier cornerbacks in the league, intercepted three Sonny Jurgensen passes.

Finally playing at home after four games on the road, the 3-1 Giants met the archrival Cleveland Browns, unbeaten in their first four games and now being coached by Blanton Collier. Though he essentially stayed with Paul Brown's system, the much more outgoing Collier proved more flexible and amenable to proposed changes, both on and off the field, even ceding to players the right to pick the pregame Saturday night movie, which Brown had always done on his own. "One of the reasons that I welcomed Blanton at the time is because he gave me an ability to truly express myself in the years he was there," said Jim Brown. "You see, coaches sometimes don't want players to have input, and great players must have input." It was easy to see that Jim Brown was talking about his own relationship with Paul Brown, at least in the last few years.

Collier also had discerned a growing racial divide on the team, of which Jim Brown was well aware. "They don't invite us to the parties and events with the pretty white girls, then we won't go to those community functions, that boring political shit, where they want to make us look like one big happy family," said Brown, never a shrinking violet. "If we can't go to all the stuff, the fake stuff, then we won't do the fake stuff. We'll play hard, dress right, carry ourselves with class, and be team people. But we don't have to kiss any ass, or take any attitude, to pacify some redneck from Mississippi."

With the former Syracuse multisport star allowed more freedom, and with the erudite mathematics whiz Frank Ryan at quarterback for the second year, Brown was to have his best year ever in 1963, leading the league in rushing attempts, yards gained, touchdowns rushing, and a remarkable 6.4 yards a carry. In addition, he caught 24 passes for 268 yards and three touchdowns. That was a vast improvement over the previous season, when Brown gained only a little more than half of the 1,863 yards he ran for in 1963 and averaged "only" 4.3 yards a carry, which would be the lowest average of his NFL career. Overall, the Browns would do much better too. After going 7-6-1 in 1962, they would improve to 10–4 in 1963. Ryan would throw for 25 touchdowns and have a 52.7 completion average, while Lou Groza, now thirty-nine years old and in his seventeenth season with the Browns—thirteen of them in the NFL—would lead the league in field-goal percentage for the fifth time by making 15 of 23 3-pointers.

In Brown's best game yet against the Giants, he ran for 209 yards and caught two touchdown passes as Cleveland beat the Giants, 35–24, leaving New York two full games back in the Eastern Conference. Back home the following Sunday, the Giants rebounded to defeat Dallas, 37–21. Among the highlights of the come-from-behind victory were Robustelli's three sacks of the extremely mobile little Eddie LeBaron and Dick Lynch's 80-yard touchdown run after he had intercepted a pass thrown by Don Meredith, who Tom Landry was alternating with LeBaron.

A week later, the Giants again faced the Browns, who were still unbeaten through six games. Playing in front of 84,213 spectators, the biggest Municipal Stadium crowd ever, New York reestablished its mastery of Cleveland. In a near-perfect display of passing and rushing offense and an overpowering defense, the Giants drubbed the Browns, 33–6. Tittle, primarily throwing short passes throughout, completed 21 of his 31 throws for 214 yards, while McElhenny, in his best game yet for the Giants, ran for 53 yards, as did Alex Webster, while Phil King gained 48 yards. Jimmy Brown, meanwhile, was held to only 40 yards running; frustrated over his inability to break through the Giants' defense, he started throwing punches in the last quarter and was ejected from the game. With the victory, the Giants cut the Browns' lead to one game with eight to play.

On a roll now, the Giants, on successive Sundays, beat St. Louis, Philadelphia, and San Francisco while the Browns lost two out of three games to enable the Giants to take a one-game lead. Over a five-game stretch, the Giants, best known for their defense in the pre-Tittle era, scored 198 points for an average of almost 40 a game. During that span, Tittle threw a remarkable 16 touchdown passes. What helped, of course, was Tittle's extraordinary number of excellent receivers in Shofner, Morrison, Walton, Gifford, McElhenny, Webster, King, and Aaron Thomas. And the Bald Eagle was connecting with a wide variety of passes: his trademark screen passes off to one side, slants up the middle, hooks to the outside, and 50- to 60-yard tosses that usually went to the fleet Shofner, the fastest receiver on the team.

The 48–14 victory over San Francisco was particularly satisfying, since Tittle's successor, John Brodie, was sacked a half dozen times, and the 49ers gained a mere 34 yards rushing. Tittle, meanwhile, threw four touchdown passes, Shofner caught seven of his throws, and the Giants piled up 568 yards on offense. By now they were the highest-scoring offense in the NFL and seemingly unstoppable.

But then, two days before their game against St. Louis at Yankee Stadium, all of the Giants were not only stopped in their tracks but stunned, as were most Americans and much of the world, when President John F. Kennedy was assassinated in Dallas on November 22.

"We had practiced that morning at the stadium, and I had driven back to my travel business in Stamford," Andy Robustelli recalled. "As I got there, one of the girls ran out screaming 'President Kennedy was just assassinated!' I, like everyone else in the office, was absolutely stunned. I didn't know if we would play on Sunday, but found out, when I went to practice on Saturday, that most colleges had canceled their games, and the AFL had canceled its games too. But the NFL decided its games would go on. From what I gathered, most of the guys agreed with the decision, even though it became very controversial. As it was, our game was not on television or on the radio, and we still had a full stadium. It was an important game, since we were tied with Cleveland and St. Louis for first place, but we lost, 24–17. A lot of people thought we lost because our hearts weren't in the game, and there's no question that it was tough to concentrate. But it was the same for the Cardinals, and they apparently handled the situation better. Still, some people, including Red Smith, never forgave Pete Rozelle for going ahead with the games that day."

Some of the Giants also thought the game should have been canceled. "I was driving back home to Queens from practice with Don Chandler when we heard the news of the assassination," said Sam Huff, who had met President Kennedy and even had campaigned for him in West Virginia in 1960. "To me, playing the game was a big mistake, and I don't know why Pete Rozelle didn't cancel all of the games. I was very upset over the president's death, and we weren't into the game at all, and neither were the Cardinals, and it was probably the worst football game I've ever been involved in."

The loss dropped the Giants to 8–3 and into a three-way tie with Cleveland and St. Louis with three games to play. Making matters worse, the Giants' next game, on Sunday, December 1, was in Dallas, where President Kennedy had been killed the week before, and where, in the past, the team's black players had to stay with black families in the city because of Dallas's segregated hotels. This time around, though, the Maras had insisted that the black players on the team—five in all— had to stay with the rest of the team in downtown Dallas, or the Giants would not play. This, even though none of the black players seemed to have complained about the previous arrangements.

"Wellington Mara always took care of it, and the people we stayed with were always nice people with nice homes," said Rosey Brown, the first player from all-black Morgan State College to play in the NFL. "And we loved it. We didn't have any curfew like the other guys, and we could do anything we wanted—drink beer and party—with no coaches checking up on us. Sometimes Charlie Conerly, Frank Gifford, and Alex Webster would come over where we were staying, and once Frank said, 'Hell, you guys got the best of two worlds.' It actually upset me when the segregation arrangements ended, and we had to stay with the rest of the players."

Still shaken by the president's assassination, the Giants had a listless week of practice, even though they knew they had to win the last three games if they were to reach the NFL championship game for the third year in a row. The team's arrival in Dallas only served to revive what had happened there only six days before. First, the Giants' charter arrived at Love Field, the airport where Air Force One, carrying the president and first lady had landed. Then the bus carrying the team passed Dealey Plaza and the Texas School Book Depository building, from where the fatal shots had been fired as Kennedy's limousine passed by. "Everybody in the bus was quiet and looked out the windows where President Kennedy had been assassinated," Huff said.

The likelihood of the Giants beating Dallas—bad as the Cowboys were, they had upset the Giants at Yankee Stadium six weeks before—and then Washington and Pittsburgh at home did not look good during the first half, when they fell behind, 27–14. But the Giants' defense stiffened and played brilliantly in the second half, holding Dallas scoreless and to 65 yards rushing and 70 yards passing, while the offense scored 20 unanswered points, the last 6 on a game-winning touchdown pass from Tittle to Shofner, during the 34–27 victory.

Back home for their final two games, the Giants' defense thrilled a capacity crowd the following Sunday by intercepting seven passes by Norm Snead and recovering five fumbles, two of them by Robustelli, as the Giants crushed the Redskins, 44–14. Now the Giants were confronted with beating a Pittsburgh team that had routed them, 31–0, in Pittsburgh. But since then, the Giants had won nine of eleven games and were the highest-scoring team in the NFL. A victory would give them their third straight Eastern Conference title and their sixth in the last eight years, a most remarkable run if it was achieved. Ironically, the Steelers, although they had won two fewer games and stood at 7-3-3, could win the conference championship by beating 10–3 New York. That was because if that were the outcome, the ties would not count, and the Steelers would have a higher winning percentage, .727 to .714, which would be the deciding factor.

As had been the case for the last eight years, in addition to the longtime Giants fans, the crowd included hundreds of broadcasting, advertising, public relations, and corporate executives, a smattering of entertainment figures, and scores of Roman Catholic monsignors and priests who were friends of the Maras and thus had jumped on the Giants bandwagon in what had become the team's most glorious and successful era. There were also, as at every home game, a number of political figures, including the mayor of Stamford, J. Walter Kennedy, a onetime sports publicity man for his alma mater, Notre Dame, and then for the Harlem Globetrotters basketball team. A close friend of Robustelli's, Kennedy was not averse to telling friends that he had once advised Robustelli to forgo a tryout with the Los Angeles Rams and instead take a teaching and coaching job at a high school in Connecticut. "I can take absolutely no credit for Andy's success," Kennedy would say often.

With Bobby Layne having retired at the end of the 1962 season, the

Steelers' quarterback was journeyman Ed Brown, who had spent eight years with the Bears before being traded to Pittsburgh in 1962. But the Steelers still had one of the league's best running backs in fullback John Henry Johnson, then in his tenth year in the NFL. Familiar faces included former Giants' guard Lou Cordileone and wide receiver Buddy Dial, a second-round draft pick by the Giants who did not make the team. One of the team's most formidable weapons was Lou Michaels, who, like Lou Groza, did double duty as a lineman—in his case, a defensive end—and as one of the league's best placekickers.

In the NFL for thirty years, the Steelers had yet to win a title since Art Rooney, a former semipro football player from the Steel City, bought a franchise with the $2,300 he had won at the racetrack one day and called the team the Pirates after the city's big-league baseball team. (The name was changed to the Steelers in 1940.) Rooney's timing was perfect, since it wasn't until 1933 that the Pennsylvania State Legislature voted to permit professional teams in the state to play on Sundays. Now, once again, they had a chance to win it all.

And until late in the third quarter, the Steelers still had a very good chance. After trailing, 16–0, Pittsburgh scored a touchdown and a field goal to pull within 6 points. Then came the most crucial play in the game. With the ball on the Giants' 23-yard line, the home team had third and 8—not an insurmountable challenge, but Del Shofner, Tittle's favorite receiver, was sidelined with an injury since the first quarter. Looking around in the huddle, Tittle knew he still had some very good receivers: Hugh McElhenny, Aaron Thomas, Joe Walton, Joe Morrison, and, of course, old reliable Frank Gifford. And it was then that Tittle suddenly remembered something that Gifford had told him earlier—that Pittsburgh cornerback Glenn Glass was playing him to the outside. "He's worrying about the down-and-out," old number 16, now one of the best flankers in the NFL, told older number 14, who then and there decided to call a play wherein Gifford would go straight toward Glass, fake an inside move but break toward the outside, and then quickly cut back across the middle. "I threw it hard into the wind, but too low," Tittle would say later.

Low it was, only a few inches off the ground, which even Gifford thought he had no chance of catching. "All I could do was to extend my right hand as far as I possibly could and just maybe be able to flip it in the air and catch it, but amazingly it stuck right in the palm of my hand—the weirdest catch I had ever made."

"I will never know how Giff caught that ball," Tittle said. "It was unbelievable, one of the best catches I've ever seen."

Steelers coach Buddy Parker agreed. "That catch was the turning point of the game," Parker said. "He shouldn't have caught that ball, but somehow he did, and I still don't know how he did it."

Needing 8 yards, the Giants had gotten 29 and a first down at the Steelers' 47. The Yankee Stadium crowd went into an uproar that could be heard across the Harlem River, where, the day before, the New York Jets had played their last game at the Polo Grounds before an announced crowd of 6,526—the smallest all season in the American Football League, and which looked even smaller than the announced figure.

With the Giants both fired up and supremely confident that Gifford's catch had nullified any chance the Steelers had of winning, Tittle then hit Gifford again, this time to the Pittsburgh 25-yard line, and then found Joe Morrison in the end zone for a touchdown. The Bald Eagle would connect with Morrison for another touchdown pass, and Don Chandler would kick a field goal to give the Giants a 33–17 victory and their third straight Eastern Conference title.

"To me, our defense never played better," Robustelli recalled. "They got down near our goal line five times, and we stopped them every time. Another time they had a foot to go on our 14-yard line, and we stopped them twice. And we intercepted three passes and recovered two fumbles. It doesn't get much better than that."

The offense wasn't bad, either. Tittle, at thirty-six, completed 17 passes for 306 yards, and 3 touchdowns, which gave him 36 for the regular season, breaking the NFL record of 33 he had set the year before. Tittle's mark would last for twenty-one years—and when it was broken by Dan Marino it would be over the course of sixteen games. Joe Morrison, filling in at fullback for Alex Webster, who had missed most of the season with injuries, again demonstrated his remarkable versatility by gaining more than 100 yards. Through the team's fourteen games, Morrison gained 568 yards on 119 carriers for a 4.8-yard average, made 31 catches, seven for touchdowns, and ran for three more for a team-leading 10 touchdowns—all while lining up at halfback, fullback, flanker, tight end, and split end. During practice, Morrison also took a number of snaps at quarterback, one of many positions he had played at the University of Cincinnati in the event he was needed there. Not to be forgotten, too, was how in 1961, Morrison, the NFL's jack-of-all-trades, also played safety during the last three regular-season games and the championship game against the Packers.

"Joe was just what you wanted in an all-around player," Robustelli said. "He wasn't big, only around one hundred ninety, and he wasn't particularly strong or fast, but he did so many things so well just when you needed him the most. I don't know of any player who ever did more for us."

On defense, Dick Lynch had a spectacular year, leading the league in three categories as he intercepted nine passes, as he also had in 1961; ran back three interceptions for touchdowns; and, in doing so, gained 251 yards, all Giants records. Lynch's number of touchdowns from interceptions still stood forty-five years later, as did his yardage gained on interceptions, which he shared with Emlen Tunnell.

Left end Jim Katcavage also had his best year yet with the Giants. Usually overshadowed by perennial All-Pro Andy Robustelli at right end, Katcavage, extremely quick and mobile like Robustelli, recorded twenty-five sacks. That was nineteen years before the NFL started keeping track of sacks, a term that denotes a defensive player breaking through to tackle a quarterback. Forty-five years later, in 2008, Katcavage's twenty-five sacks—accomplished during a fourteen-game season—were three more than the NFL record of twenty-five set by the Giants' Michael Strahan during sixteen games in 2001 (the last one of dubious nature when Strahan "tackled" a seemingly cooperative Brett Favre of the Green Bay Packers).

Next, in the title game at Chicago on December 29, would be the Bears, the Monsters of the Midway, the only team the Giants had beaten in five championship games since 1956, the year New York had demolished the Bears, 47–7, at Yankee Stadium with a team that had included a bunch of newcomers: Andy Robustelli, Sam Huff, Dick Modzelewski, Jim Katcavage, and Don Chandler, all of whom were still on the roster in 1963 and, in the opinion of most NFL coaches and players, were as good as ever, if not better.

—

For the third year in a row, the Giants found themselves playing an NFL championship game in subfreezing weather on a freezing field: 9 degrees at game time before a capacity crowd of forty-five thousand at Wrigley Field, the longtime home of the Chicago Cubs. Unlike the Packers, who had beaten the Giants in the last two title games, or the Colts, who had done so in 1958 and 1959, the Giants were convinced they were the better team when they took on the Bears in what shaped up as a classic confrontation: the NFL's highest-scoring team with the league's best passing attack against a team with the best defense both against the pass and the rush. During the season, the Giants scored a team-record 448 points for an average of 32 points a game—both NFL bests—while the Bears held opponents to league lows of 144 points and an average of 10.3 points a game. Despite that outstanding defensive performance under assistant coach George Allen, later the head coach of the Los Angeles Rams and the Washington Redskins, the Giants were 10-point favorites, mainly, it was believed, because in Y. A. Tittle they had the league's hottest quarterback.

Though the Bears had no leaders in any offensive categories in 1963, they still had placed four offensive players on the all-NFL team along with six defensive players, including all three linebackers: Bill George, Joe Fortunato, and Larry Morris. And in Mike Ditka, in his third year, Chicago had perhaps the league's best and toughest tight end, who would become the first player at that position to be inducted into the Pro Football Hall of Fame.

"I saw in the films that Ditka would elbow and or cheap-shot you," Huff recalled, "so I told Jerry Hillebrand we were going to send him a message right away. Jerry was going to belt him in the face mask as he came off the line of scrimmage and knock him toward me in the middle, and then I'd knock him back to Jerry. We did just that, and he screamed, 'What are you guys trying to do to me?' Then I told him I'd been watching him on film and saw what he had been doing to some people, and that he'd better not try any of that stuff against us and had better play by the rules. Mike was a very tough guy, even when he was starting out in the league, but we didn't have any trouble with him after that."

As it developed, what the Giants' offense did to itself, in large part because of an injury to Y. A. Tittle, decided the outcome of the game. The Giants drove downfield for a touchdown on their first possession, which was capped by a 14-yard pass from Tittle to Frank Gifford. Later in the quarter, the Giants recovered a fumble at the Bears' 31. And on the next play, Tittle hit Del Shofner in the end zone for what appeared to be a certain touchdown—only to have a frozen-fingered Shofner (players rarely wore gloves at the time) drop the ball. On the following play, Larry Morris intercepted a Tittle screen and ran it all the way to the Giants' 5. From there Bears quarterback Bill Wade went in for a touchdown. So instead of a 14–0 Giants lead, the game was tied at 7–7.

The Giants drove to the Bears' 2-yard line early in the second period, but after two sweeps called by Allie Sherman resulted in a loss of yardage, Don Chandler kicked a 13-yard field goal that gave New York a 10–7 halftime lead. But on the Giants subsequent possession, Tittle was tackled by a blitzing Bill George as he was about to throw a pass to Gifford, tearing ligaments in his left knee. Overtly upset by the injury, Tittle had to be replaced by rookie Glynn Griffing for the remainder of the half. "It was like somebody stuck a knife in my knee," Tittle said later. It would turn out to be the most critical play of a very cold afternoon at Wrigley Field.

The twenty-three-year-old Griffing, the Giants' only backup quarterback, had thrown only 40 passes during the regular season and looked totally lost when he replaced Tittle. "He wasn't doing anything," Sherman said of Griffing, who would be released at the end of the year, "and I felt if I left him in, he was going to get intercepted, so I asked Y. A. if he could go back in, and he said he could."

So, after a Novocain shot, Tittle returned in the second half, limping and with virtually no mobility. As soon as Tittle was hurt, many of the Giants wished, somewhat belatedly, that Ralph Guglielmi, the thirty-year-old journeyman, hadn't been traded to Philadelphia midway through the season, leaving the team without a seasoned backup quarterback.

"I tried to talk him out of going back out in the second half," Huff said. "I told him we could win it with our defense, which never let the Bears cross the 50-yard line on their own during the game. 'You got us the lead, Y. A.,' I told him, 'and they can't move the ball on us, so stay out.' But it didn't do any good. He said, 'Sam, this could be my last shot to win a title, so I've got to play. I want that ring.' "

Early in the third quarter, Tittle, unable to get set on his left leg, which a quarterback must do in throwing a pass, tossed a soft screen pass that defensive end Ed O'Bradovich picked off at the Bears' 24-yard line and ran back to the Giants' 14. After Wade hit Mike Ditka on a crucial 3rd-and-9 situation, the Chicago quarterback ran in for his second touchdown to give the Bears a 14–10 lead.

Still, the Giants had a chance. With only ten seconds left, and the Giants at the Bears' 39, Tittle, sending Shofner deep and getting reasonably good protection, threw a 50-yard pass into the end zone, but the ball overshot Shofner and landed in the hands of Richie Petitbon—Tittle's fifth interception of the day. Furious at himself, Tittle yanked off his helmet and banged it to the frozen turf again and again until it cracked, then stalked off the field in tears, hurting both physically and mentally, knowing that time was running out and that he might not get another chance at an NFL title.

With the Wrigley Field crowd celebrating loudly and raucously, Bill Wade dropped to one knee on the next play as time expired, and the Giants had lost their third NFL championship game in a row and fifth in eight years.

The final statistics belied the outcome. Even with Tittle's serious injury, New York gained more yards passing than the Bears—140 to 129—and more yards rushing—128 to 93. The interceptions made the difference. Once again, the Giants' defense had been brilliant; refusing to let the Bears cross midfield on their own during the game; both of Chicago's touchdowns were set up by pass interceptions. Overall, the Giants demonstrated they were the better team and, had it not been for Tittle's injury, would have won the game.

Robustelli, among other Giants, felt that having Guglielmi to relieve Tittle could have changed the outcome. "It was obvious to all of us that Tittle shouldn't have played in the second half," the Giants' defensive right end said, "but he forced himself to because he knew there was no one else. Chalk it up to poor planning."

Physically, even apart from Tittle's injury, the Giants had taken a beating. Guard Bookie Bolin had to leave with a concussion in the second half, and fullback Phil King, the Giants' leading rusher in 1963, missed part of the game because of an injury. But it was Tittle's injury that was calamitous for the Giants.

For the third year in a row, Sherman had taken the Giants to the NFL championship game, but at this point, it was small balm. Surely, with none of the players talking retirement, even though Tittle would be thirty-seven and Andy Robustelli thirty-nine in 1964, most of the Giants felt on the dreary and quiet plane trip back to New York that they were still on a roll and would assuredly break that title-game losing streak, perhaps next season.

If not, it had been a hell of a run.

EPILOGUE

By the fall of 1963, thirteen members of the Giants, more than a third of the roster, were spending the football season—and in a few cases, the entire year—in Stamford, a tribute to Andy Robustelli's persuasive come-ons to his teammates about the delights of living in the fairly affluent Connecticut suburb thirty-five miles from Yankee Stadium. The team's Stamford orientation was so strong that the *Stamford Advocate* ran a photo that September of eleven of the players in uniform with the caption "Stamford Giants Face Cleveland Opener." In addition to carpooling to practices and games, most of the players and their wives often socialized, going to dinner and parties together. Another ritual occurred on Sundays, when the Giants were playing at home, and Herb Kohn, the co-owner of a local furniture store and a civic activist in Stamford, would drive his wife, Kay, plus Ginger Walton, Adonis Patton, and Patsy King, the wives of three Giants who lived close together in Stamford, to Yankee Stadium. "After the games, the wives would go over to the Concourse Plaza to party and then go into Manhattan while my wife and I drove home," Kohn recalled. "But that's how close the team and the wives were at the time."

By the winter of 1964, though, the togetherness that had marked the Giants began to come asunder, and the team would never be the same again.

In March, Dick Modzelewski and his brother Ed were in a Cleveland restaurant they owned, when Little Mo got a phone call from Allie Sherman informing him that he had been traded to the Cleveland Browns for tight end Bobby Crespino. "I couldn't believe it, and I was stunned," said Modzelewski, who had just turned thirty-three and had played in 178 consecutive games since breaking in with the Redskins in 1953. "I was also upset because I had gotten very close to so many guys on the Giants."

Shaken by the trade and concerned about whether he too was in danger of being traded, Sam Huff, working in his off-season job with the J. P. Stevens textile firm, went to the Giants' headquarters in Manhattan to express his displeasure. Huff, then twenty-nine years old, had been named to the all-NFL team for the sixth year in a row. "I said to Wellington Mara, 'You've traded Rosey Grier, Cliff Livingston, and now Mo. Am I next?' "

"You'll never be traded, Sam," Huff quoted Mara as having said. "You're part of the family."

"A few weeks later, I was in Cleveland on business for J. P. Stevens and having dinner at the Modzelewskis's restaurant," said Huff, "when Ed got a call and came back to the table with a strange look on his face and said the call was actually for me. It was my wife, who obviously had been crying, and she told me that Allie Sherman had called to say I had been traded to the Redskins. Imagine, he tells my wife, but not me. I was shocked beyond belief. I was also very upset because the other players were more like brothers to me than my own brothers, and I loved New York and didn't want to leave. I also knew that I had been lied to by Well Mara. That really bothered me because the Maras had always been great and made us feel like we were all family. Eventually, though, Well and I patched things up, once I realized that Allie had persuaded him that trading me, Mo, and Rosey would help, even though he could have stopped any of the trades." Modzelewski agreed with Huff that Mara, had he wanted to, could have prevented their being traded. But, good natured as Little Mo was, he forgave Sherman and later even agreed to go on a weekly television show that the coach hosted in New York. Huff, nowhere near as forgiving, said, "I'll never forgive Sherman for as long as I live." Following his and Modzelewski's trades, Huff, in a bit of black humor, told what was left of the Giants' defense not to patronize Dick and Ed Modzelewski's restaurant in Cleveland if they wanted to avoid being traded.

Huff said he felt that Sherman, as the team's former offensive coordinator, was envious of the defense Tom Landry had contrived in 1956 and tried to change it. "When he did, he changed my style of play and made me less effective," Huff said. "A couple of times, when things weren't going right, I told Andy we had to go back to the old defense, because I couldn't play Sherman's, and we did, and everything worked out okay. But then after one game, which we had won, Sherman came storming into the locker room and screamed, 'I told you this is my defense, and you goddamn better play it!'"

Robustelli, who finished his career as a playing coach at his highest salary ever, $28,500, also found the trades of Huff and Modzelewski inexplicable. "We lost two key players who knew our system and played it well, which shook everyone up," Robustelli said more than twenty years after he had retired. "There was no way we could be as efficient as in past years." Like Huff, Robustelli felt that Sherman had always resented the fact that the Giants' defense had become more popular and had received more acclaim than the offense, probably the first time that had happened in the NFL. He also believed that Sherman wanted to recalibrate the Giants to his own liking even though they were still a championship team. "I feel that Sherman tore the Giants apart to satisfy the whim of being able to say he now had his team," the Giants' playing coach said. "But the record shows he did better with the team he largely inherited."

Stunningly, in the space of two years, the Giants traded away half of the Fearsome Foursome, one of the best front fours in the history of the NFL, along with Huff, the most glorified and popular—at least to most Giants fans—member of the defense, if not the entire team. Columnists and sports commentators denounced the trades—especially the Huff one—and in particular Sherman, who until then had enjoyed a good relationship with the media.

"I felt we were at a point where we had to make some changes," Sherman explained later, while neglecting to say if he thought that either Huff or Modzelewski had slowed down or if their talents had diminished in other ways. "We needed a new dimension. Some guys were getting mature, and we felt that we were losing something. And we had to strengthen our defense."

That last comment was difficult to understand, since, in trading away Modzelewski and Huff, the Giants got two offensive players and only one defensive player—and certainly no one to replace those two stalwarts. To replace Huff, they inserted rookie Lou Slaby, who lasted all of two years with the Giants and never came close to reminding anyone of Huff.

Whether those trades were a major factor in what happened to the Giants in 1964 or whether it was combined with the fact that the team was getting old, New York went into a horrendous tailspin, going from first to last in the NFL's Eastern Conference: from a record of 11–3 in 1963 to 2-10-2 in 1964, the team's worst mark to that point in its history, which would be even worse two years later. After holding opponents to an average of 20 points a game in 1963, the Giants yielded an average of 28 points in 1964. The offense also crumbled. After leading the NFL by scoring a team-record 448 points the year before, the Giants scored only 241 points in 1964 for an average of 17.2 points per game, the lowest in the league. Y. A. Tittle, though he would complete 52.3 percent of his passes, connected for only 10 touchdowns, compared with his record 36 the previous season, and would be intercepted 22 times, more than ever before in his fifteen years in the NFL.

During the following winter, much of the heart of the team was gone, as thirty-nine-year-old Andy Robustelli, thirty-five-year-old Jack Stroud, thirty-four-year-old Frank Gifford, thirty-three-year-old Alex Webster, and Tittle, thirty-eight, all retired. Of the three members of the defense who had been traded, Huff went on to play five seasons with the Redskins, the last as a playing-coach under Vince Lombardi; Modzelewski, three seasons with the Browns, who would win another NFL title during his first season with them; and Grier, four years with the Los Angeles Rams. Notably, none of the players exchanged in trades for Huff, Modzelewski, or Grier made impressions with the Giants.

New York also inexplicably traded away Don Chandler, who had emerged as one of the league's best punters and placekickers, to Green Bay, where he would play three seasons under Vince Lombardi, the man who once chased Chandler and Huff out to an airport in Vermont to persuade them not to desert the team and to get back to Saint Michael's College immediately. Also traded were halfback Phil King, the Giants' leading rusher in 1963; cornerback Erich Barnes, who had been named to the NFL All-Pro team in 1964; and guard Darrell Dess. So it was that in two off-seasons, the

Giants lost a total of eleven starters from the 1963 Eastern Conference championship team.

At the same time, Lombardi himself traded away one of his best players, center Jim Ringo, a perennial All-Pro during ten seasons with the Packers. Legend has it that Ringo showed up to talk contract with Lombardi with an agent at his side in March of 1964 at a time when most players still negotiated their contracts directly with management, and agents were still on the bargaining cusp of the NFL. Lombardi supposedly was not only taken aback by the agent's presence, but offended that Ringo, whom he liked a lot, had brought along a third party to discuss his contract. *Wasn't my word good enough for him?* Lombardi mused when Ringo introduced the agent. As the legend goes, the agent told Lombardi that his client wanted his salary increased to $25,000 for the 1964 season. Lombardi said nothing while giving both the agent and Ringo withering stares. Aware that the Philadelphia Eagles were interested in Ringo, Lombardi supposedly then picked up the phone on his desk and told his secretary to put him through to the general manager of the Eagles.

"You still want Ringo?" Lombardi is supposed to have asked to whoever picked up the phone. "Then you've got him; it's a deal."

Whereupon Lombardi said to the agent, as stunned as Ringo was, "If you want to talk about Ringo's salary, call the Eagles; he belongs to them now."

While Lombardi never disavowed that version, Packers officials in the years to come denied the Ringo trade went quite that way. Ringo was from the Philadelphia area and had indicated he'd like to finish his career with the Eagles. Lombardi, the Packers party line went, assented to his desire because he felt that Ringo, then thirty-two years old, had slowed down a bit, and he knew he could get a good young linebacker, Lee Roy Caffey, and a first-round draft choice in exchange for Ringo and backup fullback Earl Gros. But, largely because of his distaste for agents, Lombardi let the mythical version live on, perhaps as a lesson to other Packers who might be thinking of hiring agents. Most of the players may not have loved Green Bay, especially in December, but knew that with the Packers, they were playing with one of the best teams in the NFL and thus likely to make it to the championship game, and to make the extra money that came with that.

After the horrendous 1964 season, the Giants bounced back slightly in 1965, finishing at 7–7, with only Brown, Katcavage, Lynch, and Patton remaining from the team that had won three Eastern titles from 1961 through 1963. Two months before the team reported to Fairfield University for preseason training that year, Jack Mara, who had been the Giants' president for thirty-one years, died, and was replaced by his younger brother, Wellington, who had been in charge of football operations for years. Then, in July, the Giants surprisingly gave Sherman a ten-year contract that superseded a five-year contract set to expire in 1968.

In the years to come, that did not look like one of Wellington Mara's better deals.

In 1966, with Sherman set financially until 1975, the Giants fell to 1-12-1, their worst record ever—and which included a 72–41 loss to the Redskins in Washington—and the team would not record another winning season until 1970, by which time Sherman had been fired (just before the start of the 1969 season) and replaced by assistant coach Alex Webster.

Compounding matters, the Giants, with the first draft pick in 1965, passed up opportunities to draft Joe Namath, Gale Sayers, and Dick Butkus, among others, choosing instead running back Tucker Frederickson, who, during his six seasons with the Giants, was hindered by injuries and enjoyed only modest success, with a 3.4-yard rushing average.

Though he was acknowledged by his players and opposing coaches as a brilliant and innovative offensive master, Sherman, though only forty-six when he was fired by the Giants, never coached again. "I was approached by a number of head coaches about becoming an assistant and also by some ownership groups regarding head-coaching jobs in the NFL, but nothing ever materialized," Sherman said in 2008 at the age of eighty-five, looking much like he did when he was the Giants' head coach, apart that his hair had gone gray. "I also would have liked to have gotten into ownership of a club and coached, too, but that didn't materialize, either."

What did materialize was a successful career in business. Like many of his players, he had prepared for an after-football life by working during the off-season, in his case as an insurance broker and in sales, and hosting weekly television and radio shows during the football season. After leaving the Giants, Sherman was a partner in a tape-duplicating company, a consultant for a cable television network, an investment counselor, and a management consultant and then a senior vice president with Warner Communications and at Time Warner, Inc., where he was involved in a variety of sports ventures. Later, Sherman became the president of the New York City Off-Track Betting Corporation. During the 1970s and 1980s, he also was a host and co-host of a number of television and radio network programs on CBS, ESPN, and Home Box Office (HBO).

"I enjoyed the work, but all the while I missed being directly involved in football," Sherman said.

To no one's surprise, Tittle announced his retirement on January 22, 1965, at Mamma Leone's, a popular Manhattan restaurant, saying, "I don't want to come back and be a mediocre football player again. I was last fall." In a somewhat bizarre sequence, several hours later, at Toots Shor's restaurant, the Giants' favorite postgame hangout, the Jets, now playing at Shea Stadium in Queens, introduced University of Alabama star Joe Namath as their new quarterback, whom they had signed for a then-whopping $400,000 contract. It was a stark contrast—the coming and the going of perhaps the two best quarterbacks ever to play in New York—the ending of one great quarterback's career, and the beginning of another.

"Coming to New York and playing for the Giants was the best thing that ever happened to me," Tittle said forty-four years later. "My wife and I loved the city—everybody was just great, including the players. Was I finished as a player? I really don't think so. You don't go from the season I had in 1963, when I threw thirty-six touchdown passes, to not having anything left the next year. I could still throw the ball as far and as well as ever, and my arm strength was still good. The team just changed too much. The trades hurt us, and I didn't see any chance of us being a contender in the next few years. But I owe a lot to the Mara family. They traded for me late in my career when some people didn't think I had much left, and so I'm grateful to them."

To Wellington Mara, the Mara family member who had always been closest to the players, there was a subtext to the Giants' precipitous downfall: the brand-new Jets, of all things. "I think that the Jets coming in when they did contributed to our bad years because we tried to do everything for the short term rather than the long haul," Mara told Gerald Eskenazi of the *New York Times* in the mid-1970s. "We'd trade a draft choice for a player, figuring he'd give us one or two good years. We didn't want to accept how the public would react if we had a bad year or two or three. It was a question of misplaced pride. The fans would have stuck with us anyhow."

Indeed, Mara, according to some sources, became almost paranoid when the AFL was formed and established a franchise in New York, even though the Titans-Jets drew poorly during their first four years. But then the upstarts began to attract crowds comparable to those of the Giants by 1964, the year the Giants began to unravel. As for trading draft choices for players, the reverse seemed to be true. The Giants actually obtained some of their best players—Robustelli and Shofner, for example—by giving up draft choices, and did not begin to slip badly until they traded away veterans.

Perhaps because Mara primarily put the teams together, he had a particular fondness for the Giants of the mid- and late 1950s and early 1960s. "In conversations with me years later, Wellington Mara made it quite clear that he had a special place in his heart and his head for the Giants of that era," said Bill Wallace, the former *Herald Tribune* and *New York Times* sportswriter, who had covered the Giants. "He also would say that it was plain to him that those Giants teams were greater than the sum of their parts."

—

Tittle, like so many Giants of what arguably was the team's most glorious stretch, was already on the road to being very successful off the field when he retired. After starting to sell insurance door-to-door while with the 49ers, he built his own insurance and financial-services company in Mountain View, California, in the San Francisco Bay Area, and became a millionaire. The same was true of Robustelli, who, after having started his own sporting goods store business while still a player, was to become extremely successful as the head of a conglomerate that included a travel business, a sports-marketing component, a speakers' bureau featuring athletes (including a large number of NFL stars), and a video unit. At varying times, Robustelli's company employed all nine of his children—he and his wife had one more after he retired, and eventually thirty-four grandchildren and eleven great-grandchildren—

and some of their spouses. For a while, Robustelli also served as a television analyst of AFL games and hosted a radio show in New York with former New York Jets lineman Sam DeLuca. For many years, Gifford and Summerall became sportscasters, primarily of NFL games, although Summerall also broadcast the U.S. Open golf and tennis tournaments and the Masters Golf Tournament, along with becoming a familiar voice on radio, doing commercials for nationally known products after his retirement as a player. Gifford, though, found himself overshadowed in fame when he married the actress and television personality Kathie Lee Epstein in 1986—it was the second marriage for both—and began to raise a second family in Greenwich, Connecticut.

Huff also went into broadcasting, serving for two years as a radio analyst for New York Giants games and, for more than forty years, doing Washington Redskins games, while spending more than twenty years as a marketing executive with the Marriott hotel chain. Dick Lynch, the onetime Broadway cutup who, as a bachelor, squired Kim Novak around town, became a radio analyst, broadcasting Giants games for more than four decades, in addition to becoming a printing-company executive in the New York area. Lynch and his wife were dealt a devastating blow on September 11, 2001, when their first son, Richard, a bond trader, was killed in the attack on the Twin Towers of the World Trade Center in Manhattan. Kyle Rote also became a successful broadcaster, starting out with WNEW-AM radio in New York and later serving as an analyst on NFL games while also becoming involved in a number of business enterprises.

Hardly any Giants, if any, thought that Rosey Grier's guitar playing in the clubhouse would lead to anything, but it did. Late in his career and after he retired, "Ro," as the mountainous Grier was called by his teammates, performed at concerts, including one at Carnegie Hall, and in clubs with such well-known acts as Gladys Knight and the Pips, Chuck Berry, Bobby Darin, and Curtis Mayfield. That led to appearances in several movies and in a number of television shows. The multitalented Grier also parlayed his needlepoint talents into a book entitled *Rosey Grier's Needlepoint for Men.* Grier later became a minister in Los Angeles and worked for the city counseling troubled young people in and out of jail.

Grier, who along with Modzelewski kept the Giants' clubhouse loose before games and practices, also became close to Senator Robert Kennedy and accompanied him often while he was seeking the Democratic presidential nomination in 1968. It was Grier who put his thumb behind the trigger and yanked the gun out of Sirhan Sirhan's hands and then subdued him after he had fatally shot Kennedy in the kitchen of the Ambassador Hotel in Los Angeles. "Bobby Kennedy was a tremendous influence on me and my life," Grier said during the winter of 2008. "He genuinely liked me and encouraged me to express my feelings and to get out and help people, which I did. Jackie Onassis also became a close friend."

Given the Giants' collective intelligence, it is not surprising that an extraordinarily large number of Giants of the late 1950s and early 1960s became coaches, both on the college and NFL levels. That led some sportswriters to nickname the team Mara Tech, since the organization had, to a considerable degree, become a training ground for coaches, not to mention broadcasters and a few millionaires. In addition to Alex Webster, those who coached in the NFL included Harland Svare, Dick Nolan, Ed Hughes, and Joe Walton, who coached the New York Jets for seven years and, in his seventies, was still coaching at Robert Morris University near Pittsburgh well into the twenty-first century, while Joe Morrison became the head coach at the University of South Carolina. Robustelli also had a brief fling at coaching, serving as the head coach of the short-lived Brooklyn Dodgers of the Continental Football League in 1966 and later becoming director of operations for the Giants from 1974 until the end of the 1978 season. Meanwhile, he still ran his multifaceted business in Stamford and continued his involvement in a number of real estate properties in the Caribbean. Then, of course, both Tom Landry and Vince Lombardi, who began their NFL coaching careers as assistants with the Giants, went on to become legendary coaches in the league.

Those who became assistant coaches in the NFL included Robustelli, Svare, Webster, Jimmy Patton, Emlen Tunnell, Kyle Rote, Rosey Brown, Sam Huff, Dick Modzelewski, Jim Katcavage, Ray Wietecha, Bob Schnelker, Don Heinrich, Walt Yowarsky, and Allan Webb, the onetime semipro player, who later became the director of personnel for the Cleveland Browns and then the San Francisco 49ers during the Bill Walsh era.

Many others became successful in various business ventures,

ranging from insurance to positions in the corporate world. Many, if indeed not most, of the Giants of the era married young, usually to high school or college sweethearts, and the marriages tended to last. In 2008 Robustelli and Tittle and their wives celebrated their sixtieth wedding anniversaries, while Webster and Modzelewski had by then been married for more than fifty years.

Among those who had died by 2017 were Andy Robustelli and Frank Gifford, both at the age of eighty-five; Alex Webster at eighty; Dick Lynch at seventy-two; Tom Scott at eighty-four; Alan Webb at eighty; Charlie Conerly, who passed away at the age of seventy-four after undergoing open-heart surgery; Emlen Tunnell, who died of a heart attack at age fifty-three while an assistant coach with the Giants; Jimmy Patton, who was killed in a car accident when he was thirty-eight years old; Phil King, who died at thirty-seven when a rifle he was cleaning went off; Carl Karilivacz, who died at thirty-eight of a heart attack; Kyle Rote, the team's Renaissance man, who wrote poetry, fiction, and songs while also becoming an accomplished pianist and the first president of the NFL Players Association, who died at the age of seventy-three; and Joe Morrison, who died at fifty-one while coaching at South Carolina. The list also included Ray Wietecha, the brilliant no-look center; defensive backs Dick Nolan and Herb Rich; and Gene Filipski, best remembered for running back the opening kickoff of the 1956 NFL championship game 54 yards in sneakers provided by Andy Robustelli; and Allie Sherman, who coached the Giants from 1961 through 1968.

Shortly after Gifford's death in 2015, his family revealed that he had suffered from chronic traumatic encephalopathy (CTE), and that the Gifford family had decided to have his brain studied in the hope that it would contribute to medical research on the link between football and traumatic brain injury.

Of the Giants of that glorious period, eight were elected to the Pro Football Hall of Fame in Canton, Ohio, and two of those, Gifford and Tittle, had their numbers retired, as did Charlie Conerly and Joe Morrison. Neither Conerly nor Morrison made it to the Pro Football Hall of Fame, although Conerly came within two votes of being enshrined. Speaking at an NFL Alumni golf tournament in Westchester County in the early 1980s, long after Conerly had retired, Dave Anderson, the Pulitzer Prize–winning sports columnist for the *New York Times*, described Conerly as "the best quarterback not in the Pro Football Hall of Fame." Notwithstanding all of his versatile talents, it seems strange that Morrison's number was retired but not the numbers of Emlen Tunnell, Rosey Brown, and Andy Robustelli, all of whom are in the Hall of Fame. Indeed, in the year 2000, Brown was the only Giant named to the NFL's seventy-fifth all-time team. Morrison, by contrast, never even made the NFL All-Pro team, something Tunnell and Brown did nine times each, and Robustelli seven times. That Tunnell, Brown, and Robustelli—perhaps the best defensive back, offensive tackle, and defensive end ever to play for the Giants—never have had their numbers retired by the Giants seems inexplicable. In fact, Morrison's number virtually *had* to be retired because of a compliment made by Alex Webster in 1972 when he was coaching the Giants and Morrison was in his final year as a player.

"I got up to speak briefly at a team dinner at Jim Downey's restaurant in Manhattan," Webster recalled. "Joe had just had a great game and, referring to the fact that he was going to retire after the season, I said, 'When Joe retires, they ought to retire his number too.' Of course, I just meant it as a compliment, not thinking the Giants would do it. But apparently when Well Mara heard about what I had said, he felt they had to retire Joe's number at the end of the season, and they did. I don't think Well really wanted to but felt he had to because of what I said. And I really don't think Joe felt right about it."

———

Very few of the Giants of the fifties and sixties go to NFL games these days, but many do watch, at least occasionally, on television. In many cases, they do not like what they see. "I hate it," said Huff, who covers all sixteen of the Redskins' regular-season games every year and after leaving the Marriott hotel chain raised thoroughbreds on his twenty-eight-acre farm in Middleburg, Virginia. "Guys jumping up and down after they make a tackle. Hell, they're paid to make tackles."

Dick Modzelewski, a fierce tackler during his NFL career, said he sometimes cringes at the tackling and missed tackles. "The players are more athletic today, but a lot of them don't know how to tackle," said Modzelewski, who, after retiring, underwent a number of surgeries on the back he injured while with the Giants. "You rarely ever see them tackle low like you're supposed to, and everybody's hotdogging it when they do make a tackle or score a touchdown, even if they're losing by twenty points. We wouldn't dare do that. For one thing, we'd never get away with it."

Gino Marchetti, the great Baltimore Colts defensive end, agreed. "I can't stand watching all that bullshit," said Marchetti, who along with former teammate Alan Ameche launched a string of very successful fast-food restaurants with start-up money donated by Colts' owner Carroll Rosenbloom. "The league could put a stop to it, but they won't."

Harland Svare, who after serving as a playing coach with the Giants became a head coach with the Rams and the San Diego Chargers, also found the "lack of discipline" in NFL games disturbing. "I don't particularly like the celebrating between plays and some of that type of stuff," said Svare who rejoined his Giants defensive mentor, Vince Lombardi, as defensive coordinator for the Redskins in 1969, when Lombardi was the head coach. "The coaches could stop it, but they don't." Lombardi, as Svare well knows, most certainly would, as would Tom Landry.

Several other former Giants, while disdainful of some of the celebratory tactics during NFL games, said they thought that players in the twenty-first century had some notable advantages over players in the 1950s and 1960s. "They're so much bigger, faster, and more athletic," former tight end Joe Walton said in 2017. Walton also noted that, given their lucrative salaries, modern-day players do not have to work in the off-season and spend much of their time working out. "Like most players in our era, I never lifted a weight. And we all worked in the off-season because we weren't making that much money from playing football," he said. "And some guys like Andy Robustelli and Sam Huff even worked at second jobs during the season."

However, all of the former Giants interviewed agreed that most players from their era could have played today. But they felt that it was difficult, if not impossible, to compare players from past and present eras. So did Dave Anderson, the Pulitzer Prize–winning sports columnist for the *New York Times*, who often covered Giants' games in the 1950s and 1960s. "Even the linemen are more athletic today," Anderson said. "And the fact that there are so many black players in the NFL has made a difference." (By contrast, there were only a handful of black players in the league in the 1950s, including defensive back Emlen Tunnell, the first African American to play for the Giants.) Asked to compare quarterbacks from the two eras, Anderson said it was impossible. "In the fifties and sixties, quarterbacks rarely threw more than twenty passes in a game, while today some throw more than fifty in a game." Anderson also said that great players of the past would still stand out today. "Jimmy Brown, for example, was and still is the running back of all time," the former *Times* sports columnist said in referring to the former Cleveland Browns star.

Another former Giant, Bobby Simms, also thought the influx of black players was significant to the latter-day success of the NFL. "I think a lot of them are more determined," said Simms, a tight end and linebacker during his three seasons with the Giants and later head of his own investment management company.

Like so many of his old teammates, Svare attributed much of the Giants' success in the late fifties and early sixties to discipline and intelligence. "We were a very disciplined team that worked very hard and didn't tolerate anyone not taking care of themselves, and that meant no going out and drinking during the week," the former All-Pro linebacker said from his home in Castle Rock, Colorado, after a forty-minute run on a winter Sunday in 2008. "Fortunately, we had a very smart bunch of guys."

Svare's name still resonated with many Giants fans more than four decades after he retired as a player, as did so many others. Even their numbers remained in the minds of fans. While hardly anything in Andy Robustelli's office bespoke his background as a football player, his Connecticut license plate carried two initials and two digits—NY81, his old team and his old number—because even the unsentimental Robustelli knew that he was part of a team that became the toast of New York once upon a time, and had much to do with making the National Football League what it is: an integral and hugely popular thread of the American sports fabric.

ACKNOWLEDGMENTS

═══

*F*ar and away the most pleasurable aspect of researching this book was interviewing about fifteen former New York Giants who played on the team in the mid- and late-1950s and the early 1960s, along with members of other NFL teams of the era. To a man, they were friendly, cooperative, informative, and, it seemed, eager to talk about the Giants' teams of that period, and, most of all, about the teammates with whom they formed such a close bond.

Despite the low pay they received—which made off-season, and often even in-season, jobs necessary—they all agreed that playing for the football Giants of the 1950s and early 1960s was a joyful and fulfilling experience, both because of the Mara family's closeness with the players and the connection that existed among those players.

To all of the players I interviewed, I owe a great deal of gratitude. I am indebted even to Chuck Bednarik—"Concrete Charlie"—who almost ended Frank Gifford's career with perhaps the most famous, or infamous, tackle in NFL history in 1960; and Raymond Berry, the genteel and sure-handed Hall of Fame receiver for the Baltimore Colts, who was instrumental in the Colts' overtime victory over the Giants in 1958 in "the greatest football game ever played." More than four decades later, most of those Giants and many of their opponents still remained active, including Andy

Robustelli, Y. A. Tittle, Pat Summerall, Joe Walton, Dick Lynch, Sam Huff, and Gifford, either in football or in private business. If it was enjoyable talking to those players of the past, so, too, was it a delight to talk to Perian Conerly, the widow of Charlie Conerly, who provided material about the large number of players and their families who lived at the Concourse Plaza Hotel near Yankee Stadium, the postgame parties in their apartment, and the ensuing subway trips into Manhattan on the days of home games by the players and their wives, many of whom were very close. Helpful, too, was Jean Robustelli, who filled me in on details that her husband, Andy, was too modest to discuss, along with providing birth data on the Robustelli's nine children and the thrill and excitement of watching Andy play while sitting with other players' wives at Yankee Stadium and then venturing to Toots Shor's and other Giants' hangouts.

Others who were fonts of information in one way or another were Ed Clark, who helped Andy Robustelli launch a business career that would evolve into a multimillion-dollar conglomerate by convincing his boyhood friend to join him in opening a sporting goods store after Robustelli's first year in the NFL; Greg Michie, who was the right-hand man to Robustelli in his business interests for more than forty-five years and helped tweak the memory of the unassuming Robustelli on some of his feats of yesteryear, both as an athlete and a businessman; Robustelli's former Stamford High School teammates Carmine Tosches (who was also the quarterback during Robustelli's four years at Arnold College), and lifelong friends Vito DeVito and Fred "Lefty" Giuliani, both of whom became successful minor league baseball players and then as an educator and coach, and as a banker, respectively.

Of inestimable help were Bob Markowitz, the alumni relations coordinator for the Cleveland Browns, who provided clippings from Cleveland and Akron newspapers on games between the Giants and Browns when there was a New York newspaper strike in 1958; and the public relations directors of the Giants (Pat Hanlon), the Indianapolis Colts (Craig Kelley), and the Philadelphia Eagles (Derek Boyko), along with one of Boyko's predecessors, Jim Gallagher, who handled the team's public relations during the era I wrote about. Other public relations specialists who dug back into the past for me were the sports information directors of St. Michael's (Seth

Cole); Williamette University in Salem (Robert McKinney); Gustavus Adolphus College (Tim Kennedy); Fordham University (Joe DiBari); and Allie Sherman's alma mater, Brooklyn College (Alex Lang). Among the sports editors, past and present, who helped my cause were Ted Ryan of the *Burlington (Vermont) Free Press* and Jim Day of the *Salem (Oregon) Statesman-Journal*, while former broadcasters who contributed anecdotes and other material were Tony Adams, longtime sports director for WCAX-TV, and the station's current sports director, J. J. Chioffi. Liz Scott, the archivist at St. Michael's, was also helpful in providing materials from the years when the Giants trained there.

A number of sportswriters who covered the Giants also provided anecdotal material, including Dave Anderson, the Pulitzer Prize–winning sports columnist for the *New York Times*, and Bill Wallace, who covered the Giants for the *New York Herald Tribune* and then for the *Times*.

Others I am indebted to for their cooperation are Vince Lombardi Jr.; Nancy Habetz, the public relations director at Fairfield University in Connecticut, where the Giants lived and trained on campus; Vernon Biever, the esteemed photographer whose work on Green Bay Packer games earned him enshrinement in the Packers Hall of Fame, and who contributed a number of photos for the book; John Marikos, the news librarian for the *Salem Statesman-Journal;* Jennifer Spencer of the Fordham University Law School, who researched Vince Lombardi's brief tenure as a student; Bill Filipski, one of the three sons of Gene Filipski, the former Giants' halfback, kickoff, and punt returner; Lori Sherman, one of Allie Sherman's two daughters, who provided background data on photos of the former Giants' coach; Mike Daly, the managing editor of the *Connecticut Post* in Bridgeport, Connecticut, and Ray Van Stone, the paper's former sports editor, for their recollections of the Giants when they trained at Fairfield University in the late 1950s and during the 1960s; Alice Gingold of the New York Historical Society, who produced materials about the Concourse Plaza Hotel in the Bronx and information on the New York City subway system of the era when Charlie Conerly, Frank Gifford, Sam Huff, and other Giants often rode the city's subway trains; Michael Duignan, the assistant director of development at Art Donovan's alma mater, Mount St. Michael Academy in the Bronx; Jack Clary, a prolific writer of books about the NFL and its teams, and to my Bronxville friend Jim Houlihan, the onetime Fordham pitcher and a huge Giants' fan, for lending me books, magazines, and videos about his favorite football team. A friendly nod of thanks also goes to Kim Ibanez, Jim's executive assistant, who was also immensely helpful in my research.

I am also indebted to Ernie Accorsi, the former public relations director and general manager of the Colts, who later was general manager of the Cleveland Browns and the New York Giants; Frank Deford, the superb and extremely versatile writer who grew up in Baltimore as an avid Colts' fan; and John Ziemann, the president of the Baltimore Ravens marching band, which began operations in 1947 as the Baltimore Colts band and is thus the oldest band in the NFL, and who put me in touch with a number of the Colts who played in the 1950s and 1960s.

As always, libraries were a treasured source, both for their books about the Giants and other NFL teams and for obtaining microfilm of newspaper stories going back a half century and more. In this instance, I primarily relied on the New York Public Library for newspaper microfilm from the days when New York had as many as a dozen daily papers; and Connecticut libraries in Stamford (my hometown), Fairfield (both the public and the university libraries), Norwalk, Westport, and Wilton. Above all, I am most grateful to Susan Madeo at the Westport Library for obtaining difficult-to-find books from the interlibrary loan system and microfilm from newspapers in New York, Chicago, Philadelphia, and a few other cities and towns.

Helpful, too, was Jim Mullan, an English professor at Fairfield University, specializing in Irish studies, who not only could recall almost every Giants game he has seen since the late 1940s, but, when given the jersey number of a Giants' player of the 1950s or 1960s, could tell you in a flash the name of the player, no matter how obscure, who wore it. And he was probably not the only Giants fan from that glorious era who could do it.

Of immeasurable assistance was my editor, Mark Tavani, who, once again, skillfully helped guide me along on this pleasant literary journey and was a joy to work with. Thanks go out, too, to Andrew Blauner, who had great faith in this project from the start.

NOTES

1: RETURN TO WINOOSKI PARK

INTERVIEWS: Andy Robustelli, Alex Webster, Carmine Tosches, Robert Daley, Tony Adams, Seth Cole, Ed Markey, Liz Scott, Robert McKinney, Tim Kennedy, Ted Ryan, Mike Donohue, Jim Day, Rev. Raymond Doherty, John Marikos.

PUBLICATIONS: *Burlington (Vermont) Free Press, New Haven Register, Bridgeport Telegram, Bridgeport Post, New York Times, Salem (Oregon) State Journal, Burlington Daily News, Los Angeles Times, Total Football* (New York: Harper Collins, 1996), Jack Clary, *Once a Giant, Always* (Boston: Quinlan Press, 1987), Don Smith, *New York Giants* (New York: American Sports Publishing Company, Inc., 1960), Associated Press.

2: HUFF AS IN TOUGH

INTERVIEWS: Andy Robustelli, Robert Daley, Don Smith, Tony Adams, Sam Huff, Dick Modzelewski, Vince Lombardi Jr., Carmine Tosches, Ted Ryan.

PUBLICATIONS: *Burlington Free Press, Burlington Daily News, Boston Globe,* Leonard Shapiro, *Tough Stuff* (New York: St. Martin's Press, 1988), *New York Giants Information Guide 2007,* Carlo Dvito, *Wellington* (Chicago, Triumph Books, 2006), Associated Press.

3: MR. HIGH-LOW AND THE FORMER BOMBER PILOT

INTERVIEWS: Robert Daley, Pat Summerall, Andy Robustelli, Tom Scott, William N. Wallace, Don Smith, Sam Huff, Robert McKinney.

PUBLICATIONS: *New York Times, New York Herald Tribune*, Shapiro, *Tough Stuff*, Clary, *Once a Giant, Always*, Barry Gottehrer, *The Giants of New York* (NewYork: G. P. Putnam's Sons, 1963), Rosey Grier with Donald Baker, *Rosey* (Tulsa: Honor Books, 1986), Gerald Eskenazi, *There Were Giants in Those Days* (New York: Grosset & Dunlap, 1976), Dave Camerer, "Robustelli the Rock," *Sport*, November 1957, Frank Gifford and Harry Waters, *The Whole Ten Yards* (New York: Random House, 1993), David Maraniss, *When Pride Still Mattered* (New York: Simon & Schuster, 1999), Dave Klein, *The New York Giants* (Chicago: Henry Regnery, 1973), Jim Terzian, *New York Giants* (New York: Macmillan, 1973), Denne Freeman and Jaime Aron, *I Remember Tom Landry* (Sports Publishing L.L.C., 2001).

4: THE MARLBORO MAN

INTERVIEWS: Andy Robustelli, Harland Svare, Perian Conerly, Don Smith, Alex Webster, Robert Daley, William N. Wallace.

PUBLICATIONS: *New York Giants Information Guide, 2007, New York Daily News, New York Times*, Clary, *Once a Giant, Always*, Gottehrer, *The Giants of New York*, Richard Whittingham, *The Giants: An Illustrated History* (New York: Harper & Row, 1987).

5: THE MEANEST MAN IN THE NFL

INTERVIEWS: Y. A. Tittle, Andy Robustelli, Raymond Berry, Alex Webster, Tex Coulter, Jim Finks, Gino Marchetti, Joe DiBari, Patrice Kane.

PUBLICATIONS: *San Francisco Chronicle, New York Times, Chicago Tribune, Chicago Daily News*, Associated Press, Y. A. Tittle and Don Smith, *Y. A. Tittle: I Pass* (New York: Franklin Watts, Inc., 1964), Richard Whittingham, *Giants in Their Own Words* (Chicago: Contemporary Books, 1992), Jim Dent, *Twelve Mighty Orphans* (New York: St. Martin's Press, 2007).

6: PUTTING TOGETHER AN INSTANT DYNASTY

INTERVIEWS: Bob Markowitz, Robert Daley, Dick Modzelewski, Ed Modzelewski, Alex Webster, John Heisler, Sam Huff, National Football League.

PUBLICATIONS: *Total Football*, Michael MacCambridge, *America's Game* (New York, Random House, 2004), Mickey Herskowitz, *The Golden Age of Pro Football* (NewYork: Macmillan Publishing Company, 1974), *New York Daily News, New York Times, Cleveland Plain Dealer, Cleveland Press*.

7: FROM THE POLO GROUNDS TO "THE HOUSE THAT RUTH BUILT"

INTERVIEWS: Andy Robustelli, Perian Conerly, Carmine Tosches, Pat Summerall, Sam Huff, Jim Katcavage, Herb Kohn, Joe Walton, Ed Clark.

PUBLICATIONS: *New York Times, New York Daily News, New York Mirror, New York Post*, Perian Conerly, *Backseat Quarterback* (Jackson: University Press of Mississippi, 2003).

8: THE GROCERY BOY FROM THE WEST SIDE

INTERVIEWS: Tony Pia, Vito DeVito, Andy Robustelli, Carmine Tosches, Fred "Lefty" Giuliani.

PUBLICATIONS: *Stamford Advocate*, Clary, *Once a Giant, Always*.

9: THE ORIGINAL FEARSOME FOURSOME

INTERVIEWS: Dick Modzelewski, Andy Robustelli, Ed Clark, Greg Mitchie.

PUBLICATIONS: *New York Times, New York Herald Tribune, New York Daily News, New York Post, Philadelphia Inquirer*, Whittingham, *Giants in Their Own Words*, Gottehrer, *The Giants of New York*, Eskenazi, *There Were Giants in Those Days*.

10: THE COAL MINER'S SON

INTERVIEWS: Dick Modzelewski, Ed Modzelewski, Andy Robustelli, Robert Daley, William N. Wallace, Perian Conerly, Sam Huff, Don Smith.

PUBLICATIONS: *New York Times, New York Daily News, Chicago Tribune*, Whittingham, *Giants in Their Own Words*, Gottehrer, *The Giants of New York*, Jim Terzianj, *New York Giants* (New York, Macmillan Publishing Co., Inc., 1973).

11: "CAN'T ANYBODY OUT THERE BLOCK?"

INTERVIEWS: Sam Huff, Harland Svare, Rosey Grier, Alex Webster, Perian Conerly.

PUBLICATIONS: Mickey Herskowitz, *The Golden Age of Pro Football, Washington Post, Washington Times-Herald, New York Times, Total Football, New York Daily News, Chicago Tribune, Chicago Sun-Times*, NFL website.

12: THE COMPLETE FOOTBALL PLAYER

INTERVIEWS: Don Smith, Andy Robustelli, Jim Katcavage, Sam Huff, Dick Modzelewski.

PUBLICATIONS: Gifford and Waters, *The Whole Ten Yards, New York Times, New York Daily News, Cleveland Press, Cleveland Plain Dealer, Akron Beacon Journal, Total Football, Philadelphia Inquirer, Philadelphia Bulletin*.

13: ED AND ANDY'S SPORTS STORE TO THE RESCUE

Perian Conerly, Jean Robustelli, Ed Clark, Vince Lombardi Jr., Ed Modzelewski, Dick Modzelewski.

PUBLICATIONS: Gottehrer, *The Giants of New York*, Whittingham, *The Giants, New York Giants Information Guide 2007*, Eskenazi, *There Were Gi-*

ants in Those Days, New York American, New York Herald Tribune, New York Times, Chicago Tribune, Sports Illustrated.

14: THIS IS THE ARMY, MR. GRIER

INTERVIEWS: Alex Webster, Andy Robustelli, Rosey Grier, Sam Huff, Dick Modzelewski, Don Smith, Y. A. Tittle, Ed Modzelewski, Bob Moscowitz.

PUBLICATIONS: MacCambridge, *America's Game*, Herskowitz, *The Golden Age of Football*, Gifford and Waters, *The Whole Ten Yards*, National Lacrosse Hall of Fame, *New York Times, New York Daily News, Pittsburgh Post-Gazette, Pittsburgh Press, Cleveland Plain Dealer, Cleveland Press, Total Football*, Bert Randolph Sugar, *The 100 Greatest Athletes of All Time.* (Secaucus, NJ: Carol, 1995).

15: THE KICKER WITH THE WRONG-WAY FOOT

INTERVIEWS: Pat Summerall, Vince Lombardi Jr., Walt Michaels, Vince Costello, Alex Webster.

PUBLICATIONS: Pat Summerall, *Summerall: On and Off the Air* (Nashville: Thomas Nelson, Inc., 2006), Maraniss, *When Pride Still Mattered*, Eskenazi, *There Were Giants in Those Days, New York Giants Information Guide 2007, Total Football, New York Times*, Red Smith in the *New York Herald Tribune, Chicago Tribune, Cleveland Press, Cleveland Plain Dealer, Washington Post*, Dave Klein, *The Game of Their Lives* (New York: New American Library, 1976), Tex Maule, *The Game* (New York, Random House, 1963).

16: "HOW ABOUT THAT SUMMERVILLE?"

INTERVIEWS: Michael Daley, Phil Rahrig, Pat Summerall, Perian Conerly, Alex Webster.

PUBLICATIONS: *Newark Star-Ledger, Philadelphia Daily News, Philadelphia Inquirer, Cleveland Plain Dealer, Cleveland Press, Total Football, New York Giants Information Guide 2007*, Gottehrer, *The Giants of New York*, Eskenazi, *There Were Giants in Those Days.*

17: WHERE HAVE YOU GONE, OTTO GRAHAM?

INTERVIEWS: Walt Michaels, Pat Summerall, Sam Huff, Allie Sherman, Dick Modzelewski.

PUBLICATIONS: *Cleveland Plain Dealer, Cleveland Press, Akron Beacon Journal, Sports Illustrated, Total Football.*

18: "THE BEST FOOTBALL GAME EVER PLAYED"

INTERVIEWS: Ernie Accorsi, Frank Deford, John Ziemann, Gino Marchetti, Andy Robustelli, Raymond Berry, Art Donovan, Bob Wolff, Dick Modzelewski, Sam Huff, Alex Webster, Dave Anderson, George Schaefer,

Danny O'Toole, Marge Schmidt.

PUBLICATIONS: *Baltimore Sun, Baltimore News-Post, Baltimore American, New York Times,* Red Smith in the *New York Herald Tribune, Sports Illustrated, Total Football, Baseball Encyclopedia* (New York: Macmillan Publishing Company, 1990), Tex Maule, *The Best Football Game Ever* (Baltimore: William H. Shriver Jr. and Helicon Press, Inc., 1959), Robert Riger and Tex Maule, *The Pros* (New York: Simon and Schuster, 1960), MacCambridge, *America's Game,* Klein, *The Game of Their Lives,* Herskowitz, *The Golden Age of Pro Football.*

19: CHUCKIN' CHARLIE—BETTER WITH AGE

INTERVIEWS: Ernie Accorsi, Frank Deford, Raymond Berry, Sandy Unitas, Perian Conerly, Andy Robustelli, Gino Marchetti, Carmine Tosches, Ed Clark, Vince Lombardi Jr., Allie Sherman, Joan Sherman, Robert Daley, Don Smith, Dick Lynch.

PUBLICATIONS: *Baltimore Sun, Baltimore News-Post, Sports Illustrated,* Associated Press, *New York Times, Philadelphia Inquirer, New York Daily News,* Whittingham, *Giants in Their Own Words,* Eskenazi, *There Were Giants in Those Days,* Clary, *Once a Giant, Always, Total Football,* Conerly, *Backseat Quarterback,* Red Smith in the *New York Herald Tribune, Time* magazine, *New York Giants Information Guide 2007,* NFL website.

20: COLTS-GIANTS REDUX

INTERVIEWS: Perian Conerly, Dick Lynch, John Ziemann, Andy Robustelli, Sam Huff, Allie Sherman.

PUBLICATIONS: Perian Conerly for the *North American Newspaper Alliance, Baltimore Sun, New York Times, New York Herald Tribune,* Whittingham, *The Giants,* Gottehrer, *The Giants of New York,* Clary, *Once a Giant, Always, Sports Illustrated.*

21: FRANK GIFFORD, MEET "CONCRETE CHARLIE"

INTERVIEWS: Andy Robustelli, Ed Clark, Greg Michie, Sam Huff, Don Smith, Chuck Bednarik.

PUBLICATIONS: Freeman and Aron, *I Remember Tom Landry,* Eskenazi, *There Were Giants in Those Days,* Shapiro, *Tough Stuff, Cleveland Press, Cleveland Plain Dealer, New York Times, New York Daily News,* Gifford and Waters, *The Whole Ten Yards, Sports Illustrated.*

22: HIGH SCHOOL HANDBALL STAR TO COACH THE N.Y. GIANTS

INTERVIEWS: Vince Lombardi Jr., Allie Sherman, Y. A. Tittle, Don Smith, Perian Conerly, William N. Wallace, Allan Webb.

PUBLICATIONS: *Total Football,* Terzian, *New York Giants,* Tittle and

Smith, *I Pass*, Eskenazi, *There Were Giants in Those Days*, Whittingham, *The Giants*, Gottehrer, *The Giants of New York, New York Times, New York Herald Tribune*, Associated Press, *New York Daily News*.

23: "I'M IN LOVE WITH YELBERTON ABRAHAM TITTLE"

INTERVIEWS: Vince Lombardi Jr., Sam Huff, Rosey Grier, Perian Conerly, Don Smith, Pat Summerall, Y. A. Tittle, Alex Webster, Joe Walton, Allie Sherman, Jean Robustelli, Dick Modzelewski.

PUBLICATIONS: *Total Football*, Gifford and Waters, *The Whole Ten Yards*, Tittle and Don Smith, *I Pass*, Dianne Tittle deLaet, *Giants and Heroes: A Daughter's Memoir of Y. A. Tittle* (Hanover, NH: Steerforth Press, 1995), *Time* magazine, Mariness, *When Pride Really Mattered, New York Times, New York Daily News*.

24: THE LAST HURRAH?

INTERVIEWS: Rosey Grier, Alex Webster, Andy Robustelli, Y. A. Tittle, Sam Huff.

PUBLICATIONS: *New York Times, New York Herald Tribune, New York Daily News*, Mariness, *When Pride Still Mattered, New York Times Information Guide 2007, Cleveland Plain Dealer, Cleveland Press*, Associated Press, *Baltimore Sun*, Gifford and Waters, *The Whole Ten Yards, Washington Post, Stamford Advocate, Chicago Tribune, Sports Illustrated*.

EPILOGUE

INTERVIEWS: Herb Kohn, Dave Anderson, Joe Horrigan, Ernie Accorsi, Harland Svare, Dick Modzelewski, Sam Huff, Andy Robustelli, Allie Sherman, Don Smith, Greg Michie, William N. Wallace, Rosey Grier, Carmine Tosches, Ed Clark, Dick Lynch, Alex Webster, Allan Webb, Bill Filipski.

PUBLICATIONS: Clary, *Once a Giant, Always, Total Football*, Maraniss, *When Pride Really Mattered*, Eskenazi, *There Were Giants in Those Days*, Whittingham, *Giants in Their Own Words*, Terzian, *New York Giants*.

INDEX

ABOUT THE AUTHOR

JACK CAVANAUGH is a veteran sportswriter who has covered scores of major boxing bouts, along with the Olympics, the World Series, Super Bowl games, the Masters Golf Tournament, and both the U.S. golf and tennis opens. He is the author of *Tunney*, and his work has appeared most notably on the sports pages of *The New York Times*, for which he has covered hundreds of varied sports assignments. In addition, he has been a frequent contributor to *Sports Illustrated* and written for *Reader's Digest*, *Tennis* and *Golf* magazines, and other national publications. He is also a former reporter for both ABC News and CBS News. Cavanaugh is currently an adjunct writing professor at Fairfield University. He and his wife, Marge, live in Wilton, Connecticut.